College Writing

3

HOUGHTON MIFFLIN
ENGLISH FOR ACADEMIC SUCCESS

Gabriella Nuttall

California State University, Sacramento

SERIES EDITORS

Patricia Byrd

Joy M. Reid

Cynthia M. Schuemann

Houghton Mifflin Company
Boston   New York

Publisher: Patricia A. Coryell
Director of ESL Publishing: Susan Maguire
Senior Development Editor: Kathy Sands Boehmer
Editorial Assistant: Evangeline Bermas
Senior Project Editor: Kathryn Dinovo
Manufacturing Assistant: Karmen Chong
Senior Marketing Manager: Annamarie Rice
Marketing Assistant: Andrew Whitacre

Cover graphics: LMA Communications, Natick, Massachusetts

Photo credits: © James Leynse/Corbis, p. 2; Southwestern Bell Mobile Systems, LLC d/b/a Cingular Wireless, http://www.cingular.com. Copyright © 2004, Cingular Wireless. Reprinted with permission, p. 48; © Adam Woolfitt/Corbis, p. 204; © Jim Zuckerman/Corbis, p. 243; © Wolfgang Kaehler/Corbis, p. 245

Text credits: Hoyer, W. D., & MacInnis, D. J., Consumer behavior, 2nd Edition. Copyright © 2001 by Houghton Mifflin Company. Reprinted with permission, p. 11; Goff, A. & Wheeler, C. "Web Evaluation Criteria." Copyright © 2001 by WebQuest. Reprinted with permission, p. 60; Nevid, J.S., Psychology concepts and applications. Copyright © 2003 by Houghton Mifflin Company. Reprinted with permission, p. 133; Nevid, J.S., Psychology concepts and applications. Copyright © 2003 by Houghton Mifflin Company. Reprinted with permission, p. 159.

Printed in the U.S.A.

Library of Congress Control Number: 2004112230

ISBN: 0-618-23030-0

123456789-CRW-08 07 06 05 04

Contents

Houghton Mifflin English for Academic Success Series

CHAPTER 1

Chapter 1: Analyzing Print Ads

CHAPTER 2

Chapter 2: Evaluating Web Design

Houghton Mifflin English for Academic Success Series

SERIES EDITORS

Patricia Byrd, Joy M. Reid, Cynthia M. Schuemann

○ What Is the Purpose of This Series?

The Houghton Mifflin English for Academic Success series is a comprehensive program of student and instructor materials: four levels of student language proficiency textbooks in three skill areas (oral communication, reading, and writing) with supplemental vocabulary textbooks at each level. For instructors and students, a useful website supports classroom teaching, learning, and assessment. For instructors, four Essentials of Teaching Academic Language books (*Essentials of Teaching Academic Oral Communication, Essentials of Teaching Academic Reading, Essentials of Teaching Academic Writing,* and *Essentials of Teaching Academic Vocabulary*) provide helpful information for instructors new to teaching oral communication, reading, writing, and vocabulary.

The fundamental purpose of the series is to prepare students who are not native speakers of English for academic success in U.S. college degree programs. By studying these materials, students in college English for Academic Purposes (EAP) courses will gain the academic language skills they need to be successful students in degree programs. Additionally, students will learn about being successful students in U.S. college courses.

The series is based on considerable prior research as well as our own investigations of students' needs and interests, instructors' needs and desires, and institutional expectations and requirements. For example, our survey research revealed what problems instructors feel they face in their classrooms and what they actually teach; who the students are and what they know and do not know about the "culture" of U.S. colleges; and what types of exams are required for admission at various colleges.

Student Audience

The materials in this series are for college-bound ESL students at U.S. community colleges and undergraduate programs at other institutions. Some of these students are U.S. high school graduates. Some of them are long-term United States residents who graduated from a high school before coming to the United States. Others are newer U.S. residents. Still others are more typical international students. All of them need to develop academic language skills and knowledge of ways to be successful in U.S. college degree courses.

All of the books in this series have been created to implement the Houghton Mifflin English for Academic Success competencies. These competencies are based on those developed by ESL instructors and administrators in Florida, California, and Connecticut to be the underlying structure for EAP courses at colleges in those states. These widely respected competencies assure that the materials meet the real world needs of EAP students and instructors.

All of the books focus on…

- Starting where the students are, building on their strengths and prior knowledge (which is considerable, if not always academically relevant), and helping students self-identify needs and plans to strengthen academic language skills
- Academic English, including development of Academic Vocabulary and grammar required by students for academic speaking/listening, reading, and writing
- Master Student Skills, including learning style analysis, strategy training, and learning about the "culture" of U.S. colleges, which lead to their becoming successful students in degree courses and degree programs
- Topics and readings that represent a variety of academic disciplinary areas so that students learn about the language and content of the social sciences, the hard sciences, education, and business as well as the humanities

All of the books provide…

- Interesting and valuable content that helps the students develop their knowledge of academic content as well as their language skills and student skills
- A wide variety of practical classroom-tested activities that are easy to teach and engage the students
- Assessment tools at the end of each chapter so that instructors have easy-to-implement ways to assess student learning and students have opportunities to assess their own growth
- Websites for the students and for the instructors: the student sites will provide additional opportunities to practice reading, writing, listening, vocabulary development, and grammar. The instructor sites will provide instructors' manuals, teaching notes and answer

keys, value-added materials like handouts and overheads that can be reproduced to use in class, and assessment tools such as additional tests to use beyond the assessment materials in each book.

○ What Is the Purpose of the Writing Strand?

The Writing strand of the Houghton Mifflin English for Success series prepares ESL students for academic written work, particularly in the first two years of college study. Many ESL students have learned English mostly through their ears; others have studied English primarily with their eyes. Each group has unique written-language problems. The goals of the writing books are to build on the strengths of the students, to respect the knowledge they have, and to identify and teach language, content, and rhetoric that students must have to succeed in college courses. The writing strategies presented focus on confidence building and step-by-step, easy-to-learn processes for effective academic writing.

The four writing textbooks prepare students for the range of writing tasks assigned in college courses, and the solid scaffolding of skills focus on "college culture" as well as on academic writing. The high-interest, content-based chapters relate to academic work and college disciplines, and the chapter materials have been designed to appeal to a variety of student learning styles and strategies. The authentic native-English speaker (NES), ESL, and professional writing samples offer students examples of required writing in post-secondary institutions; the writing assignments have been drawn from actual college courses across the curriculum. In addition, the content of each textbook is based on the HM Writing Competencies, which in turn are based on state-designed competencies developed by hundreds of experienced ESL teachers.

Grammar and technology in the Writing strand

Because the ESL population is so diverse in its grammar and rhetoric needs, each chapter contains Power Grammar boxes that introduce structures needed by the students to write fluent, accurate academic prose. The structures are drawn from the writing required by the chapter content. Students who need additional work with the structures are referred to the Houghton Mifflin website, where high-quality relevant additional support is available.

Assignments in the writing textbooks also ask students to use the Internet: to investigate topics and to identify and evaluate sources for research. Materials about citing sources is sequenced and spiraled through the books so that students exit the writing program with substantial practice with and knowledge about using sources.

Assessment Materials Accompanying the Writing strand

This Writing strand is filled with informal and formal assessment. Students write, self-assess, and have significant opportunities for peer response and other external informal review, including teacher response. The end of each chapter contains additional writing tasks for practice or for testing/evaluation. Each chapter also asks students to self-evaluate the skills they have learned; these self-evaluations have proven surprisingly honest and accurate, and the results allow teachers to review and recycle necessary concepts. Finally, students regularly return to the revision process, revising even their "final" drafts after the papers are returned by the teacher, and receiving grades for those revisions.

More formally, the instructor website (http://esl.college.hmco.com/ instructors) and the *Essentials of Teaching Academic Writing* book offer assessment information and advice about both responding to and "grading" student writing. Information in these sources help instructors set up valid, reliable criteria for each student writing assignment in each book (which the instructors are encouraged to share with their students). These resources also contain sample student papers with teacher responses; sample topics to assess student strengths and weaknesses and to measure achievement and progress; and "benchmarked" student papers that describe the range of student grades.

Instructor Support Materials

The co-editors and Houghton Mifflin are committed to support instructors. For the Writing strand, the *Essentials of Teaching Academic Writing* by Joy Reid is an easily accessible, concise volume. This teacher resource, with its practical, problem-solving content, includes organizational suggestions for less experienced writing instructors, materials for response to and evaluation of student writing, and activities for teaching. In addition, each textbook has a password-protected website for instructors to provide classroom activities, substantial information and materials for assessment of student writing, and a "workbook" of printable pages linked to the textbook for use as handouts or overhead transparencies.

○ What Is the Organization of *College Writing 3*?

College Writing 3 prepares high-intermediate students for academic writing in U.S. colleges. After a review of the basic paragraph structure, the book introduces the academic essay and teaches students to write explaining essays on a variety of academic topics popular with ESL college students. The students learn to explain *what, why* and *how* as they follow a three-step writing process: Gathering Information, Focusing and Organizing, and Writing, Editing, and Revising. In Chapter 1, the students learn and write paragraphs about advertising methods. In Chapter 2, the students learn about web design as they evaluate commercial websites. Chapter 3 focuses on therapeutic and/or surgical techniques related to vision, hearing, and taste loss. Chapter 4 requires students to research information, interview experts, and write about the effects of college stress on first-year students. In Chapter 5, students learn about archeological and anthropological mysteries as they review the writing process and strategies they learned in the previous chapters. Throughout the book, grammar points are integrated with the writing assignments instead of being taught in isolation.

Chapter Organization

Chapter Objectives

Each chapter begins with a preview of the chapter goals. After working on the chapter, the students can go back to the chapter goals and check off the skills they learned well and those they still need to practice.

Self-Evaluation and Peer Reviews

During the writing process, students are frequently asked to evaluate their own and other students' writing. Peer review sheets are included in the Appendix.

Readings

Most of the chapters contain excerpts from textbooks or websites for introductory college courses. Key vocabulary words are defined for the students, and end-of-reading exercises help the students "unpack" the texts and select relevant information.

Student Models

Student writing samples are presented in each chapter. The samples provide concrete models for the students as well as opportunities for writing analysis and evaluation.

Power Grammar

Each chapter reviews two to three grammar points and lists some exercises. The grammar points are integral to the chapter topic and writing task and therefore more meaningful to the students. Additional work on the grammar points is available on the Houghton Mifflin website.

Web Power

This feature is found throughout the book. It reminds students that additional information and/or practice is available online.

Master Student Tips

Throughout *College Writing 3*, the students receive advice, in the form of tips, on how to best approach or complete tasks and assignments in each chapter.

Additional Practice

Each chapter ends with additional writing assignments for practice and assessment. They also provide students with an opportunity to reflect on their learning process and assess their mastery of the writing process.

Acknowledgments

Many people have contributed to this project. Special thanks go to Houghton Mifflin ESL editor Susan Maguire and developmental editor Kathy Sands Boehmer for their guidance and support. I am deeply grateful for the unwavering support of series editor Joy Reid, without whom this book would never have been written. I am also very thankful for series co-editor Pat Byrd, who patiently answered my many questions, and fellow co-author Li-Lee Tunceren, who supported me with her energy and enthusiasm. I am indebted to my faculty advisors, Tina Jordan, Catherine Hatzakos, and Deana Lewis, for their feedback and thoughtful suggestions.

The following reviewers contributed with their insightful comments to the revision and reshaping of this book:

Margaret Annen, University of Texas, Brownsville;
Maria Begemann, Wright State University, Dayton;
Leslie Biaggi, Miami Dade College;
Cheri Boyer, University of Arizona;
Dana Ferris, CSU, Sacramento;
Janet Harclerode, Santa Monica College;
Rosemary Hiruma, CSU, Long Beach;
Erin Lofthouse, City College of San Francisco;
John Miller, Southern Adventist University;
Paula Richards, Northern Essex Community College;
Deborah Stark, Queens College;
Kent Trickel, Westchester Community College;
Bob Underwood, American River College;
Susan Vik, Boston University.

I am indebted to my husband, Will, who gave me strength and encouragement when I needed them most.

Finally, I want to thank the many, many students who permitted me to use their writing in this book. They inspire me everyday with their hard work and willingness to learn.

○ What Student Competencies Are Covered in *College Writing 3*?

Description of Overall Purposes

Students develop the ability to compose (i.e., comprehend, select, plan, and draft) and produce lengthier texts on diverse general education academic topics by applying appropriate writing strategies.

Materials in this textbook are designed with the following minimum exit objectives in mind:

Competency 1:
(level/global focus)
The student will write academic texts about general education content (e.g., Houghton Mifflin secondary and some college "essentials" textbook sources, approximate readability level 9–12, and/or topics of individual interest.)

Competency 2:
(critical thinking)
The student will learn to adjust writing skills and strategies according to academic audience(s) and purpose(s), specifically in comprehending, selecting, planning, drafting, and revising.

Competency 3:
(components)
The student will develop, produce, administer, collate, and report on surveys and use such primary data (including interviews) to support and explain main ideas in their writing.

Competency 4:
(organization)
The student will practice a wide range of textual clues for academic readers to help them understand the meaning and structure (i.e., patterns of organization) of the written text, including sentence connectors, signal words, and pronoun reference,

Competency 5:
(critical thinking)
The student will learn that the main purposes of academic writing are (a) to demonstrate knowledge in academic contexts and (b) persuade the instructor/ evaluator of that knowledge. The student will practice strategies for accomplishing that purpose.

Competency 6:
(grammar)
The student will write accurate Standard English, including proofreading and editing grammar and sentence structure, appropriate to the level.

Competency 7: The student will select, discriminate, and present
(research skills) Internet and library (i.e., secondary source) materials in
specific academic reading and writing contexts.

Competency 8: The student will demonstrate the ability to apply the
(critical thinking) following critical thinking skills when writing:

A. enhance strategies for analyzing academic
audience(s) and purpose(s);

B. analyze authentic academic assignments;

C. enhance the abilities to present written perspectives
through exploration of beliefs, arguments, and
theories;

D. transfer insights gained from readings to their
writing appropriately (e.g., citing materials and
sources);

E. synthesize information gathered from more than one
source in order to write and support an informed
opinion;

F. explain and justify opinions in response to readings;

G. apply content knowledge to academic tasks (test-
taking, academic content reading, academic
interactions, comprehending and responding
appropriately to academic writing assignments).

Competency 9: The student will understand, discuss, and write about
(culture) common academic cultural references.

Competency 10: The student will continue and expand the use of study
(study strategies) skills, learning styles, and strategies necessary when
writing for academic purposes.

○ What Are the Features of the Writing Books?

The Houghton Mifflin English for Academic Success series is a
comprehensive program of student and instructor materials. The fundamental
purpose of the program is to prepare students who are not native speakers of
English for academic success in U.S. college degree programs.

The Writing strand of the Houghton Mifflin English for Academic
Success series focuses on the development of writing skills and general
background knowledge necessary for college study. It is dedicated to
meeting academic needs of students by teaching them how to handle the
writing demands and expectations of college-level classes. The goals of the
writing books are to build on the strengths of the students, to respect the
knowledge they have, and to identify and teach language, content, and
rhetoric that students must have to succeed in college courses.

Academic Content: The content of each book relates to academic subjects and has been selected because of its high interest for students and because of the popularity of these particular disciplines/courses on college campuses.

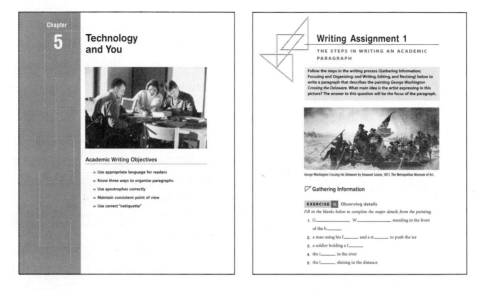

Authentic Writing Assignments: The writing assignments have been drawn from actual college courses across the curriculum. Students will find the assignments highly motivating when they realize they may receive such an assignment in one of their future classes.

Authentic Writing Models: Models provide specific examples of student writing so that students can compare writing styles, discuss writing strategies and understand instructor expectations.

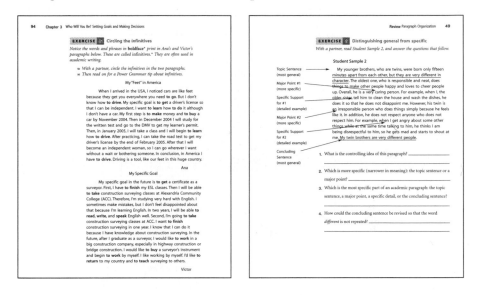

Step-by-Step Writing Process: The step-by-step writing process helps demystify the concept of "academic writing" and helps students develop confidence. The textbooks offer solid scaffolding of skills that focus on college culture as well as on academic topics and academic writing. These are supplemented by practical advice offered in the Spotlight on Writing Skills feature boxes.

Self-Assessment Opportunity: A writing course develops through assessment. Students write and revise and instructors respond and evaluate and then students write some more. The textbooks offer students opportunity for peer review, self-review, and self-evaluation.

Master Student Tips: Master Student Tips throughout the textbooks provide students with short comments on a particular strategy, activity, or practical advice to follow in an academic setting.

Power Grammar Boxes: Students can be very diverse in their grammar and rhetorical needs so each chapter contains Power Grammar boxes that introduce the grammar structures students need to be fluent and accurate in academic English.

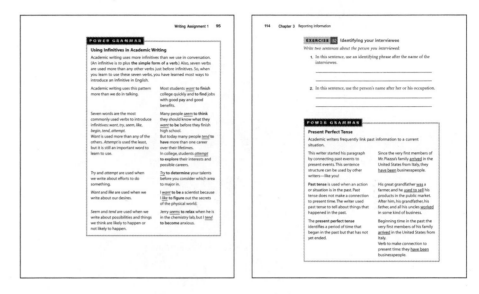

Ancillary Program: The ancillary program provides instructors with teaching tips, additional exercises, and robust assessment. Students can also take advantage of additional exercises and activities. The following items are available to accompany the Houghton Mifflin English for Academic Success series Writing strand.

- Instructor website: Additional teaching materials, activities, and robust student assessment.
- Student website: Additional exercises, activities, and web links.
- The Houghton Mifflin English for Academic Success series Vocabulary books: You can choose the appropriate level to shrinkwrap with your text.
- *Essentials of Teaching Academic Writing* by Joy M. Reid is available for purchase. It gives you theoretical and practical information for teaching writing.

Analyzing Print Ads

Marketing is the use of advertising to sell products to consumers (the people who buy and use the products). Marketing is one of the most popular majors among business college students. Knowing how to appeal to customers in order to sell a product is a very important skill for marketers, the people who design "ads."

In this chapter, you will learn about consumer behavior as you write about print advertising (ads that appear in newspapers and magazines). You will review the five basic paragraph modes used in most college writing as you write several body paragraphs by following a three-step writing process: (1) gathering information, (2) focusing and organizing, and (3) drafting, revising, and editing.

Chapter Objectives

Review this chapter's objectives before you start. Return to this chart after completing the chapter and check (✓) the appropriate box to the right.	I have learned this well.	I need to work on this.
Review the five most common paragraph modes		
Use a three-step writing process: **1.** Gathering information **2.** Focusing and organizing **3.** Drafting, revising, and editing		

Gather information by:
    Freewriting
    Reading about advertising methods
    Creating a chart
    Listing
    Clustering		

Organize your paragraph by using an outline		
Write a topic sentence with controlling ideas		
Provide main points in your paragraph that relate to the controlling ideas in the topic sentence		
Select and organize supporting details to illustrate your main points		
Write a well-developed academic paragraph		
Give and receive feedback through peer responses		
Revise and edit your paragraph		
Identify subjects and verbs in sentences		
Be aware of the differences between informal, spoken language and formal, written language		
Identify independent and dependent clauses in complex sentences		

SPOTLIGHT ON WRITING SKILLS

Paragraph Modes

Five common methods of paragraph development (also called modes) are definition, process, classification, comparison/contrast, and cause/effect. Most college courses require different types of paragraphs for different assignments. For example, a nursing student must be able to write a **definition** paragraph to **describe** a patient's symptoms. Also, a nurse might need to **compare** a patient's condition from one day to the next. In computer science, a student must be able to **explain the process** to install and use software or **how** to create programs by using a step-by-step approach.

The chart below shows the different paragraph modes, their purposes, and the types of writing assignments that correspond to the different paragraph modes.

Paragraph type	Purpose	Sample test questions	College courses that may use these test questions
1. **Definition**	To describe something in detail. Answers the question *"What?"*	What is _____? Define . . . Explain . . . Describe . . .	Biology, Chemistry, Mathematics, Economics
2. **Process**	To explain how something is made. Answers the question *"How?"*	How does it work? Describe how . . . Explain how . . . What happens . . . ?	Computer Science, Mechanical Engineering, Agriculture, Water Resources

Paragraph type	Purpose	Sample test questions	College courses that may use these test questions
3. Classification	To divide things into classes or categories. Answers the question "*What kind?*"	What types ...? List ... Categorize ...	Pharmacology, Geography, Geology, Music, Theater, English Literature
4. Comparison and/or Contrast	To show the similarities and/or differences between two things or ideas. Answers the question "*In what ways?*"	What are the differences/ similarities ...? Compare ... Contrast ...	History, Sociology, Psychology, Business, Marketing
5. Cause and/or Effect	To explain the cause or reason for something. To explain the effect or result of something. Answers the question "*Why?*"	Why _____? Discuss the effects or causes ... Explain why ...	History, Political Science, Criminal Justice, Nursing

EXERCISE 1 **Discussing paragraph modes**

Which of the paragraph types listed in the chart above seems most difficult to write? Why? Which have you written successfully before? Discuss your answers with a partner.

WEB POWER

If you need more information about writing modes or paragraph types, go to **http://esl.college.hmco.com/ students.**

SPOTLIGHT ON WRITING SKILLS

Academic Paragraph Structure

What makes an effective academic paragraph? Regardless of its purpose, a well-written paragraph must have certain characteristics that are expected by the reader.

Generally, an effective body paragraph will have the following structure:

- **Topic sentence** (a sentence that expresses the main idea of the paragraph; it contains ideas that direct and control the rest of the paragraph)
- **One to three main points** that relate to the controlling ideas in the topic sentence
- **Supporting details** for each of the main points in the paragraph, such as:

  a. Facts, statistics, and other empirical data
  b. Examples that illustrate an idea or opinion
  c. Personal experiences from your own life
  d. Expert opinions (online and print sources, interviews, surveys)
  e. Explanations

- **A concluding sentence to end the paragraph**

A paragraph is well focused and flows smoothly if keywords and phrases occur frequently in the text and refer back to the controlling ideas.

The student paragraph that follows describes the ways a jewelry ad attracts consumers. The paragraph has been marked for you so that you can see the paragraph's structure and development. <u>Keywords</u> and <u>phrases</u> are underlined.

Armandi Jewelers

Topic sentence: *topic* of the paragraph + [controlling ideas]

Main Point 1: <u>color contrast</u>

Evidence for Main Point 1: description of the (a) rings and (b) background, (c) fact: the way color contrast is achieved.

Main Point 2: <u>different textures</u>

Evidence for Main Point 2: descriptions of the (a) rings' texture and (b) background texture

Concluding sentence (summary)

The ad for Armandi Jewelers relies on [contrasting colors] and [textures] [to attract] [consumers]. The ad achieves a strong <u>color</u> <u>contrast</u> by showing two <u>white</u> gold and diamond rings against a <u>red</u> background. One ring has a <u>white</u> gold band with three small <u>white</u> diamonds in the middle while the other ring has two <u>white</u> gold bands joined together by a large <u>pale pink</u> diamond surrounded by six tiny <u>white</u> diamonds. The rings are <u>pale</u> and <u>shiny</u> while the background is <u>dark red</u>. The ad creates a strong <u>contrast</u> with the <u>dark</u> background because it makes the rings <u>stand out</u>. The <u>contrast</u> between the rings and the background is made stronger by their <u>different textures</u>. The background is a <u>velvet</u> cloth that looks <u>soft</u> and warm while the rings are obviously <u>hard</u>, <u>cold</u>, and smooth. Thus, the Armandi Jewelers ad is very <u>attractive</u> because of the <u>contrast</u> between the <u>red, soft</u> background and the <u>hard, smooth</u> diamond rings.

EXERCISE 2 **Working with paragraph format**

With another classmate:

1. Discuss why the paragraph above is an effective academic paragraph. In your notebook, make a list of effective characteristics.
2. Complete the following outline of the student paragraph so that you can practice organizing main points and supporting details (evidence). Use the information written in the left margin of the paragraph to fill out the outline.

Student Sample Outline for "Armandi Jewelers":

Topic Sentence:

_____

Main Point 1:

_____

Supporting Details: 1. _____

2. _____

3. _____

Main Point 2:

_____

Supporting Details: 1. _____

2. _____

3. _____

Concluding Sentence:

_____

SPOTLIGHT ON WRITING SKILLS

Mental Picture

Sometimes it helps to create a mental picture to understand or remember an idea better. For example, you may want to picture the typical paragraph as a **sandwich**:

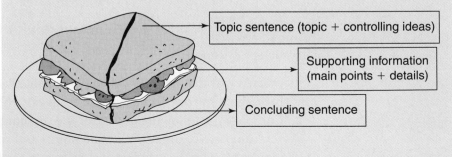

Topic sentence (topic + controlling ideas)

Supporting information (main points + details)

Concluding sentence

Writing Assignment 1

Write a paragraph that describes the ways a print ad of your choice attracts consumers. Follow a three-step writing process to compose your paragraph: 1. gathering information; 2. focusing and organizing; 3. drafting, revising, and editing.

The focus of this assignment is to *describe the ad's appeal*. The method of development you will use is *classification*.

Write your name, instructor's name, course, and section number on the front cover of a twin-pocket folder. This will become your **writing folder**. Keep all the materials, drafts, and peer reviews for this assignment in your writing folder. Bring your writing folder to class <u>every time</u> unless otherwise instructed.

○ Gathering Information

Gathering information about a topic prepares you for academic writing. Class and group discussions, freewriting, reading, and other exercises in this chapter will help you gather, select, and organize ideas for this chapter's writing assignments.

 EXERCISE 3 Discussing first impressions

With the other students in your class, answer the following questions:

1. What do you know about advertising?
2. How do you feel about advertising?
3. What <u>one word</u> would you use to describe the ad at the beginning of this chapter? Why?
4. Do you find the ad interesting? Why or why not?

EXERCISE 4 Freewriting

Freewrite for five minutes about the ways the ad catches your attention. That is, write quickly without stopping. Do not worry about grammar, spelling, or sentence structure. The purpose of freewriting is to get your ideas out on paper.

EXERCISE 5   **Sharing ideas**

With two or three classmates, discuss your freewriting. In what ways did the ad catch your classmates' attention? List them below your freewriting. When you finish, place the paper in your writing folder.

SPOTLIGHT ON WRITING SKILLS

Advertising Methods

Newspaper and magazine advertising in the United States is a huge business. The reading below is from *Consumer Behavior*, an introductory-level college textbook for marketing students. The reading discusses four ways that marketers use to make advertisements (ads) appealing for the American audience: (1) *making stimuli personally relevant*, (2) *making stimuli pleasant*, (3) *making stimuli surprising*, and (4) *making stimuli easy to process*.

Reading about advertising methods will help you with your academic writing assignments in this chapter. When you first read "Advertising Methods" (on the next page), cover the notes in the left margin with a piece of paper or a ruler.

Vocabulary you need to know for the reading "Advertising Methods":

consumer behavior: the way consumers buy and use products
relevant: important, significant
rhetorical question: a question that does not need an answer; a question asked only for effect
stimulus (plural, *stimuli*): an appeal to one or more of the human senses (seeing, hearing, smelling, and touching)
target audience: the people marketers want to attract

In most textbooks, a chapter begins with a *general heading*. It is followed by a more specific heading (a general statement or generalization that expresses an idea about the topic).

Advertising Methods

Making Stimuli Personally Relevant. Messages tend to be personally relevant when they (1) appeal to your needs, values, and goals; (2) show sources similar to the target audience; and (3) use rhetorical questions.

One of the most powerful ways for a stimulus to be perceived as personally relevant is for it to appeal to your needs, values, or goals. If you are hungry, you are more likely to pay attention to food ads and packages relevant to that need. You may pay attention to ads that show young people skateboarding or roller blading if these activities are consistent with your goals of having fun and your values regarding exercise.

You are also more likely to notice individuals whom you perceive as similar to yourself. Many advertisers use "typical customers," hoping that consumers will relate to these individuals and thereby attend to the ad.

Another way to capture consumers' attention is to ask rhetorical questions—those asked merely for effect. No one really expects an answer to a rhetorical question because its answer is so obvious. Examples include "What are you, a wise guy?" and "How would you like to win a million dollars?" These questions appeal to the consumer by including the word *you* and by asking the consumer (if only for effect) to consider answering the question. They also represent an attempt to draw the consumer into the advertisement.

A general statement contains **controlling ideas** which direct the rest of the paragraph. The controlling ideas are supported with evidence: ads featuring famous people, songs, and funny slogans.

Making Stimuli Pleasant. **People** tend to **approach things** that are **inherently pleasant**. Marketers can use this principle to increase consumers' attention to marketing stimuli.

- *Using Attractive Models.* Advertisements containing attractive models have higher probability of being noticed than those that do not because the models arouse positive feelings or a basic sexual attraction. Ads featuring popular and/or attractive individuals such as Michael Jordan, Cindy Crawford, Mel Gibson, and Christie Brinkley have been quite effective in generating attention.

- *Using Music.* Familiar songs and popular entertainers have considerable ability to attract us in pleasant ways. For example, Reba McEntire is paid to appear in snack-food commercials because of her attention-getting powers. Music relating a pleasant and nostalgic past is also used to attract attention. Commercials for Budweiser use the song "Ants," and commercials for Burger King play the song "That's the Way I Like It." Music can draw attention to an ad and enhance the attention we pay to the ad's message—provided that the music is coordinated with the ad's theme.
- *Using Humor.* Humor can also be an effective attention-getting device. Daewoo, the Korean-based car manufacturer, used humor in Britain in launching two of its new car models. The ads attracted consumers' attention with the humorous slogan "Daewho? The biggest car company you've never heard of."

Making Stimuli Surprising. Consumers are also likely to process a stimulus when it is surprising. Two characteristics make a stimulus surprising: novelty and unexpectedness.

Keywords
(important words) are used in the text to refer back to the controlling ideas. For example, notice the words that refer to the word *novelty* in this part of the reading: **novel**, **unusual**, **different**, and **new**.

- *Using Novelty.* We are more likely to notice any stimulus that is **new** or unique—because it stands out relative to other stimuli around us. Products, packages, and brand names that are **unusual** or **novel** command attention. For example, Catalyst for Men is packaged in test tubes and laboratory flasks. Because the packaging looks like a chemistry set, the product stands out from other brands on the shelf. **Unusual** looks work even for cars; for example, the Lamborghini Countach is very **different** in shape from most cars on the road.

Novel ads also command attention. To communicate that British Airways flies more people each year than the number that live in Manhattan, the carrier ran a now-famous campaign that showed the island of Manhattan flying overhead.

Although **novel** stimuli attract our attention, we do not always like them better. For example, we often dislike food that tastes different from what we usually eat, **new** clothing styles that deviate from the current trend, or **new** and unusual music. Thus the factors that make a stimulus **novel** may not be the same factors that make it likable.

- *Using Unexpectedness.* A second aspect of surprise is unexpectedness. Unexpected stimuli are not necessarily new, but their placement is different from what we are used to. Because they are different, they arouse our curiosity and cause us to analyze them further to make sense of them. 3M Company, the maker of Post-it Notes, created attention with ads that featured chickens with fluorescent notes with words like *Rush* and *Copy* stuck to their bodies. The placement of Post-it Notes on chickens was unexpected and hence attention getting.

Making Stimuli Easy to Process. Although **personal relevance**, **pleasantness**, and **surprise** attract consumers' attention by enhancing their motivation to attend to stimuli, marketers can also enhance attention by boosting our ability to process stimuli. Three things make a stimulus easy to process: (1) its **prominence**, (2) its **concreteness**, and (3) the extent to which it **contrasts** with the things that surround it.

Notice that the **main ideas** of the previous section are repeated before a new idea is introduced. The *controlling ideas* are explained and illustrated in detail. *Keywords* refer back to the controlling idea (**prominence**) and show the reader how an ad can be prominent.

- *Prominent Stimuli.* Prominent stimuli stand out relative to the environment because of their intensity. The size and length of the stimulus can affect its prominence. For example, consumers are more likely to notice *larger* or *longer* ads than to notice smaller or shorter ones. Thus a *full-page* ad has a greater chance of attracting attention than a half- or quarter-page ad. Yellow Pages advertisers have reported that *doubling* an ad's size increases sales fivefold, whereas *quadrupling* the size increases sales by a factor of 15.

Things that are moving also tend to be prominent. Attention to commercials tends to be enhanced when the ad uses dynamic, fast-paced actions. Loud sounds can also enhance prominence. Television and radio stations sometimes turn up the volume for commercials so they will stand out relative to the program.

- *Concrete Stimuli*. Stimuli are also easy to process if they are concrete as opposed to abstract. A good example of concreteness is illustrated by the brand names of some well-known dish-washing liquids. The name Sunlight is much more concrete than the names Dawn, Joy, or Palmolive and may therefore have an advantage over the others in attention-getting ability.

- *Contrasting Stimuli*. A third factor that makes stimuli easier to process is contrast. A color advertisement in a newspaper is more likely to capture attention because everything around it is black and white. A black-and-white ad on color TV is likely to stand out for a similar reason. Wine makers have found that packaging their wine in blue bottles instead of the traditional green or amber profoundly affects sales because the blue bottles stand out on the shelf. Cell phone rings that sound like Tarzan's yodel or a polka would clearly distinguish one person's cell phone ring from another's.

Source: Hoyer, W.D., & MacInnis, J.D., Consumer behavior, 2nd Edition. Copyright © 2001 by Houghton Mifflin Company. Reprinted with Permission.

WEB POWER

If you need more information about evaluating print ads, go to http://esl.college.hmco.com/students.

EXERCISE 6   Analyzing the text

Reread "Advertising Methods." As you reread, do the following:

1. In the right margin, put a question mark or write questions next to the parts of the text you do not understand.
2. Also in the right margin, write your reactions to the reading (for example, how do you feel about attractive young people advertising products?).
3. Highlight the general statements, and put a star (*) next to the examples in the reading.
4. On separate paper, list each stimulus discussed in the reading and its subcategories.

   Example:

   > Personally relevant stimuli are:
   > a. Stimuli that appeal to your needs
   > b. Stimuli that show people similar to you
   > c. Stimuli that use rhetorical questions

5. Circle *keywords* in the text that occur often and that refer to important ideas (examples: *stimuli*, *consumers*).

EXERCISE 7   Comparing your answers

Discuss your answers to Exercise 6 with three or four classmates.

1. Ask for your classmates' help with the parts of the reading you did not completely understand.
2. Discuss your reactions to the reading. Did all of you have similar opinions?
3. Did you mark the text differently? Why?
4. Compare your lists of stimuli and subcategories. Are they the same? If they are not, review the reading with your group and revise your list if necessary.
5. If you still have difficulty understanding some parts of the reading or if you disagree about some answers, ask your instructor for help.

EXERCISE 8   Finding an ad

Look through different magazines and newspapers for an ad you would like to write about in Writing Assignment 1. Choose an ad that catches your attention with images more than with words. Put the ad in your writing folder.

EXERCISE 9 **Exchanging ads**

Exchange ads with one of your classmates. Then,

1. Look carefully at the ad your classmate has chosen. What do you like about this ad? List your ideas on separate paper under the heading "Attractive Features."
2. What do you dislike about this ad? List your ideas on the same piece of paper under "Unattractive Features."
3. Write three ideas your classmate could use in her or his paragraph (examples: "The funny-looking old man in the ad is a real attention getter." "The ad wants us to think that Nike shoes are for strong, athletic women.")
4. Give your comments to your classmate.
5. Put your classmate's comments in your writing folder.

EXERCISE 10 **Creating an information chart**

Review the materials, notes, and classmate's comments in your writing folder. Then,

1. On separate paper, create four columns, one for each category in the example chart below.
2. In each column, list words or phrases that describe the ad you chose to write about. Ask yourself the questions listed in the chart to help you with specific details. Some sample answers for an ad for the cologne Eternity for Men have been completed for you.
3. Put the completed chart in your writing folder.

Information Chart			
Images	**Words**	**Stimuli**	**Layout**
(Who/What is in the ad? Objects? People? What are they doing?)	(Does the ad contain any words? What do they say? How do the words relate to the images?)	(What types of stimuli are used in the ad? Is the ad relevant to you? Surprising? Funny?)	(How are the images organized? Are they grouped together? What is the main focus of the ad? What is in the background?)

Images	Words	Stimuli	Layout
Example = a young, attractive man and a little boy, most likely his son	Example = your loved ones are the most important thing in life and beyond (Eternity)	Example = relevant stimuli. We all have someone we love—mom, dad, siblings, etc.	Example = the image of the man and son takes up two pages

EXERCISE 11   **Thinking about your readers**

Form a group with two other classmates. Then, on separate paper, answer these questions. Place your answers in your writing folder.

1. Who are your readers? That is, who is going to read your paragraph?
2. What are your readers like? Consider age, gender, education, and interests.
3. What do you think your readers already know about the ad?
4. What might your readers like to know about the ad?

EXERCISE 12   **Revising your chart**

Review your information chart. Add more words and phrases to each category to describe the ad more clearly for your readers.

○ Focusing and Organizing

> **Master Student Tip**
>
> Put Exercise 12 in your writing folder. Review the assignment occasionally as you plan and compose your paragraph to keep your readers in mind.

In the first step of the writing process, you collected information for Writing Assignment 1 through a variety of activities. In the second step, you will focus and organize your materials in preparation for writing the paragraph. This is an important stage in the writing process. By selecting your topic sentence, main points, and supporting details (evidence) carefully, you will write a more effective, well-organized paragraph.

SPOTLIGHT ON WRITING SKILLS

Topic Sentences

In an academic paragraph, the **topic sentence** is a general statement that announces the main idea of the whole paragraph. The **controlling ideas** in the topic sentence are words and phrases that direct and control the paragraph as in the "Armandi Jewelers" paragraph. Readers can ask questions about the controlling ideas that they expect will be answered in the paragraph. To write an effective paragraph, anticipate the questions your readers may ask. By answering these questions, you can explore the topic more deeply and provide support for your readers.

In Exercise 13, you will practice with a variety of topic sentences by identifying and asking questions about the controlling ideas. This practice will help you learn how to select ideas effectively.

EXERCISE 13   **Studying controlling ideas**

Read the following topic sentences about ads and advertising methods. Then,

1. Underline the topic and circle the controlling ideas.

2. With a small group of classmates, write WH- questions about each topic sentence that can help the writers develop their paragraphs (**who**, **what**, **where**, **when**, and **why**, as well as **how**, **how much**, **in what ways**). Write your questions below each topic sentence.

Example:

The Wrangler ad conveys the idea that blue jeans will never go out of style.

- **What** does the ad look like? **Who** is wearing the jeans in the ad?
- **How** does it give the idea that jeans will not go out of style?
- **Where**? All over the world? In the United States?
- **What** proof is there? Are statistics given in the ad?
- **Why** won't blue jeans go out of style?

1. The Nike ad shows a pretty model because beautiful people attract the readers' attention.

   _____

   _____

   _____

   _____

2. Ads that rely on images are more appealing than ads that contain a lot of written information.

   _____

   _____

   _____

   _____

3. Sometimes, the most successful advertisements are often the most annoying.

   _____

   _____

   _____

   _____

EXERCISE 14 **Selecting a topic sentence**

Review your information chart. Then,

1. Write three possible topic sentences for your paragraph, based on the details listed in your chart. Leave half a page under each topic sentence for questions.
2. Circle the controlling ideas in each of your topic sentences.
3. Under each topic sentence, write two or three WH- questions for each controlling idea, just as you did in Exercise 13. Leave some space under each question.
4. Identify supporting details in your information chart that answer your questions. List the details under each question. Add more details to your list if necessary.

5. Review your three topic sentences, the questions, and the supporting details. Highlight the topic sentence for which you have the strongest support. This will be the topic sentence for your paragraph.

6. Put your topic sentences, WH- questions, and information chart in your writing folder.

SPOTLIGHT ON WRITING SKILLS

Supporting Details

The **supporting details** provide proof (support) for the controlling ideas in the topic sentence. Why is this evidence necessary? Think about the "Armandi Jewelers" paragraph you read earlier in the chapter. After reading just the topic sentence, do you have a clear mental picture of the ad? Do you know exactly what the contrasting colors are? Can you understand why this ad would attract consumers? By the time you finish reading the paragraph, the supporting examples and details answer these questions, and you have formed a clearer idea of why the ad is effective.

A variety of supporting details is available to academic writers: **facts, expert opinions, examples, descriptions, observations, personal experiences**, and **explanations**. You can review some of these supporting details in the "Armandi Jewelers" paragraph and in the other student paragraphs in this chapter.

EXERCISE 15   Analyzing a paragraph

The paragraph that follows is an interesting, effective student paragraph written for Writing Assignment 1. Read the topic sentence, which is underlined. Then,

1. Circle the controlling ideas in the topic sentence (follow the "Armandi Jewelers" example).

2. Use the controlling ideas to write three questions you expect will be answered in the paragraph. Write the questions on separate paper.

3. Read the rest of the "Durable Jeans" paragraph. Then, answer the questions that follow the paragraph.

Durable Jeans

Topic Sentence

Evidence for Main

Point 1: _____

_____

_____

Evidence for Main

Point 2: _____

_____

_____

The Genuine Article ad is very attractive because it shows a simple, pleasant black and white photograph and a few convincing words. The ad shows an attractive image: a black and white photograph of three children jumping on a trampoline. Behind the children, we can see a little bit of the roof and the back of a house. In the background we can see a yard and some trees. The whole picture is very simple, and it has no colors in it, but the photograph of the children is very pleasant. The children are having fun, and they look healthy and happy. Under this image, on the right, the ad shows the brand of jeans, Genuine Article. On the left, a simple statement says that children are active and need durable clothes like the Genuine Article jeans. This is a straightforward message, and consumers will agree that children need sturdy clothes. Therefore, the Genuine Article marketers successfully capture the readers' attention with a simple but attractive ad.

4. What are the writer's main points? Circle them.
5. What types of supporting details (evidence) does the writer use? List them in the space provided next to the student paragraph.
6. Reread the three questions you wrote about the topic sentence. Were the questions answered by the paragraph? If not, do you still think the author has written a successful paragraph?

EXERCISE 16 Organizing evidence

Review your topic sentence, controlling ideas, and supporting details. Organize your material by completing the outline below. The controlling ideas from your topic sentence will be the main points in the body of the paragraph. Be sure to have at least two supporting details for each of your major points. Identify the categories of support you use.

Below is the way Hoang, the writer of "Durable Jeans," organized the evidence for her paragraph. Notice that Hoang used words and phrases, not complete sentences, to list her main points and supporting details.

Durable Jeans	Your paragraph
Topic Sentence: The Genuine Article ad is very attractive because it shows a simple, pleasant black and white photograph and a few convincing words.	**Your Topic Sentence:** _____ _____ _____ _____

A. Main Point 1: Pleasant image **Evidence:**
1. Physical Description: children jumping on trampoline, back of house, trees
2. Fact: Children playing
3. Observation: healthy, happy children having fun
	A. Main Point
	1: _____
	   Evidence:
	1: _____
	   _____
	2. _____
	   _____
	3. _____
	   _____

B. Main Point 2: Simple statement **Evidence:**
1. Summary of the caption
2. Observation: sturdy clothes for children
	B. Main Point
	2: _____
	   Evidence:
	1. _____
	   _____
	2. _____
	   _____
	3. _____
	   _____

Hoang did not have a third point. If you do, write your information on separate paper.	**C. Main Point** **3:** _____

W E B   P O W E R

To learn about descriptive words and phrases, go to the
website: **http://esl.college.hmco.com/students**.

○ Writing, Revising, and Editing

Experienced academic writers know they will follow the process of
writing and revising more than once. In this step of the writing process,
you will write the "rough draft" of your paragraph. Then, you will improve
your paragraph by **revising**. Revision means "looking again." For academic
writers, it means reading and rereading their writing and making changes
to improve it.

While revision focuses on the development, organization, and
structure of your paragraph, **editing** means correcting grammar, spelling,
and sentence structure errors. Editing is usually the last step of the
writing process.

Both experienced and inexperienced academic writers know what
they mean to say, so they cannot always see their weak points or language
errors. For this reason, **asking for a response** from readers is very
important. Since writing is a way to communicate with others, even
professional writers ask for feedback from friends, reviewers, and editors.
Asking readers for their opinions about the clarity and effectiveness of
your writing is a major step in the writing process. In this class, you will
receive feedback from your peers and your instructor. Keep an open mind,
and carefully consider their advice.

EXERCISE 17 Drafting your paragraph

*You have generated ideas and planned your paragraph. Now you are ready
to write a first draft of your paragraph about the ad's appeal.*

1. Write your topic sentence at the top of a piece of paper. (Did you
   remember to indent?)
2. Write each major point, and follow it with supporting details. As
   you write, think about what your readers need to know in order to
   "see" the ad. Remember that your purpose is to describe two or
   three ways the ad persuades the target audience. Use a variety of
   words and phrases (e.g., *luxurious, funny, very modern*) to describe
   the ad and create a clear image for the reader.

SPOTLIGHT ON WRITING SKILLS

The Concluding Sentence

In addition to having a topic sentence, main points, and supporting details, an effective academic paragraph usually has a **concluding sentence**. The closing or concluding sentence completes the paragraph by:

- Summarizing or restating the controlling idea
- Giving a recommendation, suggestion, or invitation
- Proposing a solution to a problem explained in the paragraph
- Making a prediction based on the paragraph's information

The "Armandi Jewelers" paragraph ends with a summary. Here are two other possible concluding sentences for that paragraph:

1. Thus, the contrasting colors and textures of the ad will attract consumers and probably bring new customers to the Armandi Jewelers store. (Prediction)
2. Therefore, people who can afford to buy jewelry should consider this ad and choose to shop at Armandi Jewelers. (Recommendation)

EXERCISE 18   **Writing a concluding sentence**

Reread your paragraph, and write a concluding sentence by using one of the four techniques for writing concluding sentences.

POWER GRAMMAR

Subjects and Verbs

Generalizations are statements that express broad ideas or opinions about a topic. The verbs in general statements are often in the simple present tense. Topic sentences are generalizations, so the verbs in topic sentences are also in the simple present tense. When using this tense, make sure each subject in your sentences agrees with its verb.

Consider the examples on the next page from the professional reading in this chapter. The *subjects* are in italics and underlined, and the **verbs** are in boldface.

Sentences	Explanations
No one really **expects** an answer to a rhetorical question.	*No one* is the subject. It is a singular pronoun, so the verb that relates to it ends in "s" (**expects**).
Novel *ads* also **command** attention.	*Ads* is the main subject. It is a plural noun, so the verb **command** does not not end with an *s*. The word *novel* describes the noun *ads*. Therefore, *novel ads* is the complete subject.
Familiar songs and popular entertainers **have** considerable ability to attract us in pleasant ways.	The complete subject of the sentence is *familiar songs and popular entertainers*, so the verb is plural (**have**).
One of the most powerful ways for a stimulus to be perceived as personally relevant **is** for it to appeal to your needs, values, or goals.	*One of the most powerful ways for a stimulus to be perceived as personally relevant* is the complete subject. The verb **is** refers to *one*, which is the main subject. Notice that the main subject and the verb are not close together in the example on the left. When descriptive words and phrases come between the subject and verb, the writer may forget to make the verb agree in number with the subject. To practice recognizing subjects and verbs, do the following exercise.

EXERCISE 19 **Studying subjects and verbs**

Circle the ⟨main subject⟩ and <u>underline</u> the verb in the following sentences. Some sentences have more than one subject and one verb. They are marked with an asterisk (*). If the subject and verb do not agree, correct the errors.

Example:

show

<u>Many</u> ⟨ads⟩ in magazines ~~shows~~ attractive young people.

1. Some marketers attempt to grab consumers' attention by using funny images.
2. Attractive young people often appears in perfume ads.
3. A surprising image in print advertisements attract readers.
4. *Many people read newspapers, but they do not pay attention to the print ads.
5. Some print ads catch readers' attention with bold colors.
6. The stimuli in the Coca-Cola ad is pleasant stimuli.
7. *My sister reads women's magazines all the time and look at all the ads.

EXERCISE 20 **Comparing information**

Share your answers with a classmate. Discuss the answers that differ. Which sentences in Exercise 19 were difficult for you? Why? Ask your instructor for help if you are confused or unsure about the subjects and verbs in the exercise.

WEB POWER

For more practice with subjects and verbs, go to the website **http://esl.college.hmco.com/students**.

EXERCISE 21 Revising and self-editing

Before asking others for feedback, academic writers review, revise, and edit their writing. They reread their writing, make decisions about improving their writing, edit their grammar, and correct their punctuation errors.

1. Reread your paragraph carefully, and look for words or ideas to revise. Ask yourself these questions:
   a. Do I need to add or change any details?
   b. Does my paragraph need to be organized differently?
   c. What unclear sentences or words do I need to improve or change?
2. Edit your grammar and correct your punctuation. Ask yourself these questions:
   a. Did I indent the first sentence of the paragraph?
   b. Did I capitalize after each period?
   c. Are all of my sentences complete?
   d. Did I use the simple present tense for the topic sentence?
   e. Do the verbs in the paragraph agree with their subjects?

EXERCISE 22 Working on peer response

Exchange your paragraph with one of your classmates. Use the form "Peer Response 1-1" (Appendix 1, p. 252) to give feedback about her or his paragraph.

1. When you are finished, return the paragraph and the response sheet to your classmate.
2. If you have questions about your classmate's response, ask your classmate.
3. Thank your classmate for the feedback.

EXERCISE 23 Writing the final draft

Reread your paragraph, and consider the peer response suggestions from your classmate:

1. Which suggestions will improve your writing?
2. What did you learn from reading your classmate's paragraph that can be applied to your writing? How can you incorporate her or his suggestions in your paragraph?
3. Rewrite your paragraph.
4. When you have completed your final draft, place it in a folder with your previous drafts, your classmate's feedback, and all the other materials you developed for Writing Assignment 1. Give the folder to your instructor.

EXERCISE 24 **Responding to instructor response**

When your instructor returns your paragraph, read her or his comments carefully:

1. What did your instructor like about your paragraph? List your strengths on an index card or a piece of paper.
2. What did he or she say you need to improve? List your weaknesses on the other side of the index card or paper. Keep the card or paper in your writing folder.
3. If you are confused about your instructor's feedback, circle the comments you don't understand. Make an appointment with your instructor or go to her or his office during office hours to ask for help. Remember to bring your writing folder with you.

POWER GRAMMAR

Speaking versus Writing

Grammatically, speaking and writing are different. If you wrote down a casual conversation with a friend, you would see the differences. Some typical characteristics of spoken and written English are listed below.

Spoken English	Written English
• incomplete sentences (*'cause I'm tired*)	• complete sentences (*I did not go to the party because I was tired*)
• many short, simple sentences (*I see, I'm sure*)	• many complex sentences (see pp. 38–39)
• many coordinating conjunctions (*and, but, so*)	• many dependent clauses (see pp. 38–39)
• more questions (?) and exclamations (!)	• more statements ending with periods (.)
• more personal pronouns (*I, we, you, they*)	• few personal pronouns
• more informal vocabulary (*kids, yeah, ok, y' know*)	• more formal vocabulary (*children, I agree with . . ., it is common knowledge that . . .*)
• use of contractions (*don't, I'm, can't*)	• no use of contractions (*do not, I am, cannot*)

Academic writing requires more formal written English. Usually, contractions are seldom used, and informal vocabulary is avoided. Do the exercises below to review some vocabulary differences between informal spoken English and more formal written English.

EXERCISE 25 Circling the errors

In each sentence, circle the underlined word or phrase that is more appropriate for academic writing. After you finish, compare answers with two classmates'.

Example:

Health magazines should <u>get rid of</u> / (remove) their food ads.

1. The Taco Bell ad shows <u>a bunch of</u> / <u>many</u> young people eating chicken soft tacos.

2. The Ferrari ad is <u>way cool</u> / <u>very striking</u>.

3. Marketers should not crowd their ads with too much written <u>stuff</u> / <u>information</u>.

4. Some ads are very eye-catching, but they advertise useless <u>junk</u> / <u>products</u>.

5. It is <u>OK</u> / <u>acceptable</u> to use attractive people in ads as long as they are appropriately clothed.

6. Little <u>kids</u> / <u>children</u> usually pay attention to ads that show toys or baby animals.

EXERCISE 26   **Identifying the errors**

The sentences below contain contractions, which are inappropriate in academic writing. Circle the contractions and write in the complete verb. Compare answers with one of your classmates.

Example:

should not

Clothing ads (shouldn't) show scantily dressed people.

1. The Genuine Article ad is very attractive, but it doesn't have any bright colors.

2. It's difficult to find a magazine that does not show any ads.

3. Many consumers can't afford the rings in the Armandi Jewelers ad.

4. Some very creative ads haven't been very successful.

5. Fast-food ads do not appeal to me if I'm not hungry.

6. Some ads aren't very attractive because they don't contain any eye-catching images.

WEB POWER

For more information about informal vs. formal English, and for more exercises, go to **http://esl.college.hmco.com/ students.**

Writing Assignment 2

Follow the three steps of the writing process (gathering information; focusing and organizing; drafting, revising, and editing) to write a paragraph in which you describe two or three marketing stimuli that result in an effective magazine or newspaper ad of your choice. Do not analyze the same ad you used for Writing Assignment 1.

(Focus of the assignment: *describe the effects of the stimuli*; paragraph development: *effects*)

Keep all the materials for this writing assignment in your writing folder as you did for the previous writing assignment. After you finish the assignment, give the folder to your instructor.

◯ Gathering Information

EXERCISE 27 **Analyzing the assignment**

With another classmate, discuss your answers to the following questions:

1. Who will read your paragraph?
2. What is the purpose of this assignment? What will you learn about academic writing by completing this assignment? What will your readers learn about advertising?
3. What does the assignment ask you to do? Circle the words in Writing Assignment 2 that give specific directions.
4. What else do you need to know about this assignment? (examples: When is the assignment due? Does it need to be typed, or can it be handwritten?)
5. How formal should your language be? Should you worry about using formal language and sentence structure?

EXERCISE 28 Listing ideas

What stimuli are used in the ad? What details relate to each stimulus? What else can you describe that can help your readers understand how the ad is effective? Answer these questions as you do the following:

1. List the different stimuli used in the ad.
2. Leave some space under each stimulus for details.
3. List supporting **details** under each stimulus.
4. **Select** the most relevant details for your paragraph.

If you prefer, you can use clustering instead of listing for this exercise. For an explanation of clustering, read the "Spotlight on Writing Skills" that follows this exercise.

This is how Ramona, who wrote about a Carl Jr.'s fast-food ad, listed some of her ideas. She selected ideas 1 and 2 for her paragraph because she had more supporting details for those. Notice that she used words and phrases, not complete sentences, to list her ideas.

Ramona's List of Ideas

Idea 1: Pleasant stimulus: appetizing food

Details: freshly baked bun, not soggy
well cooked, juicy meat patty
fresh, crisp lettuce
red, ripe tomato
crunchy white onion
melted cheese dripping over the meat patty

Idea 2: pleasant stimulus: attractive model

Details: healthy, with shiny brown hair and perfect skin
wearing make-up?
young, probably in her twenties
slender
her face and arms are thin, not chubby

Idea 3: personal relevance: I'm a student with a limited income
and limited time

Details: cheeseburger is inexpensive
affordable for students
quick meal

SPOTLIGHT ON WRITING SKILLS

Clustering

Some writers prefer to generate ideas by clustering them first before organizing them in a list. To cluster your ideas, begin with one central idea and use bubbles and arrows to connect it to related ideas and details. When you are finished, number your ideas in order of importance and cross out unimportant ideas or details. See how Mary clustered the ideas for her paragraph in the example that follows.

Notice that Mary crossed out *prominence* because she only had one supporting detail for this idea. She also crossed out other unimportant details.

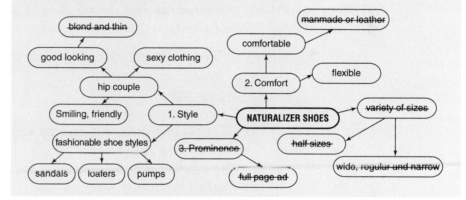

SPOTLIGHT ON WRITING SKILLS

Outlining

Outlining is not just a way to generate ideas; it is also a way to organize your ideas from general to specific. In outlining a paragraph, a writer begins with the most general statement, the topic sentence. Then, the writer lists the main points, which relate to the controlling ideas in the topic sentence. The main points are more specific than the topic sentence but are more general than the supporting details, which are the most specific part of the paragraph. These supporting details can be *facts, expert opinions, examples, descriptions, observations,* and *personal experiences.* Make sure to list all your supporting details in the outline.

Tina, a student who took this class, created the outline below for her paragraph. Notice how she refers to the controlling ideas in the main points and details.

Tina's Outline

<u>Topic sentence</u>: The Acura MDX ad effectively attracts readers with three
different stimuli.

<u>Main Point 1</u>: The ad uses surprising stimuli to attract readers.
  <u>Supporting details</u>:
    <u>Physical Description</u>
    The Acura surprisingly drives up the steep slope of a snow-
    capped mountain without any difficulty.
    The car does not have snow chains, and this is definitely
    unexpected because a car would normally have snow chains in
    a similar situation.
    <u>Example</u>
    My friend has this car and it really drives easily over hills
    and mountains.

<u>Main Point 2</u>: The ad also uses pleasant stimuli to attract the
              readers' attention.
  <u>Supporting details</u>:
    <u>Description</u>
    The body of the Acura is painted metallic silver.
    The sky is a deep azure.
    The weather is sunny above the misty clouds.
    <u>Personal experience (reaction)</u>
    When I first saw the ad, I really liked the color of the
    car and how it reflected the blue of the sky. It gave
    me a sense of freedom.

<u>Main Point 3</u>: The ad relies on prominent stimuli to make the Acura
              stand out.
  <u>Supporting details</u>:
    <u>Facts</u>
    The photo of the Acura is in color.
    The large photo of the mountain and the sky is in black
    and white.
    The small color photo is part of the larger photo.
    The color contrast between the two photos makes the
    car more noticeable.

<u>Concluding sentence</u>: The surprising, pleasant, and prominent stimuli in
                  this ad all combine to attract the readers'
                  attention.

✍ **EXERCISE 29** Creating an outline

Create an outline for the ideas you generated by listing or clustering. Write your topic sentence first, then your main points and supporting details, and finally your concluding sentence. After writing your outline, review it to make sure each of your controlling ideas is clear and well supported.

◯ Focusing and Organizing

EXERCISE 30 Developing paragraphs

The paragraph below was written by a student in response to Writing Assignment 2 and is about the effects of both pleasant and relevant stimuli in a Naturalizer shoes ad. Read the paragraph carefully, and then complete the steps that follow.

Naturalizer Shoes

Supporting details for Main Point 1 (pleasant stimuli):

Young, good looking

couple

_____

_____

_____

Supporting details for Main Point 2 (relevant stimuli):

_____

_____

_____

Concluding Sentence:

_____

_____

_____

The Naturalizer shoe ad uses two approaches to convince its customers to buy the shoes. First, the ad uses some pleasant stimuli to show that the shoes have style. In the first picture on the left side of the ad, a young, good-looking couple is dressed in fashionable clothes. Below this picture, three pictures of different shoes show potential buyers the variety available. The first picture shows a pair of elegant pumps, and the second picture shows a pair of trendy loafers. The last picture shows a pair of red sandals with chunky heels. The stylish photos are pleasant so that consumers interested in fashion will pay attention to the ad. Next, the ad makes the product relevant to consumers by describing how comfortable the shoes are. On the right side of the picture, the ad gives a description of the "Fit 4 U" system: 1) cushy padding; 2) flexibility; 3) softness; 4) perfect fit. Then, the ad describes each point. The cushy padding is for shock absorption while the sole flexibility allows easy foot movement. The softness of the upper shoe enhances flexibility, and the perfect fit is met by providing a variety of shoe sizes. This detailed description attracts those readers who want practical, comfortable shoes. As we have seen, the Naturalizer ad gets the attention of potential customers by focusing on the shoes' style and unique features.

1. <u>Underline</u> the subject and <u>double underline</u> the verb in the topic sentence in the paragraph on the previous page.
2. Circle the controlling ideas in the topic sentence.
3. Draw lines between each controlling idea in the paragraph and the sentences that support it.
4. In the left margin, list the supporting details for each main point as shown in the example.
5. Highlight the keywords and phrases that refer to the controlling ideas.
6. Which concluding technique does the writer use? Write it in the left margin of the paragraph, below the words "Concluding Sentence."
7. What have you learned about writing effective paragraphs by doing this exercise?

EXERCISE 31 Giving peer feedback

Exchange your listing or clustering and outline with one of your classmates. Then,

1. Answer these questions about your classmate's ideas on separate paper.
   a. Does the topic sentence clearly respond to Writing Assignment 2?
   b. Does the topic sentence state what the ad is about?
   c. Does the topic sentence have clear controlling ideas?
   d. Do the controlling ideas refer to the stimuli the ad uses to attract consumers?
   e. Does the outline mention two or three main points that refer to the controlling ideas?
   f. Does each main point have at least one supporting detail?
2. On the same paper, suggest one or two changes your classmate could make to her or his outline.
3. Give your suggestions to your classmate.
4. Read your classmate's suggestions carefully.
5. Ask questions about suggestions you do not fully understand.
6. Thank your classmate for her or his feedback.
7. Place your classmate's suggestions in your writing folder.

POWER GRAMMAR

Complex Sentences

Earlier in this chapter, you studied and discussed the differences between spoken and written English. In your academic writing, you will use more formal English. First, you will use appropriate vocabulary. Next, you will write complex sentences.

When you speak, you do not have to pay attention to sentence structure and punctuation because your listeners cannot "see" what you say. In addition, they can always ask you questions if they need clarification during a conversation. However, when you write, your readers have only your written language; you will not be there to answer their questions. Therefore, your sentences need to be clear and grammatically correct.

A **complex sentence** combines two or more clauses: at least an **independent clause** and a **dependent clause**, which is also called a **subordinate clause**.

Sentences	Explanations
(S) (V) **1.** Consumers pay attention to ads. (S) (V) **2.** Marketers will use beautiful women in their ads. (S) (V) **3.** Some marketers use surprising stimuli in magazine ads. (S) (V) **4.** Most consumers prefer colorful ads.	An **independent clause (IC)** is a group of words with at least a subject (S) and a verb (V), and it expresses a complete idea or thought.

Sentences	Explanations

1. ... when they contain the word SALE.
 	
2. If they want to attract a male audience, ...
 	
3. ... because they want to grab the readers' attention.
 	
4. While a few consumers prefer black and white ads, ...
	A **dependent clause (DC)** is a group of words with at least a subject and a verb, but it is **not** a complete sentence. DCs are used by writers to show that they are less important than ICs in sentences. That is, DCs provide additional information and ideas, but they do not provide the most important information or ideas in the sentence.
	
	    DCs often begin with a word that makes them less important. Here are some of those "dependent" words, which are called **subordinating conjunctions:**
	
	since *because*
	although *after*
	before *while*
	when *until*
	if *unless*
	
	    Notice that often a DC can become an IC if the first (dependent) word is removed.

1. Consumers pay attention to ads **when** they contain the word SALE. 2. If they want to attract a male audience, marketers will use beautiful women in their ads. 3. Some marketers use surprising stimuli in magazine ads **because** they want to grab the readers' attention. 4. **While** a few consumers prefer black-and-white ads, most consumers prefer colorful ads.	For a DC to be complete, it needs to be connected to an IC. For example, if you connect the four dependent clauses to the independent clauses listed in this chart, their meaning becomes clearer (the DC's are underlined). Notice that the DC can come before or after the IC. **When** the DC comes before the IC, it is followed by a comma. Notice the **dependent words** in boldface that begin the DCs.

EXERCISE 32 **Identifying dependent clauses**

With a classmate, underline the DCs in the sentences that follow. Remember that a DC starts with a "dependent word" (see list in the previous Grammar Power box) and can come before or after an IC.

1. When marketers use attractive people in print ads, consumers are more likely to notice the ads.

2. Many marketers use colorful print ads because they want to attract the readers' attention.

3. If an ad contains written information and no images, readers probably will not notice it.

4. The Carl Jr.'s ad shows a woman eating a cheeseburger while the 7-Up ad shows a woman drinking a soda.

5. Unless people complain about the number of ads in newspapers and magazines, marketers will increasingly rely on print ads to advertise their products.

6. The Genuine Article ad is very attractive even though its only image is a black-and-white photograph.

EXERCISE 33 **Finding dependent clauses**

With two or three classmates, underline all the DCs in the paragraph below. The first DC has been identified for you.

1. To help you identify the DCs, circle the dependent word at the beginning of each DC: **although, even though, when, because, if.** Remember that a DC can come before or after an IC.

2. **After** you finish, compare your paragraphs with two classmates'. Did you underline the same clauses? Discuss any differences. **If** you are not sure about the clauses you underlined, ask the instructor for help. (Did you notice the DCs in these directions?)

Carl Jr.'s Cheeseburgers

The Carl Jr.'s ad uses two pleasant stimuli to tempt young consumers, an appetizing cheeseburger and a sexy young woman. The cheeseburger is big and looks very appetizing <u>**while** the meat appears to be well cooked and nicely browned</u>. Although the meat patty is well done, it looks juicy. The lettuce, onion, and tomato look fresh, and the melted cheese is dripping over the meat patty. This suggests the idea that the cheese is still hot and the cheeseburger has just been assembled. With this image, the ad succeeds in making the cheeseburger look delicious. The second pleasant stimulus in the ad is the gorgeous model eating the cheeseburger. In the ad, she is about to take a big bite out of the sandwich. Even though she is eating a huge cheeseburger, she appears to be healthy and slender. This image gives the message to young women like me that we can eat a lot and still look great. Many people gain weight when they eat fast food on a regular basis, but the ad does not show that. It only shows the beautiful model because she is very attractive and creates a positive image about eating at Carl Jr.'s. Also, the attractive model appeals to young men because they like to eat at fast-food places and meet attractive young women. The ad seems to suggest to young men that they'll meet good-looking women if they eat at Carl Jr.'s. Thus, the Carl Jr.'s ad is very successful at targeting young people by using pleasant stimuli.

W E B   P O W E R

For more information and practice with DCs and ICs, go to
http://esl.college.hmco.com/students.

○ Writing, Revising, and Editing

EXERCISE 34 Drafting your paragraph

Reread Writing Assignment 2, your prewriting, and your outline. Then,

1. Consider the feedback from your classmate, and revise your outline.
2. Draft your paragraph by following your revised outline. Be sure to explain clearly how the ad effectively attracts consumers. Give many details.
3. Check your draft for formal academic vocabulary and complex sentences. Make sure your paragraph has at least three complex sentences.

EXERCISE 35 Responding to paragraphs

For this exercise, work with two classmates. Make two copies of your paragraph, one for each member of your group. Use the form "Peer Response 1-2" (Appendix 2, p. 254).

EXERCISE 36 Revising and self-editing

Review the feedback you received during peer reviews. Make changes to your paragraph to improve its communication for the reader. Check your sentence structure. Check the spelling, punctuation, and capitalization.

EXERCISE 37 Responding to instructor's response

After your instructor hands back your paragraph, read your instructor's comments. If one or more comments seem confusing to you, go to your instructor's office during office hours or make an appointment with her or him to discuss your paragraph.

EXERCISE 38 Writing the final draft

Write the final draft of your paragraph if your instructor requires it. Place your paragraph in your writing folder. Include your prewriting, peer feedback, and all previous drafts. Give the folder to your instructor.

EXERCISE 39 **Reviewing chapter objectives**

Review the objectives at the beginning of this chapter, and complete the checklist. Which objectives do you still need to work on? Discuss with a friend or a classmate how you will improve in these areas.

○ Additional Writing Assignment for More Practice and Assessment

Write a paragraph in which you compare and contrast two or three major stimuli used in two print ads of your choice. The ads must compare similar products, for example two brands of soft drinks, two sports cars, or two perfumes. Decide which ad is more effective than the other.

(Focus of the assignment: *Describe the stimuli*; paragraph development: *Compare/Contrast*)

Use the three-step writing process to develop and organize the ideas for your paragraph.

Keep all the materials you develop for this writing assignment in a writing folder. Turn in your writing folder to your instructor after you finish the assignment.

○ Gathering Information

EXERCISE 40 **Making a comparison chart**

Choose two print ads for your comparison paragraph. Then, create a chart similar to the one on the next page. For each stimulus, list the corresponding details. Then,

1. Review your chart.
2. Circle three of the most important ⬭similarities.⬭
3. Bracket three of the most important [differences].
4. At the bottom of the chart, write which ad you prefer and why.
5. Place your chart in your writing folder.

This example chart shows some ideas about two different cake mixes made by Duncan Hines. Each ad shows a cake in the top half of the ad, and an attractive model in the lower half of the ad, so the models appear to be wearing the cakes on their heads. In one ad, the model has a light complexion and wears a white cake; in the other ad, the model has a dark complexion and wears a chocolate cake.

Ad 1 (Chocolate Cake)	Ad 2 (White Cake)
Relevant Stimuli A young woman with a dark complexion wearing a chocolate cake as a hat. I have a dark complexion, and I am in my early twenties, like the model in the ad. I also like chocolate cake!	**Relevant Stimuli** A young woman with a pale complexion wearing a cake as a hat. She is about my age or a little older. I don't care for white cakes (angel food or coconut).
Pleasant Stimuli A beautiful dark-skinned woman Her hair is dark brown, curly, most of it pulled back Her lips are full, but she doesn't seem to be wearing dark lipstick Her eye makeup is very dark She has a serious expression on her face She is facing the camera, but her body is turned away Elegant photo	**Pleasant Stimuli** A beautiful fair-skinned woman Her hair is dark brown, straight and long She is wearing dark lipstick that makes her lips look like the cherry on top of the cake Her eye makeup is very light She looks serious, not smiling She is facing the camera Hip photo, not as elegant as Ad 1
Surprising Stimuli The cake worn by the model as a hat Model is not smiling, as if wearing a cake is a normal thing	**Surprising Stimuli** Same as Ad 1 Her lips are a bit strange because of the cherry shape. Reminds me of Japanese geishas The model looks serious, just like the model in Ad 1
Easy to Access Stimuli Clearly the ad stands out because of the unusual image Nothing else clutters the photograph. The Duncan Hines logo takes very little space, just a tiny corner in the upper right side of the ad	**Easy to Access Stimuli** Same as Ad 1 Color contrast is more prominent in Ad 2 Cake stands out more

○ Focusing and Organizing

SPOTLIGHT ON WRITING SKILLS

Compare and Contrast

The purpose of a comparison and/or contrast paragraph is to show how two ideas, persons, or things are alike or different. By **comparing** two ideas, persons, or things, the writer shows how they are **similar** in one or more ways. By **contrasting** two ideas, persons, or things, the writer shows how they are **different** in some way or ways.

Generally, in academic writing the word *comparison* is used to mean both comparison and contrast. For instance, if the writing assignment asks you to "Compare the authors' points of view in these two articles," it is telling you to find similarities (compare) and differences (contrast) between the two points of view.

The two ways of organizing comparison and/or contrast paragraphs are as follows:

1. **Discuss first one (A) and then the other (B).**

   Topic Sentence about A and B:

   > The Duncan Hines ads are very attractive, but the ad for the white cake mix is more striking than the other because of its color contrast.

   - Give all the information about A, point by point (the ad for the white cake mix).
   - Give all the information about B (the ad for the chocolate cake mix). Arrange the information, point by point, in the same order as for A.

2. **Discuss both A and B point by point.**

   Topic Sentence about A and B:

   > The Duncan Hines ads are very attractive, but the ad for the white cake mix is more striking than the other because of its color contrast.

- Point 1 about both A and B (both ads show an attractive model)

- Point 2 about A and B (ad A shows a model with a lighter skin tone; ad B shows a model with a darker skin tone)

- Point 3 (ad A shows a more striking color contrast than ad B)

Use sentence connectors when writing a comparison and/or contrast paragraph. Examples of connectors are listed below.

To Introduce Comparison	**To Introduce Contrast**
Compared to ————,	However,
In much the same way,	In contrast,
Similarly,	On the other hand,

In the student example below, notice the paragraph organization. The connectors are underlined.

Duncan Hines Ads

Topic Sentence (topic + **controlling ideas**)

Description of both ads.

All about B: simpler, no color contrast. Details: dark skin tone, dark cake, moist lips, moist cake.

All about A: color contrast. Details: red lips, cherry on top of cake, model's dark hair.

Concluding sentence

The <u>Duncan Hines ads</u> are **very attractive**, but the ad for the **white cake mix** (A) **is more striking** than the other ad (B) because of the **color contrast**. Each ad shows a model wearing a cake on the head. Ad A shows a pale-skinned model wearing a white cake, and ad B shows a dark-skinned model wearing a chocolate cake. Both of the Duncan Hines ads are effective print ads because they appeal to readers who like cakes and readers who are attracted to beautiful models too. Ad B is elegant but simpler because it does not use color contrast as much as ad A. Ad B relies on the natural skin tone of the model, and it includes dark tones to look like chocolate and appeal to consumers. The model's moist lips remind readers of a moist chocolate cake, and this makes the ad appealing. However, ad A is more noticeable than ad B because it has color contrast. The model's dark lipstick is similar to the red cherry at the top of the white cake. The model's dark straight hair makes her face and the cake stand out. The color contrast helps draw attention to the cake without taking away from the beauty of the face. Therefore, ad A is more prominent and effective than ad B even though they both rely on attractive models.

EXERCISE 41 **Writing a topic sentence**

Write a topic sentence that states the main idea of your paragraph. (See the examples below for paragraphs about the Duncan Hines ads.)

_____

_____

Examples:

1. The Duncan Hines ads are very attractive, but the ad for the white cake mix is more striking than the other ad because of the color contrast.
2. Although both Duncan Hines ads are equally effective, the ad for the chocolate cake mix has a stronger visual impact.
3. The Duncan Hines ad for the chocolate cake mix looks more sophisticated and eye-catching than the ad for the white cake mix.

EXERCISE 42 **Developing an outline**

Choose one of the two methods of paragraph development for your compare/contrast paragraph. Create an outline based on your topic sentence. Use the chart below as a model.

Outline A	Outline B
topic sentence	topic sentence
all about A	point 1 for A and B
all about B	point 2 for A and B
	point 3 for A and B

○ Writing, Revising, and Editing

 EXERCISE 43 Drafting your paragraph

Follow your outline to write your comparison paragraph. Use appropriate sentence connectors to compare and contrast the two ads.

 EXERCISE 44 Revising and editing

Follow the steps you used for Writing Assignment 2 to revise and self-edit your paragraph. Then,

1. Ask a classmate or a friend to read your paragraph and suggest improvements.
2. Reread your paragraph, and use your classmate's suggestions to revise it.
3. Write the final draft of your paragraph, and place it in your writing folder. Give the folder to your instructor for feedback.

> **WEB POWER**
>
> You will find additional exercises related to the content in this chapter at http://esl.college.hmco.com/students.

Evaluating Web Design

In Chapter 1, you reviewed the five basic paragraph types used in most college writing, and you learned about the three steps of the writing process: (1) gathering information, (2) focusing and organizing, and (3) writing, revising, and editing.

In this chapter, you will use the writing process to write a two-page expository essay (approximately 500 words) in which you evaluate the design features of commercial websites. Web design has become very important as more and more companies rely on the Internet as one way to introduce their products to consumers.

Chapter Objectives

Review this chapter's objectives before you start. Return to this chart after completing the chapter and check (3) the appropriate box to the right.	I have learned this well.	I need to work on this.
Become familiar with authentic college writing assignments		
Use the three-step writing process introduced in Chapter 1		
Learn the structure of an effective academic (explaining) essay: **1.** Introduction and thesis statement **2.** Background paragraph **3.** Body paragraphs **4.** Conclusion		
Learn about commercial website design		
Develop Web evaluation criteria		
Gather information by using the World Wide Web		
Summarize information about Web design		
Organize your essay by using an essay map		
Write a "working thesis"		
Select and organize supporting evidence for your body paragraphs		
Write a well-developed academic essay with an introduction, a thesis statement, body paragraphs, and a conclusion		
Learn a variety of concluding techniques		
Use in-text citations (quotation) and provide citation information by following APA format		
Write end-of-text references according to APA format		
Understand the grammar of quotations		
Respond to and evaluate other students' essays about effective webpages		

Essay Assignments

The **explaining essay** is an extended piece of writing that explains an idea, a project, or a process. Explaining papers are often between two and four pages long (500–1000 words), but they can be much longer, depending on the assignment and the class level. Academic writing assignments usually require students to explain *what*, *how*, and/or *why*.

Below are some real essay questions from introductory college courses:

1. **Political Science:** Write a two-page essay that **describes the ways** a candidate's stand on the legalization of drugs **might affect** her or his chances in an election this spring.

   [Explain *what* (ways); paragraph development = **effects of candidate's stand**]

2. **Civil Engineering:** In countries with a high degree of government control of the economy, the use of state companies or authorities for infrastructure management is common. One example is a state-owned electricity company such as Electricité de France or Eletrobras (Brazil). **Discuss** the **potential advantages and disadvantages** of privatizing these companies.

   [Explain *what* (advantages and disadvantages); paragraph development = **comparison and contrast of advantages and disadvantages**]

3. **Economics:** Is it **feasible** to make the Russian ruble a convertible currency? **Why or why not?** Write a two- to three-page response.

   [Explain *why/why not* (feasibility); paragraph development = **causes/reasons for converting currency**]

**Master
Student Tip**

▼ For a review
of the different
paragraph types,
go to Chapter 1.

EXERCISE 1 **Analyzing real writing assignments**

*With two classmates, read the following authentic explaining essay
assignments and identify the following:*

1. What WH- questions (*what*, *how*, or *why*) the students must answer
   to complete each assignment

2. What method of paragraph development is required by each
   assignment

   a. **Modern U.S. History:** What were President Truman's other
      options regarding the war in the Pacific? What would have been
      the impacts and reasons supporting those options?

   b. **Agriculture:** As the manager of a cattle operation, you have
      found Brucellosis in your herd. Write a two-page report that
      explains the means of eradicating this disease and preventing
      its occurrence.

   c. **Adolescent Psychology:** Examine the statistics of student
      cheating in high schools and then discuss the reasons why
      students cheat in school.

   d. **History of Science:** Place Darwinism in a contemporary light
      examining some of the contemporary theoretical debates
      pertaining to the evolutionary theory, such as selection vs. drift,
      punctuated equilibrium theory, the reemergence of
      catostrophism, or the units of selection controversy.

   e. **Food Science:** Discuss the relationship of fatty acids and/or
      cholesterol to heart disease or cancer. Select specific fatty acids.

Chapter Essay Assignment

Select and describe three or four characteristics of an effective commercial webpage and compare and contrast two commercial webpages that advertise two brands of the same product. Explain which one is more effective and why.

As you did in Chapter 1, keep all the materials, drafts, and peer reviews for this assignment in your **writing folder**. Bring your writing folder to class every time, unless otherwise instructed.

To complete this assignment, you need to:

- Complete an Internet search
- Select three or four characteristics of a successful commercial website
- Select two commercial websites to evaluate
- Write an essay by following a three-step writing process

Your essay must include:

- An introductory paragraph
- A background paragraph
- Two or three additional body paragraphs
- A concluding paragraph
- Two in-text references (one for each website)

Master Student Tip

 If you are unsure about any of the information above, consult your instructor.

EXERCISE 2 **Analyzing the chapter assignment**

With three classmates, analyze this chapter's essay assignment. Discuss the following:

1. What is the purpose of this assignment?
2. What level of formality is appropriate for this assignment? For example, is it acceptable to use slang or contractions?
3. How will your instructor evaluate the assignment?
4. What questions (*what, how,* and/or *why*) will you answer in your essay in response to the essay assignment? (*Hint:* Underline the words in the assignment that tell you what to do.)
5. What concerns or questions do you have about this assignment?
6. Share your answers with another small group of classmates.

SPOTLIGHT ON WRITING SKILLS

The Explaining Essay

Academic writing assignments often require students to write a two-to three-page typed and double-spaced explaining essay. An essay of that length usually contains an introductory paragraph, a background paragraph, two or more body paragraphs, and a concluding paragraph. Most academic writing has a similar framework. Longer assignments have more body paragraphs and somewhat longer paragraphs.

Most explaining essays also require students to cite information from print or online sources. The sources cited in an essay are usually listed on a separate page titled "References." In this book, each student example that cites sources is followed by a reference list.

Below is a visual framework for most academic explaining essays of two to three pages. Notice the similarities and differences between the essay structure and the body paragraph structure (which you also reviewed in Chapter 1).

[centered; important words capitalized]

[length of introduction: about 50–75 words]

[length of background paragraph: 125–175 words]

[each topic sentence relates to one or more ideas in the thesis]

Title of the Essay

Introduction

- A general introduction of the topic to the reader
- A small amount of information about the topic that will interest the reader
- The thesis statement (the main idea of the <u>essay</u>)

Background Paragraph (immediately follows the introduction)

- Necessary information about the topic; for example,
  - a brief history of an object or idea or issue
  - definitions of key terms about the topic
- Explanation of why and/or how you researched the topic
  - describes a survey you designed/administered
  - describes an interview you designed/conducted

[each body
paragraph explains,
defines, and/or
illustrates one or
more ideas in the
topic sentence]

[length of each
body paragraph:
125–175 words]

[length of
conclusion: about
50–75 words]

Body Paragraphs (2–4 total): Each contains:

- A topic sentence (the main idea of the paragraph)
  - 1–3 sentences about main points (each relates to one of
    the ideas in the topic sentence)
  - evidence and support for each main point
    (facts, examples, descriptions, personal experience, expert
    opinions)

- a concluding sentence

Conclusion (summarizes, predicts, recommends, and/or offers
a solution)

EXERCISE 3 Evaluating essay structure

*With three or four classmates, read Vera's essay below. Cover the notes in
the right margin of the essay with a ruler or a piece of paper. Then,
complete the steps that follow.*

Bridal Shoes Websites

The main topic
(wedding shoes
websites) is
introduced in the
first sentence.
"Attention-grabber":
her sister's story.

The introduction
gradually leads to the
thesis statement.

Thesis Statement:
the most specific
sentence in the
introduction. For the
websites you
evaluate, give the
URL in an in-text
citation.

    Last week, I went on the World Wide Web to look for
wedding shoes. It all started because of my sister. Her wedding
day was getting closer every day. Almost everything was ready.
She had her dress, tiara, and wedding veil; however, she had not
found the "right" wedding shoes. I wanted to help my sister, so I
went on the Internet, and I found hundreds of websites
advertising wedding shoes. How could I choose the best shoes
among so many? I thought carefully about the criteria I needed
to use to evaluate the website carefully. After I developed my
criteria, I went on a "website hunt." After some work, I narrowed
down my search to two websites: Bridal Shoes, Website A
(bridalshoes.com), and Bridal People, Website B
(bridalpeople.com). In the end, I decided that Website A had
better images, clearer organization, and easier text than the other
website.

Bridal Shoes Websites (cont.)

<table>
<tr>
<td>

Topic Sentence: the most general sentence in the paragraph.

Background Paragraph:

1. Description of Web search process
2. Definition and reason for each criterion

</td>
<td>

After I selected the evaluation criteria, it was easy to select the right websites. To find all the websites about bridal shoes I went to *google.com*. In the search space I typed "wedding shoes," and I clicked on the search button. Then I saw hundreds of websites about bridal shoes. I looked at the top 10 websites and chose the two websites that fitted my criteria the most. The reason I chose images as one of my criteria is that pictures help to evaluate a product. In fact, one Internet source stated, "The right picture or image can instantly convey the fundamental qualities that make your product or service better than your competition" ("Effective Website," 2002). The other criterion I selected is organization because the way the images are presented and grouped together helps in navigating the website. The text is also very important in a website because if the product descriptions are difficult to read, then it is hard to get the necessary information. Therefore, images, organization and text are the criteria that helped me choose Website A as the best website.

</td>
</tr>
<tr>
<td>

Body Paragraph 2

1. Description and evaluation of A's images
2. Contrast with B and evidence about "other products" on B
3. Description and evaluation of A's colors
4. Contrast with B and evidence of distracting colors on B
5. B's NEW!
6. A's easy-to-focus page

</td>
<td>

In fact, Website A had very nice images that grabbed my attention. Images are very important on a website. I saw shoes of all kinds, with high heels, medium heels, low heels; sandals, boots and more. The photographic images were very nice and detailed. Website B had many photographs too, but some of the images did not include shoes, and it was confusing to see other products on the page for shoes. For example, photos of dresses, tiaras and veils were shown along with the photos of shoes. In addition, Website A had a blue background that made the images stand out and contrasted well with the purple text. On the other hand, Website B had many colors: green, blue, red, purple and brown. All the colors distracted me from the images. Also, Website B had the word NEW that changed colors and made the website look too busy whereas Website A did not have any scrolling images or text, so it was easier to focus on the page.

</td>
</tr>
</table>

Bridal Shoes Websites (cont.)

Body Paragraph 3:

1. Description and
   evaluation of A's
   layout
2. A's clean look and
   options
3. Contrast with B
4. B's messy look

Concluding sentence

Body Paragraph 4:

1. Reference to
   research
2. Description and
   evaluation of A's
   font (cursive),
   boldfacing,
   underlining, and
   captions
3. Contrast with B.

Concluding sentence

Conclusion:
Summary of the
essay's main idea

Prediction

   Another aspect that made Website A more effective was its organization. All the important information was given in a few clear words on the left side of the page. That made a favorable impression because the Website gave details without too much text. Furthermore, the shoe images were all placed in the middle of the page so that customers could spot the product they wanted right away. Also, the lack of distracting information and images about other products made the site look cleaner and better organized than Website B. In addition, Website A had many options (links, search, tips, order/shipping and FAQ's) all at the bottom of the webpage. Instead, Website B had some options at the top and some on the right of the page, and this type of organization looked very messy and confusing. Therefore, Website A had a much better overall organization than Website B.

   Besides the organization, Website A also had better text. The article "Five Tips for Effective Websites" mentioned that text "should be clear and concise. Overall color of text and images should be a balanced contrast" ("Five Tips," 2000). Website A achieved this contrast by using cursive. This font seems more appropriate for wedding products since it is more old-fashioned and romantic. In addition, Website A had bold and underlined words that attracted the customers to the most important products and discounts. Finally, the captions were brief and easy to understand. On the contrary, Website B used print and bolded every heading, so it was difficult to tell what information was more important. The captions were difficult and sometimes too technical. Thus, Website B's text was overall inferior to Website A's text.

   In conclusion, it was challenging to identify the right criteria for judging the websites. However, taking the time to evaluate the websites carefully helped me find the perfect shoes for my sister. By looking at the images, organization, and text I was able to find the best website, Bridal Shoes. When I get married, I will use this website to buy my wedding shoes.

The word *References* is centered.

All entries are double-spaced. After the first line, each entry is indented by 5–7 spaces.

List websites in alphabetical order.

Include the date when you retrieved the information.

No period at the end of the URL (web address).

References

Bridal people website. (2004). Retrieved October 9, 2004 from
        http://www.bridalpeople.com

Bridal shoes website. (2004). Retrieved October 9, 2004
        from http://www.bridalshoes.com

Five tips for effective websites. (2000). *White Clay Multimedia*.
        Retrieved October 15, 2004 from http://www.wcmmc.com/
        wcmmc/5tips.htm

Making an effective website. (n.d.). *Dragonscale Design*. Retrieved
        October 9, 2004 from http://www.dragonscale.com/
        useful/effective.html

1. On separate paper, draw two columns to compare the essay and paragraph **structures**. How is the overall explaining essay structure similar to the structure of a single body paragraph? (*Hint*: Think about their parts and what each part does.) Write the similarities in the right column.

2. How are the two structures (paragraph and essay) different? List the differences in the left column.

3. Discuss why the introduction and the conclusion in the academic essay are shorter than the background and body paragraphs. (*Hint*: Think about supporting evidence.)

4. Then, read the notes in the right-hand margin. What do you learn from them about essay structure and essay organization? Add the information to your list.

5. Ask your instructor for help if you are confused about steps 1 through 4 in this exercise.

○ Gathering Information

Before evaluating Web design in your essay, you need to learn more about this topic. The exercises below will help you recall what you already know, learn more about Web design, and select the Web evaluation criteria you will use in your essay.

EXERCISE 4   **Writing first impressions**

Freewrite for five minutes about the websites you usually browse on the Internet. What websites do you like? What design qualities make them appealing?

EXERCISE 5   **Comparing ideas**

Discuss your freewriting with two or three classmates. Then,

1. Look at the website on the first page of this chapter. Do you find it attractive and/or interesting? Why or why not?
2. Share your answers with another group. Do you agree or disagree with the judgments of that group? Why?

SPOTLIGHT ON WRITING SKILLS

Evaluation

You practice the skill of evaluating every day: "<u>Nice</u> shirt." "That movie was <u>awful</u>!" "I <u>love</u> chocolate chip cookies." "<u>Excellent</u> website."

To make these judgments, you unconsciously develop a set of characteristics and judge those qualities positively or negatively. For example, in an evaluation of three brands of chocolate chip cookies, you would do the following:

1. Select three brands, all without nuts (they should be as similar as possible).
2. Select three to five **characteristics** by which you will judge the chocolate chip cookies, such as
   a. cost per serving,
   b. number of chocolate chips in each cookie,
   c. level of sweetness, and
   d. texture.

The characteristics you select are called **criteria** (singular = criterion).

3. Select three to five **evaluative words** to judge each of the characteristics you selected as positive or negative, such as
   a. cost per serving:
      - too expensive
      - not too expensive
      - inexpensive
   b. texture:
      - soft
      - average
      - crunchy
      - very crunchy

When a writing assignment requires you to evaluate something, it is important to establish specific criteria. Here is a list written by Katie, a student in this course, to compare the websites of two famous soft drink brands, Coca-Cola and Pepsi.

Katie's List
  Websites: Coca-Cola and Pepsi
  Product: Cola
  Reason for choosing this product: I am a big soda fan! I drink it every day.

Criterion 1: Layout
  Definition: How the website is set up and designed for functional purposes.
  Reason: The websites should be clearly formatted.

Criterion 2: Graphics
  Definition: The artistic quality of the design, including images and animation.
  Reason: The page should be visually appealing.

Criterion 3: Informative
  Definition: The website should have information relevant to the product advertised.
  Reason: Users should be able to learn as much as possible about the product so that they can make an informed choice.

Criterion 4: Easy to Use

   Definition: The information on the website is easy to find, so even those who do not use the Internet often can find it.

   Reason: If the website has plenty of information but is difficult for the user to find, what is the point of having a website?

EXERCISE **6** **Analyzing Katie's list**

Answer the questions below on separate paper. At the end of the exercise, put the paper in your writing folder.

1. Which of Katie's criteria is most interesting? Could you use it in your essay?
2. Which of Katie's criteria seems the least interesting for a reader? Why?
3. Katie defines four criteria in her outline. Two of her definitions are complete sentences, and two are not. Which of Katie's definitions are incomplete sentences? Highlight or underline them. (*Hint*: Remember that a complete sentence can stand alone and has at least one subject and one verb.)
4. How can Katie's incomplete sentences be made into complete sentences? Revise them.
5. How can studying Katie's list help you with your essay?

SPOTLIGHT ON WRITING SKILLS

Web Evaluation Criteria

You have already begun gathering information for your essay by briefly evaluating two websites and by reviewing Katie's list of criteria. Now, continue to gather information by reading what experts write about Web design. The excerpt below about Web evaluation criteria comes from an Internet page that discusses Web design. The two lists of criteria include *CARP* (contrast, alignment, repetition, and proximity) and *TILT* (text, images, links, and tables).

Web Evaluation Criteria

CARP — This evaluation concept was developed by Robin Williams and John Tollett and is a major component in their book, *The Non-Designer's Web Book.*

(C) *Contrast* is what draws your eyes into a page. The contrast might be type that is bolder, bigger, or a very different style. It might be different colors, graphic signposts, or a spatial arrangement. To be effective, contrast must be strong. A key component when evaluating contrast is to determine the focal point or main dominating feature of the page.

(A) *Alignment* simply means that the items on the page are lined up with each other. Some pages align to the left, others to the right, and still more are centered on the page. Beware of sites that mix alignments throughout their pages.

(R) *Repetition* refers to the repeated elements that unify the website. Each page in a website should look like it belongs to the same website and portrays the same concepts. Repetition is what makes this happen.

(P) *Proximity* refers to the relationships that objects develop when they are close together, in close proximity. When objects are placed close together, they appear to have a relationship, and the opposite is also true. When two items are separated by space, they appear to have no relationship to each other.

Another concept that is very useful when evaluating websites is the *TILT* concept, developed by Jeff Peach.

(T) *Text* refers to the size, color, font, and font style, which are all contributing factors of Web design. The majority of information on most webpages is still delivered through text. The qualities of the text are an important component to the website.

(I) *Images* are essential to our visually oriented society. More and more websites are incorporating pictures and images. The placement, size, format, and resolution of the images are important components in website design.

(L) *Links*, or more specifically hyperlinks, can be located anywhere on a webpage. A picture, image, or string of text can be set to be a hyperlink. Hyperlinks tell the Web browser to connect to another site or folder and either display another webpage or download a file. Links are what allows users to navigate a website.

(T) *Tables* allow web designers to organize and group information. The use of tables has also developed into a tool that plays a major factor in page design.

Web Evaluation Criteria (cont.)

References

Williams, R. & Tollett. J. (2000). *The non-designer's web book.*
Second Edition. Peachpit Press: Berkley, CA.

Peach. J. (2001). TILT. A simple approach to web design. Retrieved
from California State University, Sacramento website August
29, 2001 http://www.csus.edu/indiv/p/peachj/edte230/
activites/tilt/tilt.htm

WEB POWER

You will find more information about Web design
terminology at **http://esl.college.hmco.com/students**.

EXERCISE 7 Marking the text

Reread the CARP and TILT lists. Then,

1. Underline or highlight any words that are unfamiliar to you in the two lists.
2. Write at least two questions or comments in the margins about the unfamiliar words.
3. Discuss the lists with two classmates, and ask about the unfamiliar words. If your classmates cannot help you with the unfamiliar words, ask your instructor for help.
4. Take notes about your discussion and keep them in your writing folder.

EXERCISE 8 Selecting evaluation criteria

Number each criterion in the combined CARP and TILT lists in order of importance. Then,

1. Write your first three choices on separate paper.
2. On the same paper, explain why you chose these criteria.
3. Compare your criteria with a classmate's. Did you choose the same criteria from the reading? Why or why not?
4. Place your answers to this exercise in your writing folder.

SPOTLIGHT ON WRITING SKILLS

Summarizing

Summarizing is retelling something in fewer words. We summarize all the time in our everyday life: when we quickly retell a movie plot to a friend, when we go over our qualifications during a job interview, or when at a party we sum up the highlights of our latest vacation.

Academic work often includes summaries. Instructors often summarize the main points of a lecture at the beginning or end of class, and most textbooks include section and/or chapter summaries. Students are often asked to write summaries. For instance:

In a history course, students may be required to summarize the major events that led to a war.

A civil engineering course may require that students summarize the main characteristics of modern suspension bridges.

A computer science course may ask students to write an abstract (summary) of the program they will create as their senior project.

The topic of each summary may vary greatly, but an effective summary usually follows these guidelines:

1. It retells only the <u>main ideas</u> of the original source.
2. It is considerably <u>shorter</u> than the original.
3. It is <u>complete</u>. It reflects all the main points of the original text.
4. It is <u>objective</u>. It does not include the summary writer's comments or evaluations.
5. It is <u>balanced</u>. It gives each idea the same value given by the author of the original.

Here are strategies for writing an effective summary:

1. Read the text once to get the general meaning.
2. Read the text again, and mark the most important ideas. You may want to circle or highlight the keywords that refer to these ideas in the text.
3. Read the text a third time to review the main points and the key terms.

Master Student Tip

It helps to cover the text you are summarizing so that you are not tempted to look at it.

4. Begin your summary by giving the title of the reading and the name of the author (if available).

5. As you write the summary, try to retell the main ideas without looking at the original text. Of course, you will use some of the *keywords* and *phrases* used by the writer, but the other words and the sentence structures should be different from the original.

6. Once you are finished, compare your summary to the original text to make sure you summarized all the main ideas and gave each idea the same importance given by the author.

Note: Plagiarism is copying someone else's words without giving the author credit. In the academic world, plagiarism is considered a very serious offense because a writer owns the ideas and words he or she uses in his or her writing. Each writer has a unique style and voice, and you should not borrow words, phrases, or sentences that you would not normally use in your writing. If you want to use someone else's words, use quotation marks and reference information to show which words are not your own.

EXERCISE 9 **Writing a summary**

Read the following paragraph about Web design. Then, follow the strategies for effective summaries you read earlier. Because the paragraph is about 176 words long, try to make your summary only about 50 words or at least half as long. When you finish writing your summary, compare it to the original paragraph. Did you forget to list one or more main ideas? Add them to your summary. How long is your summary? If it is too long, cross out words or phrases that do not seem very important.

VISUAL APPEAL AND COLOR

A webpage should be aesthetically attractive, which means it should be pleasing to the eye. To achieve a pleasant appearance, Web designers use images that can attract users, such as good-looking models, funny cartoons, and other eye-catching graphics. Animation has also become a popular design element. Moving or flashing text and icons, scrolling images, and video clips are used to enhance a website and attract attention. However, color remains one of the most effective Web design tools. A webpage is considered most attractive when the color scheme is well balanced and consistent. The colors on the webpage need to complement each other well. They also need to match the webpage theme. For example, the webpage of a cancer support group may use pastel or muted colors because of the serious subject matter whereas the color scheme of a party supply store will rely on bright colors to create a feeling of excitement. Ultimately, all the visual elements used in Web design should combine to create a webpage that is visually appealing. [176 words]

EXERCISE 10 **Evaluating a summary**

Read the student summary below. Then, answer the questions that follow.

Summary introduces article and author.

Only the main ideas are included.

In "Visual Appeal and Color," Rachele Monte states that Web designers make a webpage attractive by using interesting graphics, text, and especially color. The colors on a webpage need to blend together well and should go with the webpage content. [40 words]

1. What key terms from the original text did the student use? Highlight or underline them.
2. Are the sentences in the student summary the same as the sentences in the original text? Identify subjects (S) and verbs (V) in the student sentences.
3. What have you learned from evaluating the student summary that can help you write more effective summaries?

EXERCISE 11 **Comparing summaries**

Form a group with two classmates. Take turns reading each other's summary. Then, discuss the summaries by asking these questions:

1. What do the summaries have in common?
2. How are the summaries different?
3. Why are they different?
4. Which is the most effective summary? Why?
5. What have you learned about writing effective summaries?
6. Why is summarizing an important academic skill?

EXERCISE 12 **Developing evaluation criteria**

Review the three criteria you selected from the CARP and TILT lists. Review your summary. Select four to six criteria you might use in your writing assignment.

1. On separate paper, write a one-sentence definition for each of your selected criteria.
2. Discuss your criteria and the definitions of those criteria with two or three classmates. Take notes about the discussion on separate paper.
   a. Can your classmates help you improve your definitions? Can you help your classmates with their criteria?
   b. Is one or more of the criteria your classmates have listed interesting enough to use in your essay? If so, add it to your list.
3. After the discussion, place your notes in your writing folder.

EXERCISE 13 **Selecting a product**

To choose a product for your explaining essay,

1. Make a list of three to five products you are interested in. You will select one of these products when you evaluate two websites that advertise the product. For example, if you like to ski, you may want to look for websites that advertise skis or ski clothing.
2. Next to each product, write in parentheses the brand names you already know that sell that product.
3. Select one of the products that especially interests you.

EXERCISE 14 Searching the Web

Select from the Internet two websites that advertise two brands of the product you selected. Then, on the computer,

1. Open the browser Google or another browser and type the name of the website you want to find (example: "Kellogg's cornflakes"). Visit four to six websites before you select the two you want to compare. *Note*: Choose official company websites for the product you selected. Official websites generally state "Official Website" on the homepage (the main webpage) or include the company's name in the website address, which is called URL (Uniform Resource Locator). Example: http://www.honda.com/index

2. Print a copy of the homepage of each website you chose. Label one copy "Website A" and the other "Website B." Be sure to choose two websites of **similar quality** that advertise **two brands** of the **same product**.

3. Place the copies in your writing folder.

EXERCISE 15 Revising evaluation criteria

Now that you have chosen your websites, look at them carefully. Then, revise and/or add to the list of criteria you made earlier. Be sure to give a definition and a reason for each criterion you add. Put your revised list in your writing folder. You will narrow your list to three or four criteria when you begin to organize your essay.

> **Master Student Tips**
>
> Use quotation marks every time you copy information directly from another source.

EXERCISE 16 Studying Tyler's chart

With a classmate, study Tyler's Evaluation Chart on the next page. Then, answer the questions that follow.

1. List Tyler's five criteria in what you think is their order of importance. How does your list differ from Tyler's?

2. What do you consider the most creative and interesting parts of Tyler's chart? Why?

3. Tyler's reasons are notes he wrote to himself, so they contain incomplete sentences and informal language. Underline three examples of language that Tyler should not use in his formal academic essay.

4. If you could suggest one more criterion to Tyler, what would it be? Why?

Tyler's Evaluation Chart

Scoring System:				
Very poor	Poor	Average	Above Average	Excellent

Website A: Nike's athletic shoes, Airmax Tailwind

Website B: Saucony's athletic shoes, Grid Omni 3

Criterion	Score		Reasons
	Site A	**Site B**	
1. Layout			Website A is extremely well laid out—very compartmentalized. More options at bottom of page. Seems to work better. Site B has options on the top/sides, all over. Includes almost the same options—shoe info, colors, other shoes (similar products).
2. Visual Appeal			Colors more soothing and appealing on site A (blues and greens) while site B used mostly bright orange. Overall "feeling" of B: cluttered. But A is easy to look at, evenly put together although right side lacks visual appeal.
3. Graphics			Pictures of the main product are comparable. However, site B allows a look at the sole of the shoe and a 360° view. Site A doesn't offer this.

Criterion	Score		Reasons
	Site A	Site B	
4. Readability	🥾🥾🥾🥾	🥾🥾🥾	Site A offers a scrolling text box, and because of its layout it is more readable. The grouping makes it easy for the eyes to follow. Site B is hard to follow with the eyes—like the information was splatter-painted on the page.
5. Information	🥾🥾🥾	🥾🥾🥾🥾	Both sites give shoe information and statistics, but the "technology section" for site B is like a foreign language! Site A gives more and better shoe info + ratings in easy terms.

EXERCISE 17 Evaluating two websites

Return to your writing folder and review your list of criteria. Select three or four criteria to use in the evaluation of your chosen websites:

1. On separate paper, create an evaluation form like Tyler's. Use a star system for your evaluation icons (or create your own icons):
    * = very poor   ** = poor   *** = average
    **** = above average   ***** = excellent
2. Complete your evaluation form. Base your answers on your personal opinion about each website. Remember to give reasons and details for your evaluation.
3. Which website did you prefer? On the back of your evaluation sheet, write two or three sentences that explain why you selected that website.
4. Return your evaluation form to your writing folder.

POWER GRAMMAR

Quotations

As you write your essay for this chapter, you will quote one online source about Web design. **Quoting** means writing down exactly what a person said or wrote. To show that you are quoting somebody else's words, use quotation marks.

Quotations	Explanations
According to William and Tollett, "The placement, size, format, and resolution of the images are important components in website design" (William and Tollett, 2000). The authors state, "A key component when evaluating contrast is to determine the focal point or main dominating feature of the page" (William and Tollett, 2000).	1. The introductory phrase (*according to*) and report verb (*state*) are followed by a comma (,) 2. The words inside the quotation marks are exactly the same as the original text. 3. The last quotation mark comes after the period (."). 4. When the quotation is a complete sentence, it begins with a capital letter ("The ..." "A ..."). 5. If available, the **page number** and **publication date** of the cited source are put in parentheses at the end of the quotation. 6. If the authors are not introduced before the quotation, their last names are included in the parentheses. 7. The period comes AFTER the closing parenthesis.

Quotations	Explanations
The authors affirm that one of the most important elements in contrast is "the focal point or main dominating feature of the page" (William and Tollett, 2000).	When the quotation is a phrase, not a complete sentence: **1.** The first letter of the first word is not capitalized (<u>t</u>he focal point . . .)
When evaluating websites, we should consider "the placement, size, format, and resolution" of graphics and images (William and Tollett, 2000). period	**2.** The report verb (**affirm**) is generally followed by **that**. When the quotation is in the middle of a sentence, no period is necessary before the last quotation mark (. . . resolution").

EXERCISE 18 **Analyzing quotations**

Read the quotations below and answer the questions that follow. The first two examples have been completed for you.

Examples:

                   S   V

The article "Five Tips for Effective Websites" <u>mentions</u> that text "should be clear and concise. Overall color of text and images should be a balanced contrast" (2000).

<u>As explained by</u> Chuck Letourneau, a ⟨Web design expert⟩,

     S   V

accessibility means that "anyone using any kind of Web browsing technology must be able to visit any site and get a full and complete understanding of the information contained there, as well as have the full and complete ability to interact with the site" (Letourneau, 2003).

A. One internet source maintains, "The right picture or image can instantly convey the fundamental qualities that make your product or service better than your competition" ("Making an Effective Website," 2002).

B. According to an internet article, Berners-Lee invented both "the HTML markup language and the HTTP protocol used to request and transmit webpages between Web servers and Web browsers" ("Who Invented the World Wide Web?" 2003).

C. *The Oxford American Dictionary of Current English* explains, "Hypertext allows words or graphics on a page to be connected to other webpages" (1999, p. 385).

D. InetDzine, a dot com firm , suggests, "Make it easy to explore your site, yet always have access to home and featured pages readily available."

1. Identify the main subject (S) and verb (V) that come before the quotation in each sentence.
2. Underline the report verb or phrase that introduces each quotation. List them on separate paper, and put the list in your writing folder.
3. Notice that in two sentences some words are circled. These words provide information about something. With a classmate, discuss the following:
   a. What is the information about?
   b. Where is the information located in the sentence? That is, what comes immediately before the circled words?
   c. What is the purpose of the information?

EXERCISE 19 dentifying errors

With a classmate, read the quotations below. Then, complete the steps that follow. The example has been corrected for you.

Example:

As Goff and Wheeler explain, "Tables allow Web designers to organize and group information."""

A. According to Jeff Peach, a well-known Web design expert, "The placement, size, format and resolution of the images are important components in website design".

B. As William and Tollett state, A key component when evaluating contrast is to determine the *focal point* or main dominating feature of the page."

C. The authors affirm that one of the most important elements in contrast is "the *focal point* or main dominating feature of the page.

D. When evaluating websites, we should consider the placement, size, format, and resolution of graphics and images.

1. Identify and correct the errors. (Note: To identify the errors in D, compare it to A in this exercise.)
2. Underline the report verb or phrase in each sentence.
3. Add the report verbs and phrases in this exercise to the list you wrote in Exercise 18. How can this list help you write your essay?

WEB POWER

For more practice with direct quotations, go to
http://esl.college.hmco.com/students.

○ Focusing and Organizing

You have already selected Web evaluation criteria to evaluate websites for your essay. In this phase of the writing process, you will begin to shape and organize your ideas by writing a "working" thesis statement, preparing an essay map, and drafting your introduction and background paragraphs. You can avoid a lengthy revision process if you map (plan and organize) your essay well.

SPOTLIGHT ON WRITING SKILLS

The Thesis Statement

Academic writing differs from novel or mystery writing. One difference is that the goal of academic writing is to communicate clearly and directly, without mystery or literary language. Consequently, most academic writing has a thesis statement. The function of a thesis is to state the main idea of the essay.

The thesis statement:

1. Is the most general statement in the essay.
2. Contains "controlling ideas" (words and phrases) that guide the direction of the essay and the formation of the topic sentences.
3. Is usually written at the end of the introduction.

The thesis statement is important because:

1. It helps the writer focus the essay (as a camera can focus a photograph)
2. It helps the writer create the topic sentences for the body paragraphs (each topic sentence will be about one or more of the controlling ideas in the thesis).
3. It tells the reader early in the essay the main idea of that essay.
4. It gives the reader enough information to predict the main ideas of the body paragraphs by asking questions the writer is expected to answer.

Think of the thesis statement as the roof of a house: the rest of the essay must fit under the thesis just as a house must fit under the roof. If the roof is too big, the house will look too small. A too-broad thesis would make an essay look underdeveloped. If the roof is too small, some of the rooms will not be covered; likewise, if the thesis is too narrow, some of the body paragraphs will seem off topic (outside the roof).

Here is a sample thesis statement about evaluating websites:

Most college students prefer the bright colors and good organization of the Skippy website to the Jif website.

What's the essay about?

The Skippy Website

What does the writer want to communicate to the readers?

Why college students prefer this website

What can readers predict will occur in the body paragraphs?

The writer will explain why students prefer it, why the bright colors make the website preferable, what "good organization" means, why the other website was not preferred.

Writing a thesis statement that fits your essay "just right" can be difficult. Even experienced writers cannot write a perfect thesis on the first try. Assume that your first thesis statement is a "work in progress," a "working thesis." Later, when your essay takes shape, you will review and perhaps revise or even rewrite your thesis statement.

EXERCISE 20 Analyzing thesis statements

With one of your classmates, read the three thesis statements below. Circle the (controlling ideas), and predict what questions the body paragraphs will answer. An example has been completed for you.

Example:

The Adidas website (**A**) and the Nike website (**B**) are

equally (appealing) (visually), but the Adidas website provides

(more information) and is (more user friendly).

Questions the writer will answer in the body paragraphs:

- What makes a website visually appealing?
- How are both websites visually appealing?
- Why is website information important?
- What information is given by both websites?
- What additional information does Website A provide?
- How is a website user friendly?
- How is Website A more user friendly than Website B?

1. Although the Apple computer website (**A**) is more informative, the Dell computer website (**B**) has better graphics and more interesting links.

   Questions the writer will answer in the body paragraphs:

   _____

   _____

   _____

   _____

2. The Wendy's website (**A**) has a better layout, is more user friendly, and gives more useful information than the McDonald's website (**B**).

   Questions the writer will answer in the body paragraphs:

   _____

   _____

   _____

   _____

3. Both guitar websites, Martin's (**A**) and Gibson's (**B**), have a great layout and are easy to navigate; however, Martin's website has better links and more detailed information about the guitars.

Questions the writer will answer in the body paragraphs:

_____

_____

_____

_____

EXERCISE 21   **Writing your "working thesis"**

Look again at the materials in your writing folder, especially your evaluation chart. Use the main ideas you developed to write a "working thesis." Circle the controlling ideas in the thesis statement. Then, make a list of three to five questions you plan to answer in the paragraphs that follow your introduction.

SPOTLIGHT ON WRITING SKILLS

The Essay Map

Now you need to organize the information that will go in the body paragraphs by creating an **essay map**. The essay map will help you decide what ideas you want to discuss in your essay and what evidence can best support these ideas. If you prepare your essay map carefully and thoughtfully, the actual essay will be easier to write and organize.

In the example below, Tyler identified the product and brand names of the two websites. Then, he wrote his working thesis, working topic sentences, and a concluding sentence.

Under each topic sentence, Tyler left about half a page of space and wrote WH- questions he could think of that might help him develop his controlling ideas. For each question, he listed the supporting details that answered that question. He did not always use complete sentences in his essay map.

Note: In Tyler's essay map, notice the relationship between controlling ideas in the thesis statement and controlling ideas in the topic sentences.

Tyler's Essay Map and Questions

Product: Running Shoes Brands/Websites: Nike (A) and Saucony (B)

Thesis statement's
controlling ideas

Thesis Statement: Nike, brand A, <u>better markets</u> its <u>product</u> to consumers through <u>increased visual appeal</u>, <u>readability</u>, <u>layout</u>, and <u>product information</u>.

Topic Sentence 1:
The controlling idea
"four criteria" is a
synonym for the four
qualities in Tyler's
thesis statement—
"visual appeal,
readability, layout, and
product information."

Topic Sentence 1 (Background Paragraph): These four criteria are essential in evaluating commercial websites.

Questions:

WHAT is visual appeal? Something attractive to the eye.

WHY is it important? Images are the first thing we notice in a webpage.

WHAT is readability? Easy to read (explain western reading patterns: left to right, top to bottom).

WHY is it important? Makes it easier to access information (example of website reader program for the blind).

WHAT is layout? How images are organized on the webpage.

WHY is it important? Mention information from summary.

HOW much product information should a website provide? Share personal experience.

HOW do you know consumers care about these criteria? Quote Online Source 1.

[The controlling
ideas "excited
visually" and
"visually appealing"
refer to "visual
appeal" in the thesis
statement.]

Topic Sentence 2: Most consumers want to be excited visually by a website, and Nike's website markets its shoes better than Saucony's by making the site visually appealing.

Questions:

HOW does the Nike's website attract consumers visually? Details about color, number of images (5 shoe types), quality of images (sole is shown along with upper shoe).

HOW is Saucony's visual appeal? Details about color and images (3 shoe types, shoe sole not shown).

Tyler's Essay Map and Questions (cont.)

WHY isn't Saucony's website as good as Nike's website? Saucony's images are less appealing (color comparison with Nike's), fewer in number and less complete.

[The controlling ideas "readability" and "easy to read" refer to "readability" in the thesis statement.]

Topic Sentence 3: Saucony's website scored low on readability whereas Nike's was easy to read.

Questions:

WHAT makes Saucony's readability level lower? Competing headings of equal size. Eye movement is slowed down, harder for the eyes to go from left to right (mention shoe picture at the bottom of the page, isolated from the rest of the page).

HOW is Nike's readability better? Headings of different sizes makes it easier for the eye to identify main info, smoother eye movement from left to right.

[The controlling ideas "layout," "symmetrical," and "grouped" refer to the criterion "layout" in the thesis statement.]

Topic Sentence 4: Nike's website layout was more symmetrical and grouped than Saucony's website layout.

Questions:

WHAT is symmetry? Define symmetry, give example of Nike's website (equal space is taken up by images and writing).

WHY is symmetry important? The human eye is attracted to symmetrical shapes (example from the Nike's website).

WHAT is grouping? Give definition. Explain the way images can be organized on the page. Give example of Nike's website.

WHY is layout important? Give reason: easier to distinguish and identify images and information.

[The controlling ideas "product information" and "greater quality of information" relate to "product information" in the thesis statement.]

Topic Sentence 5: The comparison of product information between the Nike's and Saucony's websites showed that Nike shared a greater quality of information.

Questions:

HOW MUCH information does the Nike's website provide? Shoe's characteristics—cushioning, motion control, stability, weight—are easy to understand.

WHY is Nike's website better than Saucony's in these areas? Saucony's website doesn't list each shoe's weight, gives less info.

HOW MUCH information does the Saucony's site provide? It lists shoe's characteristics but uses technical terminology (example: "medial midsole post").

WHY is the additional information given by Nike important? Weight is important to runners. Heavy shoes affect performance and endurance (personal example).

Conclusion: The needs of most consumers are better met by the qualities of the Nike website.

EXERCISE 22 Creating an essay map

Review your "working" thesis statement and the questions you expect to answer in your essay. On separate paper, rewrite your working thesis. Then,

1. On additional paper, write topic sentences for two or three of your body paragraphs in response to the questions about your thesis statement.
2. Leave the rest of the page empty after each topic sentence so that you can list the supporting details from your collected materials.
3. Remember: Use keywords and phrases for the controlling ideas in your topic sentences that refer to the ideas in the thesis statement.

EXERCISE 23 Listing evidence

Review your essay map. Then,

1. Under each topic sentence, write three to five WH-questions (who, what, when, where, why, and how) you will answer in the paragraph that follows that topic sentence. Use Tyler's chart as a model.
2. Answer the questions for each body paragraph. If you cannot answer some of your questions, (a) change your topic sentence or (b) find additional support by generating more ideas.
3. Put your essay map in your writing folder.

SPOTLIGHT ON WRITING SKILLS

The Introduction

Academic writing is a complex task that requires many decisions. Effective writers understand that there are as many "rules" to successful writing as there are decisions to be made. That is, academic readers have expectations about what the writing will "look like": what will come first, how it will be written, where the thesis will be, how the topic sentences will relate to the thesis statement, and even what supporting examples and details will come after a topic sentence. Many of these "rules" or reader expectations are not written; they are simply expected, and they are called "writing conventions."

Take the introductory paragraph—the first paragraph in an academic essay—as an example. The functions of the introduction are in this order:

1. To introduce readers to the topic
2. To present some interesting information about the topic to engage the readers
3. To present the thesis statement, usually the last sentence of the introduction

Notice that the introduction of an academic essay or report is shorter than the body paragraphs because it does not "conventionally" (typically) present any support or evidence.

You can make the introduction interesting by starting with a well-known fact or detail about the topic that the reader will agree with, and then follow with some less familiar information to engage the reader. You might ask a thought-provoking question or begin with a brief dialogue. Some writers like to call these different devices "hooks." Just as fishermen use baited hooks to lure their prey, writers use interesting introductions to capture their readers' attention so that the readers will want to read the rest of the essays.

Here are two examples of interesting introductions. Read both introductions before reading the comments in the left margin.

Attention-grabber or *hook*: personal experience with the topic (*Web design* and *websites*).

The introduction provides general information about the topic (*websites*) and gradually leads to the thesis.

In the thesis statement, the controlling ideas focus on three aspects (*layout*, *readability*, *quality of information*) of the general topic (*attractive websites*).

The websites compared in the essay are listed:
1. name of website,
2. date website was last updated (if given), and
3. retrieval date.

Introduction 1: Sam Goody

When I was a senior in high school, I liked to go on the Internet to download music and chat with my friends. I did not pay much attention to such things as "layout" or "links." I used links, but I had no idea how they worked. I did not even know the words "Web design" until my best friend convinced me to take an elective in high school called Elements of Web Design. Before taking the class, I had never realized before how much careful planning and work go in creating a webpage. Now I know that many companies try to attract consumers by creating colorful and eye-catching websites. Therefore, consumers must develop a set of criteria to evaluate websites more effectively. For this essay, I chose to evaluate the effectiveness of two music company websites, Sam Goody (samgoody.com) and Tower Records (towerrecords.com). Sam Goody is the best website because of its layout, readability and quality of information.

References

Sam Goody website (2003). Retrieved October 2, 2004 from
http://www.samgoody.com

Tower Records website (2003). Retrieved October 2, 2004 from
http://www.towerrecords.com/Default.aspx

Introduction 2: Head & Shoulders

The introduction begins with general information about the purpose of websites.

Hook: Reference to expert opinion about the most important characteristic of a successful website.

Thesis statement: the controlling ideas focus on more specific aspects (user friendliness, easy access, information) of the general topic (successful websites).

Websites are listed in alphabetical order

Reference begins with the title: no author available.

Nowadays everyone is using webpages for one reason or another. Webpages are a great way for companies to advertise their products and for people to shop and buy products without spending hours in stores. Some people do not know much about the different ways webpages can be designed. However, they do know when a certain page is frustrating to use or access. InetDzine, a *Dot Com* firm that specializes in website design for the AEC (Architecture, Engineering & Construction) industry, stresses the importance of making websites easy to navigate ("What Makes," 2003). Users need to be able to move easily between pages, and the homepage and featured pages should be easily accessed from any page on the website. Therefore, when I evaluated two websites that advertised two brands of shampoo, I looked at their user friendliness, easy access, and information; based on these criteria, the Head & Shoulders website (headandshoulders.com) proved superior to the Herbal Essence website (herbalessence.com).

References

Head & Shoulders website. (2004). Retrieved October 4, 2004 from http://www.headandshoulders.com/usa/main.asp

Herbal Essence website. (2004). Retrieved October 4, 2004 from http://www.herbalessences.com/home.asp

What makes a website successful. (2003). *InetDzine*. Retrieved October 4, 2004 from http://www.inetdzine.com/success.asp

EXERCISE 24 **Analyzing introductions**

Reread Introductions 1 and 2. Then, answer the following questions:

1. How does each writer capture the readers' attention?
2. Are outside sources cited? Is the author's name mentioned with each citation? Are page numbers given for each citation?
3. Which introduction did you find more interesting? Why?
4. Share your opinion with two or three classmates. How are your opinions different? Why?

EXERCISE 25 Drafting your introduction

Write an introduction for your essay. Be sure to:

1. Introduce the topic to your readers. A good way to do this is to write a general statement about Web design that your readers will agree with.
2. Capture the readers' attention with a question, a personal anecdote, surprising statistics, or some interesting piece of information about Web design.
3. Write your thesis statement.

EXERCISE 26 Evaluating an introduction

Exchange introductions with one of your classmates and do the following:

1. Read your classmate's introduction carefully. Then, answer the following questions:
   a. Does the introduction begin with a general statement about the essay topic?
   b. Does the introduction contain a "hook" that makes the reader want to continue reading? Put an asterisk (*) in the margin where you find the hook.
   c. Does the introduction contain a thesis statement?
2. Circle the controlling ideas in the thesis statement.
3. Review the essay assignment. Do the controlling ideas in the thesis statement answer the essay assignment?

SPOTLIGHT ON WRITING SKILLS

The Background Paragraph

In most academic essays and reports, the background paragraph comes right after the introductory paragraph. Its purpose is to help readers understand the essay topic and to prepare them for the rest of the essay. Another goal of the background paragraph is to give you the opportunity to demonstrate your ability to collect and organize information from outside sources.

Not all assignments require you to provide a background paragraph, but it is generally a good idea to write one. Without the information provided in the background paragraph, the reader may not be able to fully understand the essay topic, the writer's point of view, or the controlling ideas of the other body paragraphs.

The information you include in your background paragraph depends on the assignment, the audience, and the data collected. This information may include one or more of the following:

1. Definitions of key terms (example: *Alignment* means that the items on the page are lined up with each other.)
2. A brief description of the topic (example: When creating a website, designers focus on the way a website is structured, where the images and text are placed on each webpage, what font is used, and what links are provided.)
3. Scientific or technical information essential for reader understanding (example: "jpeg" images are faster and easier to download than "bmp" images because they take less computer memory.)
4. Current relevant information or research about the topic (example: According to Johnson-Eilola, "Web sites normally offer users a wide range of options for navigating the text.")
5. Evidence that a problem exists (example: In a recent study, researches found that inexperienced website designers tend to include more text in their webpages than experienced designers.)
6. Historical information about the topic (example: Tim Berners-Lee invented the World Wide Web in 1991.)

EXERCISE 27   **Evaluating background paragraphs**

The background paragraphs that follow were written by two students for this chapter's essay assignment. Read the paragraphs, but cover the notes in the left margin with a ruler or piece of paper. Then, with a classmate answer the questions that follow.

The Best Four-Wheeler

Topic sentence →

The quotation is introduced by the phrase "according to," followed by the author's name.

No page number is available for the quotation. Author and date are given.

I selected three criteria to evaluate the websites for the Daimler Chrysler Jeep Liberty (website A) and the Landrover Freelander (website B). The first criterion is accessibility. According to Chuck Letourneau, accessibility means that "anyone using any kind of Web browsing technology must be able to visit any site and get a full and complete understanding of the information contained there, as well as have the full and complete ability to interact with the site" (Letourneau, 2003). The second criterion I chose is appearance. In order for a website to be successful, it must first appeal to users on a visual level. Links is the last criterion that I selected. A good website will connect to other webpages or websites through hypertext (links). Links provide important information about the product on the main website and about other company products.

References

Daimler-Chrysler website. (2004). Retrieved October 1, 2004 from http://www.daimlerchrysler.com/dccom

Landrover website. (2004). Retrieved October 1, 2004 from http://www.landrover.com/default.htm

Letourneau, C. (2004). *Accessible Web design*. Retrieved October 1, 2004 from http://www.starlingweb.com/webac.htm

Double-spaced, end-of-text reference includes author, date, title, and date of retrieval.

Web Design

"Web design" and "Web browser" are words we use all the time nowadays, but they would not exist without Tim Berners-Lee. The basic Web design was invented by Tim Berners-Lee, Marc Andreessen, and Jamie Zawinski. Berners-Lee wrote the first Web design program to introduce data to other researchers throughout CERN (European Organization for Nuclear Research). The name of his first program was called World Wide Web or WWW (**Wingfield, 1997**). Furthermore, Berners-Lee invented both "the HTML markup language and the HTTP protocol used to request and transmit webpages between Web servers and Web browsers" ("Who Invented," 2003, p. 1). HTML means Hypertext Mark Up Language and HTTP means Hypertext Transfer Protocol. The modern Web browser was developed first in March of 1993 by Marc Andreessen and Jamie Zawinski. They created this browser to be able to access the WWW created by Berners-Lee. Their browser was the first browser available to Microsoft Windows users. Andreessen and Zawinski later created Netscape, a popular Internet browser (2003). Therefore, without Berners-Lee, Andreessen, and Zawinski, I would not be able to write this essay about evaluating websites because the World Wide Web would not exist.

The summary of the information from an Internet article is followed by an **in-text citation**. Page number is not necessary for summaries.

Because the author is not identified in the original article, the title is given for the quotation.

Same author is cited again: only the date is given in the in-text citation.

References

End-of-text references are double spaced. Notice that only the first line of each reference begins at the margin. The other lines are indented.

Who invented the World Wide Web? (2003, June 30). *Boutell International*. Retrieved October 15, 2005 from Boutell.Com, Internationalhttp://www.boutell.com/newfaq/basic/invented web.html

Wingfield, N. (1997, March 3). Still netting after all these years. *CNET News*. Retrieved October 2, 2005 from http://news.com.com/ 2009-1082_3-233721.html

1. What questions are answered in the paragraphs above?
2. What is the purpose of each background paragraph?
3. What key terms are defined in each paragraph?
4. The student who wrote the second paragraph used many technical terms related to Web design. Can you guess what his major is?
5. Read the notes in the right margin about citing sources. What rules about citing sources are discussed? List these rules on separate paper. Put the paper in your writing folder.
6. Which paragraph do you find more interesting? Why?

SPOTLIGHT ON WRITING SKILLS

In-text Citations and Sources

Your background paragraph is likely to contain one or more ideas from other sources. Remember that any information you did not know when you selected your topic <u>must</u> be "cited." That is, you must give credit to the author of the information.

To follow APA citation format:

1. For information you copy from the source, use quotation marks, and follow the quotation with the information source in parentheses. As you learned earlier, this method of citing sources is called **quoting**.

Examples:

(Last, 2000, page)   (Monte, 2005, p. 15)

2. For information that you summarize from another source, you do not use quotation marks, but you still need to cite the source of your information at the end of the summary.

Examples:

(Last, 2000)   (Monte, 2005)

Here are examples of in-text citations in five student writing samples:		
Student samples	**Information about source**	**Source of information**
1. The *Oxford American Dictionary of Current English* states, "Hypertext allows words or graphics on a page to be connected to other webpages" (Oxford Dict., 1999, p. 385). [quotation]	No author: use major words from title. Give date and page number.	dictionary
2. "anyone using any kind of Web browsing technology must be able to visit any site and get a full and complete understanding of the information contained there, as well as have the full and complete ability to interact with the site" (Letourneau, 2003). [quotation]	No page number available	website
3. "the HTML markup language and the HTTP protocol used to request and transmit webpages between Web servers and Web browser" ("Who Invented," 2003, p. 1) [quotation]	When available page number is given after the date.	website
4. Berners-Lee wrote the first Web design program to introduce data to other researchers throughout CERN (European Organization for Nuclear Research). The name of his first program was called World Wide Web or WWW (Wingfield, 1997). [summary]	No page number is necessary for summaries. Give last name of author and date.	website

Here are examples of in-text citations in five student writing samples:		
Student samples	**Information about source**	**Source of information**
5. The modern Web browser was developed first in March of 1993 by Marc Andreessen and Jamie Zawinski. They created this browser to be able to access the WWW created by Berners-Lee. Their browser was the first browser available to Microsoft Windows users. Andreessen and Zawinski later created Netscape, a popular Internet browser ("Who Invented," 2003). [summary]	No author: use major words from title	

EXERCISE 28 Evaluating in-text citations

Review the in-text citations in the student samples above. Then, answer these questions on separate paper:

1. What is the purpose of in-text citations?
2. Who are the authors of the information cited in the five paragraphs? How do you know?
3. Why is the title given instead of the author in sample 1's citation?
4. What punctuation is used in each citation?
5. What does "Wingfield, 1997" mean in sample 4's citation?
6. Writers do not use whole titles because they interrupt the text. How did the writer select the major words of titles for the citations in samples 1 and 3?
7. How does citing outside sources strengthen your academic writing?

○ Writing, Revising, and Editing

Now it is time to begin putting your essay together. Remember: Academic writing requires you to make decisions. The exercises in this stage of the writing process will help you effectively draft your essay.

EXERCISE 29 Writing your background paragraph

Reread this chapter's essay assignment (p. 52). Then,

1. Review your essay map and the other materials in your writing folder. Make sure they answer the essay assignment.
2. Begin writing your background paragraph. In your paragraph, provide at least two of the following:
   a. A definition of the Web evaluation criteria you will use in your essay
   b. Additional information you think will help the reader understand your essay's main idea
   c. A brief description of the major way(s) you gathered information for your essay
3. After you finish writing your background paragraph, place it in your writing folder.

EXERCISE 30 Reviewing a paragraph

Exchange your background paragraph with a classmate. Then,

1. Read the background paragraph. Circle the controlling ideas in the topic sentence of that paragraph.
2. In the margin, identify two ways it prepares readers for the essay, and draw a line to each.
3. At the end of the background paragraph, write one question you think your partner should also answer in her or his background paragraph.
4. Return the materials to your classmate, and thank her or him for the feedback.
5. Discuss your comments with your classmate, and ask any questions you have about the comments.

EXERCISE 31 Writing topic sentences

In Exercise 20, you developed questions for the controlling ideas in three thesis statements. With two or three classmates, read the example and the same thesis statements (on the next page) from Exercise 20. Then, complete the steps that follow.

   a. The Adidas website (A) and the Nike website (B) are equally
      appealing visually, but the Adidas website provides more
      information and is more user friendly.
   b. Although the Apple computer website (A) is more informative,
      the Dell computer website (B) has better graphics and more
      interesting links.
   c. The Wendy's website (A) has a better layout, is more user
      friendly and gives more useful information than the McDonald's
      website (B).
   d. Both guitar websites, Martin's (A) and Gibson's (B), have a great
      layout and are easy to navigate; however, the Martin's website
      has better links and more detailed information about the guitars.

1. Circle the controlling ideas in each statement.
2. On separate paper, write topic sentences for the controlling ideas in
   each thesis statement.
3. Decide which development structure would suit each body
   paragraph (definition, process, classification, comparison and/or
   contrast, cause and/or effect).
4. Explain which of these types of paragraph development interests
   you most.

EXERCISE 32 Revising your essay map

*Read this chapter's writing assignment carefully one more time to make
sure you fully understand your instructor's expectations. Then,*

1. Review your essay map:
   a. Does your thesis statement still fulfill the assignment?
   b. Do your topic sentences directly relate to your thesis statement?
   c. Do you use key words for your topic sentences' controlling ideas
      that refer to the ideas in the thesis statement?
2. Revise your topic sentences as necessary by adding or changing
   keywords and phrases.

EXERCISE 33 Reviewing supporting materials

*Look carefully at the questions and supporting materials that follow each of
the topic sentences in your essay map.*

1. Are the questions you asked about each topic sentence still directly
   related to the thesis statement?
2. What supporting details are you using? Do they truly answer your
   questions?

3. Are you using a variety of details, such as definitions, examples, descriptions, personal experiences? Are you using evidence from experts or library sources?

4. Does each piece of evidence have an in-text citation? <u>Remember</u>: Any information you did not know when you began your assignment must be followed by an in-text citation:

    a. Will you summarize information from a source? If so, put an in-text citation right after the summary: (Monte, 2005).

    b. Will you quote directly from a source? If so, add page numbers to your in-text citation: (Monte, 2005, p. 15).

5. Do you need more information to answer one or more of the questions? If so, look for more details in the research you have already gathered or visit the Internet again.

6. Would some of your supporting material "fit" better in your background paragraph? In your introduction? If so, make the changes now.

7. Is some of your supporting material no longer relevant to your essay? If so, take it out.

EXERCISE 34   **Reviewing essay organization**

Make the necessary changes to your essay map as you answer these questions:

1. The background paragraph will come right after the introduction. Which body paragraph should come immediately after the background paragraph? Why? Which should come next? Why?

2. How will you present the supporting evidence? Which detail or example should come first? Why?

3. What method of development will you use for each body paragraph? Why? Label that method in the margin. <u>Remember</u>: Each body paragraph will be organized in one of several ways: definition, process, comparison and/or contrast, classification, <u>or</u> cause and/or effect.

4. Check the citations of the supporting information in each of your body paragraphs.

SPOTLIGHT ON WRITING SKILLS

Body Paragraph Conventions

The purpose (function) of the body paragraphs is to explain and support the paragraph's main idea as stated in the topic sentence. In academic essays, the topic sentence has controlling ideas that (a) relate directly to the controlling ideas in the thesis statement, (b) direct the paragraph that follows, and (c) help the reader predict what the paragraph will discuss. Remember that the supporting evidence that follows explains, defines, and gives examples and evidence for the controlling ideas in the topic sentence.

Note: You may want to review Vera's essay, which you read and analyzed in Exercise 3, to see how her body paragraphs successfully develop and support the thesis statement.

EXERCISE 35 **Writing your body paragraphs**

Review the writing assignment, your revised essay map, your introduction, and your background paragraph. Then, compose your body paragraphs. Use this checklist.

—— Each body paragraph has a clear topic sentence.

—— The controlling ideas in the topic sentences of the body paragraphs correspond to the ideas in the thesis statement.

—— The main points in each body paragraph correspond to the controlling ideas in the topic sentence of that paragraph.

—— The supporting details clarify and explain each main point in the body paragraphs.

—— The in-text citations in each body paragraph support the paragraph's main points.

—— The quotations are followed, in parentheses, by the author's last name, the date of publication, and the page number of the cited information.

—— Each body paragraph ends with a concluding sentence.

—— Place your body paragraphs in your writing folder.

SPOTLIGHT ON WRITING SKILLS

The Conclusion

The final paragraph in an expository essay is the **conclusion**, which usually begins with a concluding phrase (see the chart and Chinh's example below). The conventions of a concluding paragraph in an academic essay are as follows:

1. It does not contain any new ideas that need to be supported.
2. It is at least as short as the introduction.
3. It typically begins with a transitional word or phrase that signals to the reader that the end of the essay is coming.
4. It usually gives a <u>very</u> brief summary of the <u>main</u> idea of the essay.
5. It contains one or more of the following concluding techniques:
   a. A recommendation to readers about the issue in the essay
   b. A prediction about future developments of the essay topic
   c. A solution to the major problem presented in the essay
   d. A final evaluation of the major ideas discussed in the essay

POWER GRAMMAR

Transitions Commonly Used in Conclusions

To begin conclusions	• In conclusion, • To conclude, • As this report shows, • In summary,
To show consequence or result	• As a result, • Consequently, • As a consequence,
To make a prediction	• If . . . , then . . . • Unless measures are taken, there will be . . . in the future. • It is possible that in the next year, . . . • As a consequence of . . . ,

Transitions Commonly Used in Conclusions (cont.)

To offer solutions	• One solution is . . . • In order to solve (the problem of, the issue discussed), • It is possible that . . . is a first step toward solving . . .
To provide a recommendation	• The research suggests that . . . • As _____ (name of the expert) states, " . . ." • We must . . . • I recommend that . . . • Clearly, a recommendation for _____ must be made.
To evaluate	• Actually, • In contrast to . . . , • Although . . . ,

EXERCISE 36 Analyzing two conclusions

With a classmate, read the two conclusions below. Then, answer the questions that follow.

Conclusion 1

In conclusion, an effective website must provide clear and accessible information, eye-catching graphics, and "freebies." The website for L'Oreal makeup products follows these criteria successfully. As a consequence, it is more effective than the Maybelline site, which does not always give clear information and does not offer any free samples. If the Maybelline website were to give out some "freebies" and improve the quality and quantity of its product information, then it would become as effective as L'Oreal's website.

References

L'Oreal website. (2004). Retrieved October 5, 2005 from
http://www.loreal.com/us/index.asp

Maybelline website. (2004). Retrieved October 5, 2005 from
http://www.maybelline.com/home.aspx?res=true

Conclusion 2

In summary, the Skiershop website is superior to Al's Ski Equipment Barn website because of its user friendliness and excellent links. Skiershop's attractive layout and color choice also make this website stand out more compared to Equipment Barn's website. I recommend that Equipment Barn improve its website by adding more links and updating them regularly. To attract more users, this company should also simplify the website's layout and change its color scheme. Purple just does not seem to work with ski equipment! I am sure that these changes would attract more shoppers.

References

Al's ski equipment barn website. (2004). Retrieved October 2, 2004 from http://www.untracked.com/

Skiershop.com website. (2004) Retrieved October 2, 2004 from http://www.skiershop.com/catalog/index.php

1. What transitions are used in the two conclusions? Circle them. Use the transition chart in Power Grammar for help.
2. What concluding techniques does each writer use? (*Hint*: Look at the words and phrases you circled.) List the concluding techniques in the margin, next to where each occurs.
3. Write a possible thesis statement for her essay. Base the statement on the ideas summarized in the first conclusion. Do the same for the other conclusion.
4. Why are these conclusions effective?

EXERCISE 37 Comparing introduction and conclusion

With a partner, reread Katja's introduction (below). Then, read her conclusion. After you read, answer the questions that follow.

Introduction

Nowadays everyone is using webpages for one reason or another. Webpages are a great way for companies to advertise their products and for people to shop and buy products without spending hours in stores. Some people do not know much about the different ways webpages can be designed. However, they do know when a certain page is frustrating to use or access.

InetDzine, a *Dot Com* firm that specializes in website design for the AEC (Architecture, Engineering & Construction) industry, stresses the importance of making websites easy to navigate ("What Makes," 2003). Users need to be able to move easily between pages, and the homepage and featured pages should be easily accessed from any page on the website. Therefore, when I evaluated two websites that advertised two brands of shampoo, I looked at their user friendliness, easy access, and information; based on these criteria, the Head & Shoulders website (headandshoulders.com) proved superior to the Herbal Essence website (herbalessence.com).

Conclusion

Shopping online is a great way to find different products in different stores just by sitting at home on a comfortable chair and "clicking away" on the computer. When consumers know what qualities make a webpage effective, then they will know which webpages to explore and which ones to pass when shopping online. If a website is user friendly, easy to access, and informative, then it is a site worth exploring. The Head & Shoulder website is an example of this type of website. People can save time and avoid frustration by going to this effective website because the designers worked hard to make this website as accessible as possible to their customers.

1. Circle the keywords that appear in both the introduction and the conclusion.
2. What concluding technique(s) are used in the conclusion? List them in the margin, next to where each occurs.
3. Why is the conclusion effective? List your reasons here:

   _____

   _____

EXERCISE 38 **Writing your conclusion**

Reread your essay carefully. Then,

1. Begin your conclusion with a concluding word or phrase.
2. Write a sentence that connects to the last sentence of the last body paragraph.
3. Add the two sentences that summarize the essay's main idea and controlling ideas.
4. Add a prediction, a solution, a recommendation, or an evaluation.
5. Set your essay aside for a few hours or even a whole day if possible.

SPOTLIGHT ON WRITING SKILLS

The References Page

For every source you cite in your essay, you must write a complete reference. Your in-text citations refer your readers to the References page, which is the last page of your essay.

Your research for this essay was from the Internet. Here is the basic form for a complete end-of-text reference from the Web:

Last name of the author

First name's initial

Date of publication (if available)

No capitalization except for the first word.

Date you retrieved the information from the Internet.

URL (no period at the end)

If the URL is too long to fit in one line, divide after any slash (/) or a period (.).

Wingfield, N. (1997). Still netting after all these years. *CNET*

News. Retrieved October 2, 2004 from http://news.

com.com/2009-1082_3-233721.html

Below is a sample References page. It contains three examples of end-of-text references for online sources that show you how to solve problems related to gathering data for your citations:

Two authors.
Titles of articles are NOT italicized.
NO caps except for first word.

Write (n.d.) if no date is given.
Begin with title if no author is given.

Title of website is italicized.

References

Goff, A. & Wheeler, C. (2001, August 29). Web evaluation criteria. *WebQuest*. Retrieved September 19, 2004 from http://imet.csus.edu/imet2/wheelerc/webquests/ |web_evaluation_criteria.htm

The WDG reference section. (n.d.) Retrieved August 30, 2004 from http://www.htmlhelp.com/reference/

Who invented the World Wide Web? (2003, June 30). *Boutell International*. Retrieved October 10, 2004 from http://www. boutell.com/newfaq/basic/inventedweb.html

EXERCISE 39 **Analyzing end-of-text citations**

With two or three classmates, identify the punctuation used in the end-of-text citations above by doing the following:

1. Circle each form of punctuation. Is there a period at the end of the URL?
2. What words are capitalized in the citations? Circle each capital letter.
3. Write four rules for writing an end-of-text citation for Internet sources.
4. Share your rules with another group.

EXERCISE 40 **Writing your end-of-text citations**

Write a References page for your essay. List all the sources you used in your essay. Follow the guidelines you have been given in this chapter.

W E B P O W E R

For updated information on APA style for online sources, go to **http://esl.college.hmco.com/students**.

EXERCISE 41 **Revising your first draft**

Reread Writing Assignment 2. Reread your essay and use the checklist in Appendix 3 ("Revision Checklist," pp. 256–257) to revise your draft. After you are finished, type your essay neatly (follow the format in Appendix 4, "Essay Format," p. 258.) Print four copies of your essay: one for your writing folder, and three for your classmates.

EXERCISE 42 **Participating in a read-around peer response**

Sit in a circle with three classmates. Give each classmate a copy of your essay. Each classmate reads a different part of your essay. Use the form in Appendix 5, "Read-around Peer Review" (pp. 259–260). Then, collect the copies of your essays from your classmates and thank your classmates for reviewing your essay.

EXERCISE 43 **Revising**

Reread your essay and consider the peer response suggestions from your classmates.

1. Which suggestions will improve your writing? How can you incorporate their suggestions in your essay?
2. What did you learn from reading your classmates' essays that can be applied to your writing? Change the parts of your essay that are confusing.
3. Add information or explanations to make your ideas clearer to the reader.

EXERCISE 44 **Self-editing**

Read your essay again, but this time focus on sentence clarity and grammar:

1. Read each sentence carefully to make sure it has a clear subject and a verb.
2. Make sure you use formal language. If you are not sure you are using a word correctly, look it up in a dictionary to make sure it matches what you want to say.
3. Check for subject-verb agreement. Remember that plural verbs do not take the -s (example: "People think . . ." "Some students feel").
4. After you have completed your final draft, place it in a folder with your previous drafts, your classmates' feedback, and all the other materials you developed for Chapter 2 Essay Assignment. Give the folder to your instructor.

EXERCISE 45   **Reading instructor response**

When your instructor returns your essay, read her or his comments carefully:

1. What did your instructor like about your essay? List your strengths on an index card or a piece of paper.
2. What did he or she say you need to improve? List your weaknesses on the other side of the index card or paper. Keep the card or paper in your writing folder.
3. If you are confused about your instructor's feedback, circle the comments you do not understand. Make an appointment with your instructor or go to her or his office during office hours to ask for help. Remember to bring your writing folder with you.

EXERCISE 46   **Writing one more draft**

If your instructor assigns another (final) draft, follow your instructor's feedback to make final changes to your essay. Print your final draft, and place it in your writing folder with the other essay materials. Give it to your instructor.

EXERCISE 47   **Reviewing chapter objectives**

Review the objectives at the beginning of this chapter, and complete the checklist there. Which objectives do you still need to work on? Discuss with a friend or classmate how you will improve in these areas.

⭘ Additional Writing Assignments for More Practice and Assessment

Assignment 1: Create an Essay Map

Reread Katja's introduction and conclusion (Exercise 38). Then,

1. Write an essay map for her essay. Base your map on the ideas you listed in Exercise 38.
2. Borrow keywords from the thesis statement and the conclusion to write the topic sentences. Leave space (four or five lines) under each topic sentence.
3. Circle the controlling ideas in the topic sentence, and list supporting details for these ideas.

Assignment 2: Summarize an Article

Choose an online or print article about an aspect of Web design you do not know well. Write a one-paragraph summary of the article.

Assignment 3: Write about Writing

What was it like to write this chapter's essay assignment? Write a one-page response in which you explain your experience. What was easy? What was hard? Why? What have you learned about your strengths and weaknesses as a writer? For help with this assignment, review the chapter objectives checklist you completed in Exercise 47.

WEB POWER

You will find additional exercises related to the content in this chapter at **http://esl.college.hmco.com/students.**

Reporting about Sensory Loss

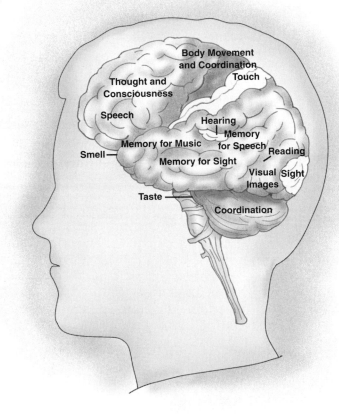

In Chapter 2, you learned about the explaining essay and its parts: the introduction and thesis statement, the body paragraphs and topic sentences, and the conclusion. You also learned about summarizing information and quoting sources. In this chapter, you will apply what you have learned about writing reports.

Many courses in the applied sciences require college students to write reports about concepts and techniques explained in class lectures. In this chapter, you will use the three-step writing process you learned in the previous chapters to write a two- to three-page report about sensory loss and the techniques used to treat it. You will use in-text citations as part of your supporting evidence.

Chapter Objectives

Read the following chapter objectives to preview the chapter content. After you complete the chapter, return to this chart and check (✓) the appropriate boxes on the right.	I have learned this well.	I need to work on this.
Analyze research-based essay assignments		
Apply the three-step writing process to report about sensory loss		
Gather information by brainstorming ideas		
Practice note-taking skills		
Search the World Wide Web		
Evaluate website content		
Gather information at the campus library		
Prepare and give an oral report		
Select appropriate supporting evidence about sensory loss		
Write an essay map to organize your report		
Write a well-developed, well-organized report		
Paraphrase information		
Use paraphrase in your report		
Support your essay with a variety of in-text citations		
Use a diagram to illustrate sensory perception and/or sensory loss		
Prepare a References page		
Use report verbs and phrases to introduce cited information		
Use transition words and phrases to connect ideas		
Learn the difference between quotations and paraphrase		

Chapter Essay Assignment

In each assignment below, a person has been partially deprived of one of her or his senses. You will select one assignment to research and report about. For this research report, you will investigate the topic on the World Wide Web.

1. A person whose vision is impaired decides to have LASIK surgery. In a three-page research report, write:
    A. A background paragraph that describes refractive eye problems; use a diagram to show the biology of (impaired) vision
    B. Two to four body paragraphs discussing the advantages and disadvantages of LASIK surgery.

2. What happens when a person loses her or his sense of taste? Select one reason why a person may partially or completely lose the sense of taste. Write a three-page research report that includes:
    A. A background paragraph describing one to three reasons why a person could lose part or all of her or his sense of taste
    B. Two to four body paragraphs that:
        (a) Discuss the short-term and/or long-term effect(s) of losing all or part of one's sense of taste for your selected reason(s); use a diagram to show how we taste food
        (b) Explain way(s) of restoring or improving one's sense of taste.

3. A person who is hard of hearing can often be helped by using a hearing aid. Select one way a person may become hard of hearing and need to use a hearing aid. In a three-page research report, write:
    A. A background paragraph that explains the way a person can become hard of hearing; use a diagram to show how we hear or what happens when a person loses some of her or his hearing
    B. Two to four body paragraphs discussing the process used by digital hearing aids to help a person who is hard of hearing.

Keep all the materials, drafts, and peer reviews for this essay assignment in the writing folder you used for the essay assignment in Chapter 2, or you may use a new two-pocket folder. Ask your instructor for guidance.

To complete this assignment you need to:

- Search the Internet and the library
- Write a report by following a three-step writing process

Your essay must include:

- An introductory paragraph
- A background paragraph
- Two or three additional body paragraphs
- Two or three in-text references (quotations, summaries, and/or paraphrases)
- A diagram illustrating sensory perception/loss
- A concluding paragraph
- A References page at the end of the paper.

EXERCISE **1** Analyzing the essay assignment

Reread the chapter essay assignment. Then, with three classmates, answer the following questions:

1. What is the **purpose** of this chapter's report assignment? What will you learn by writing a report?
2. Who will **read** your essay? How much knowledge of the topic can you expect your readers to have?
3. Where can you find information about LASIK, taste loss, or hearing aids?
4. What level of formality is appropriate for this assignment?
5. Circle the keywords in the three choices for this chapter essay assignment. What WH- questions (*what, how, why*) will be answered by each? Write them below:

Essay Assignment Choice 1

Examples:

How does the human eye work? What are "refractive eye problems"?

_____

_____

_____

Essay Assignment Choice 2

Examples:

How do we taste food? What happens when a person has a "partial loss" of taste?

Essay Assignment Choice 3

Examples:

How does the human ear process sounds? What does a hearing aid do?

> **Master Student Tip**
>
> If you are unsure about your answers to any of the exercises in this chapter, consult your instructor.

○ Gathering Information

The essay assignment choices in this chapter require you to gather information about three main topics: (1) vision, hearing, or taste; (2) refractive eye problems, taste loss, or hearing loss; and (3) LASIK, ways of restoring taste, or digital hearing aids. This section of the chapter contains many exercises to help you gather and organize this information.

EXERCISE 2   Recalling previous knowledge

Observe the picture at the beginning of this chapter. Then, answer the following questions on separate paper:

1. What comes to mind when you look at it?
2. Which areas of the brain control the five senses? Can you tell from the picture?
3. Which of the five senses do you think we use most often?
4. Which sense do we use least often?
5. What do you know about the five senses? In your notebook, write five sentences about each of the five senses.

EXERCISE 3 Making a list

Create three columns on a sheet of paper. Quickly list what you know about each of the three topic choices in this chapter essay assignment. Then, write down any questions that come to your mind related to each topic. Review your three lists and questions and your answers to Exercise 2, and choose the topic you will write about. Put your lists in your writing folder.

SPOTLIGHT ON WRITING SKILLS

Brainstorming

Brainstorming is a way to generate as many ideas as possible in a short amount of time. *Group brainstorming*, brainstorming with other people, is often used in the business world to generate solutions to difficult problems. In your case, brainstorming with other students will help you share knowledge and ideas. During brainstorming, everybody in the group should participate and share information with the other group members. No idea should be criticized during brainstorming. You will be able to evaluate and select ideas on your own after your brainstorming session.

EXERCISE 4 Brainstorming ideas

Form a group with three or four other students who have chosen the same essay choice. Then, do the following:

1. Share what you know about the topic with your group, especially the list you wrote in Exercise 3.
2. Take notes during the brainstorming session.
3. Review your notes with your group. Reread the assignment and the questions you listed in Exercise 2. What information does your group lack? What do you need to learn more about in order to write your essay?
4. Write more questions that you need to answer in your essay (*examples: What does the human ear look like on the inside? What is good about LASIK? Does smoking affect a person's ability to taste?*).
5. Put your notes and questions in your writing folder.

SPOTLIGHT ON WRITING SKILLS

Websites

You are probably familiar with a variety of search tools or engines. For academic research, the most reliable are Google, AltaVista, Yahoo, and Excite. As you search the Internet, you will have to modify your search, add words or delete them, to get a reasonable number of results. For example, you can begin a broad search by using the word *sight* or *human eye* and then narrow your search by adding words, such as *loss* or *color blindness*. Leave out unimportant words like articles (*a/an*, *the*) and prepositions (*in*, *to*, *with*).

Examples of effective student searches:

1. *General subject*: Taste
   Narrowed topic: Taste buds
   Specific topic: Taste buds sour salty sweet bitter

2. *General subject*: Hearing
   Narrowed topic: Eardrum
   Specific topic: Eardrum loud noises

3. *General subject*: Sight
   Narrowed topic: Eyesight problems
   Specific topic: Myopia nearsightedness

When you searched the Internet for Chapter 2's essay assignment, you looked for commercial websites that advertised a product. In this chapter, you will search for accurate scientific information. Therefore, you will have to pay close attention to the websites you choose.

Not all websites are the same. In fact, there are at least four major types of websites. Each is recognizable by the domain, which are the letters that appear at the end of the **web address**, called **URL** (Uniform Resource Locator):

1. .com = a **commercial** website. It is created by a person or a company. Generally, the reader (you) needs to evaluate carefully the information on .com websites. The goal of a commercial website is to sell a product or an idea. Therefore, the information provided may be incomplete or even biased; it may mention only the good points about a product. In some cases, the information may be incorrect.

2. .edu = the websites of <u>educational</u> institutions, such as colleges and universities. The information provided by these websites has educational purposes: information about the campus, courses offered, faculty, and student services. Official faculty websites generally end in .edu.

3. .gov = <u>government</u> websites. These sites provide accurate information about government services and offices. They also provide accurate information and statistical data about specific cities or counties: population, economy, weather, and so forth. Some government sites report about government-sponsored research.

4. .org = a nonprofit <u>organization</u>, such as the Public Broadcasting Company or the American Heart Association. The main purpose of these sites is to provide information for the public. Therefore, the information is generally accurate and objective.

EXERCISE 5 Evaluating websites

With your classmates, discuss the websites listed in the Spotlight on Writing Skills box about websites. Which seem(s) more reliable? Why? How will this information help you search the Internet?

Master Student Tip

<u>Select your sources carefully</u>. If you cannot retell the main idea of the article in your own words, then it is not a good choice. It will be very difficult to summarize and cite something you find confusing. Select sources that may contain some difficult terminology but that are generally clear.

WEB POWER

You will find more information about evaluating sources at **http://esl.college.hmco.com/students**.

EXERCISE 6 Searching the World Wide Web

Go on the Internet and find information about the essay topic you chose. Consider your group's questions to help you decide what information to select. Be careful about the websites you select.

1. Search specific words that can help you find information about your topic (examples: *partial loss of vision, causes of hearing loss, olfactory glands, taste buds*).

2. Print the first page of the Internet information you want to use in your essay. Place the printed webpages in your writing folder.

3. If the URLs are not already on the printed pages, write them down. You will need this information for your References page.

EXERCISE 7 Searching the library

With a classmate who is researching the same topic, go to the library to gather information:

1. List words and phrases for your search as you did for the Internet search.
2. If you are unfamiliar with the computerized catalog, ask a librarian for assistance.
3. Try to find the most recent sources to use in your report, because the newest information will be best.
4. After you select a source, write in your notebook the information listed in the References Information chart (below). Most of this information will go on your References page, so it is important that you record it carefully (see the examples that follow the Reference Information chart).
5. Photocopy the articles or chapters you have located that contain useful information. Place the copies in your writing folder.

References Information

Information needed for ALL sources	Library call number
	Name of the author
	Date of publication
Information for books	Title of the book
	Place of publication
	Publisher
Information for magazines and journals	Title of the article
	Title of the journal or magazine
	Volume number
	Inclusive page numbers

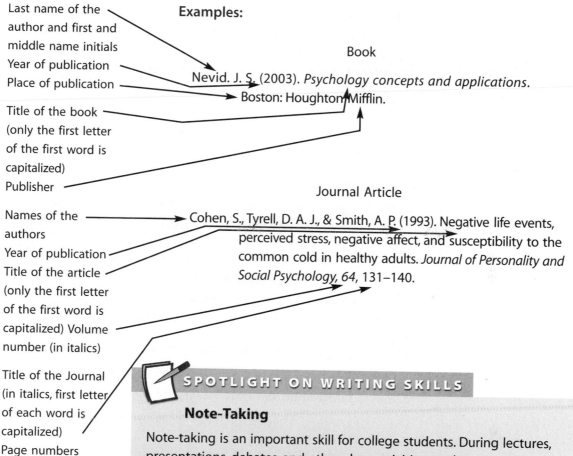

Examples:

Book

Last name of the author and first and middle name initials → Nevid. J. S. (2003). *Psychology concepts and applications.*

Year of publication →

Place of publication → Boston: Houghton Mifflin.

Title of the book (only the first letter of the first word is capitalized)

Publisher →

Journal Article

Names of the authors → Cohen, S., Tyrell, D. A. J., & Smith, A. P. (1993). Negative life events, perceived stress, negative affect, and susceptibility to the common cold in healthy adults. *Journal of Personality and Social Psychology, 64,* 131–140.

Year of publication →

Title of the article (only the first letter of the first word is capitalized) Volume number (in italics)

Title of the Journal (in italics, first letter of each word is capitalized)

Page numbers

SPOTLIGHT ON WRITING SKILLS

Note-Taking

Note-taking is an important skill for college students. During lectures, presentations, debates, and other class activities, students must be able to write down important information without falling behind. It is impossible to write everything a speaker says, so it is better to use mostly words or phrases, not complete sentences, and to write down only the most important information. For example, if the speaker says, "The human ear has three main parts: the outer ear, the middle ear, and the inner ear," a student's notes may say: "human ear, 3 parts: outer, middle, inner." Some people use symbols when taking notes, such as:

an arrow→ to show a relationship between ideas
an equal sign = to mean that two things or ideas are the same

& for *and*   temp for *temporary*
w/ for *with*   diff for *difference* or *different*
w/o for *without*   sthg. for *something*
bc for *because*

If you use symbols and/or abbreviations in your notes, be sure to use them consistently so that you do not forget what they mean.

Here is a student example of note-taking. Notice that the student, Marco, used some of the abbreviations and symbols mentioned on the previous page in order to write as much information as possible during a group presentation. Later in this chapter, you will take notes as your classmates report information.

Marco's Notes

Tongue tastes four things: sweet, sour, salty, bitter
nose does the rest

> example: raw potato & apple taste sweet crunchy
> tongue can't tell diff nose can

nose helps us taste food gone bad so →

> we don't get food poisoning
> people have good mem 4 smells
> e.g. smell rotten egg once, you remember forever!

allergies can stop smell bc nose swells, stuffy →

> not safe to smell sthg. we don't know
> could hurt our nose, health, kill us

olfactory → anything about smell

> olfactory receptors = nose's smell cells
> cilia = tiny hairs

nose sends smells to brain w/ olfactory nerves

causes of partial/total loss of smell (olfactory sensation)

> brain tumors, surgery, old age, working w/ chemicals, smoking

causes of temp loss:

> cold, flu, allergies, strong chemicals

EXERCISE 8 Evaluating Marco's notes

With two or three classmates, reread Marco's notes. Then, answer these questions:

1. What information surprised you in Marco's notes? Why?
2. What information interested you? Why?
3. List up to four topics the writer could use for a single paragraph and the paragraph development structure the writer could use for each topic (use the chart below).

Paragraph Topic	Method of Development
Examples: a. The way(s) the nose's smell cells recognize different odors	a. Process (explain how the cells work)
b. The effect(s) of brain tumors on olfactory nerves	b. Effects (explain what damage tumors cause)
1.	
2.	
3.	
4.	

POWER GRAMMAR

Verbs for Reporting Information

Many college courses require students to report information in a variety of written assignments—for example, when describing a laboratory experiment, evaluating a product, solving a problem, or discussing a controversial issue.

Report verbs are used to introduce information from a variety of sources as shown in the examples below.

Sentences with Report Verbs	Explanations
1. In this report I will <u>discuss</u> the negative effects of sound pollution on young children. [The author conveys his thesis statement.]	Writers use a variety of report verbs to: 1. Communicate their ideas and opinions.
2. Dr John S. Thyne, M.D., <u>recommends</u> *that* children under 5 years of age listen to classical music every day. [The author relates advice of an expert.]	2. Cite experts in the field by quoting and/or paraphrasing their words.
3. The research results <u>indicated</u> *that* teenagers can lose up to 50% of their hearing when exposed to very loud music one hour a day over a period of six months or longer. [The author reports the results of a study.]	3. Relate the results of an experiment or research study.
4. Many studies on the effects of cigarette smoke <u>show</u> *that* smoking causes a temporary loss of taste sensation.	4. The author summarizes the results of many research studies.

Choose carefully among report verbs because they usually indicate to the reader the level of conviction of the expert cited or the strength of the data provided. Below are some examples of reporting verbs:

Forceful	Less Forceful	Weak
argue	state	suggest
assert	explain	imply
claim	find	indicate
contend	recommend	propose
insist	demonstrate	observe
maintain	investigate*	mention
	report	predict
	note	hypothesize
	show	

Master Student Tip

Most report verbs are followed by the word *that*. The exceptions to this rule are followed by an asterisk (*) in these lists.

Another important distinction occurs between verbs reporting the results or effects of something (for instance, an experiment) and verbs reporting opinions or information not necessarily related to results or effects. Here are some of these verbs:

Results	Information and Opinions
demonstrate	allege
indicate	argue
investigate	describe*
observe	discuss*
predict	examine*
report	explain
show	present*
suggest	reveal

EXERCISE 9 **Preparing to report**

Reread the essay assignment you chose. Review your online and print information carefully. Then,

1. Highlight or underline the most important information that would help you complete the essay assignment.
2. On separate paper, write notes about the parts you highlighted. You will be the only one reading the notes, so you may use informal language, abbreviations, and symbols.
3. Compare your notes to the original text to make sure you did not forget any important information you could use in your essay.
4. Rehearse for your oral presentation by reciting your notes to yourself or by reporting to a friend. Time yourself so that you do not go over two minutes.
5. Place your notes in your writing folder.

EXERCISE 10 **Reporting to your group**

Form a group with two or three other students who chose the same essay topic. Then,

1. Give a two-minute oral report to your group about the information you found on the Internet and at the library.
2. Take notes about the information you learn from your group. Use a different page for each classmate's presentation.
3. For each presentation, create a suggestion chart similar to the one for Marco's notes. Give your suggestions to your classmates.
4. With your group, reread the essay assignment and revise the list of questions you wrote in Exercise 2. Think of more questions you and your classmates need to answer in your essays.
5. Place your classmates' suggestions in your writing folder.

EXERCISE **11** **Evaluating freewriting**

After reading her notes, a student, Hoang, did some freewriting to check her knowledge and understanding of the topic. With a classmate, read Hoang's freewriting about hearing loss. Then, complete the steps that follow.

Hoang's Freewriting

Hearing—we use our ears, obviously but what do they look like inside? I think there is something like a hammer in our ear and hairs that move with sound. Sound waves, actually. And what is the use of the part of the ear we can see? Probably the external ear collects sound. However, our ears are very small compared to most mammals; even our pets (dogs, cats, hamsters) have bigger ears than humans! During brainstorming Tom said that his grandfather can't hear well because his ear drums are damaged. Tom explained that the ear drum is a menbran or membrane (?) that moves when the sound waves come inside the ear. Apparently a big, loud explosion during the Vietnam war damaged Tom's grandpa's ear drums. They just popped (gross!) So very loud noises can cause hear loss. Can't something like that be fixed? Tuang said eardrum damage can be fixed sometimes, but he didn't know how. He talked about traditional hearing aids and said that they can help make noises louder but not always clearer. I remember reading in the newspaper that a new hearing aid that uses computer technology can help people who never heard a sound in their lives. These people are "profoundly deaf" and can finally hear for the first time by using this technology. Something to do with the brain and the nerve system. Not sure what or how. My grandaunt lives with us, and she cannot hear very well. My mom said it is because she is very old, so old age can cause hearing loss. My grandaunt wears a hearing aid in her right ear; I know because I have seen it. It is not nice looking, and I wouldn't want to wear one.

1. Circle the keywords that refer to important information.
2. Put an asterisk (*) in the margin next to the most interesting information.
3. Bracket [ ] the incomplete sentences in Hoang's freewriting.
4. Highlight words or phrases that are too informal for academic essays.
5. For two of the informal words or phrases, write more formal *synonyms* (words with similar meaning) that Hoang could use in her report (example: "what is the use of the part of the ear we can see?" = "what is the function of the external ear?")

EXERCISE 12   Freewriting

Reread the essay assignment you chose. Review all your notes and materials about the assignment, including your classmates' suggestion charts. Then, on separate paper, freewrite for fifteen minutes about what you have learned so far about the topic. Remember that when you freewrite, you may use informal language and incomplete sentences.

1. Write what you remember from your notes.
2. Write anything else you remember reading in books, newspapers, and magazines about this topic.
3. Write anything you remember about people you know who have experienced this sensory loss.
4. After you finish, read your notes and circle keywords that refer to the essay topic.
5. Put an asterisk in the margin next to the information that you could use in your essay.
6. When you finish, put your freewriting in your writing folder.

EXERCISE 13   Evaluating Hoang's questions

Read Hoang's questions, which she wrote after reviewing her freewriting. What other questions does Hoang need to answer in her essay? Add two or three questions to her list.

Hoang's Questions

What are sound waves?
What part of the ear is the hammer?
How does it work?
What is the ear drum?
How does it work?
What does "eardrum damage" mean?
What does a human ear look like?
How does it work?
What does it mean to be "profoundly deaf"?
How do old age and loud noise cause hearing loss?

_____

_____

_____

☞ **EXERCISE** 14 **Revising your questions**

Review your notes, your freewriting, and your list of questions once again. Add more questions that can be answered in your essay. Put your revised questions in your writing folder.

POWER GRAMMAR

Transitions

In academic writing, ideas must flow smoothly and be well organized. You have already learned about using keywords and complex sentences to show the relationship between ideas. Another way to show the logical connection between ideas is to use **transitions** between sentences. The examples below are from student essays about sensory loss.

Sentences with Transitions	Explanations
Smoking can cause a temporary loss of taste sensation. In addition, it can cause a loss of appetite. The largest sensory organ in our body is the skin. It senses touch, texture, pressure, and temperature (warmth and cold). Furthermore, the skin allows us to feel pain.	In addition and furthermore are used to *add* information. Other common transitions that show *addition*: Also, Moreover, Additionally,
RGP lenses are similar to the old-fashioned hard lenses; however, the lenses have to be worn at night time when the person is sleeping. We associate the smell of freshly baked bread to something good. Conversely, we associate the smell of sour milk to something disgusting.	However and conversely show *contrast* between two sentences. Other common transitions that show *contrast*: Nevertheless, On the other hand, On the contrary, In contrast,

Sentences with Transitions	Explanations
LASIK is generally permanent, but it does not always work well. <u>Therefore</u>, people have to choose carefully what method to use. Smoking has been shown to cause temporary taste loss up to one hour after smoking; <u>consequently</u>, chain smokers experience consistent taste loss.	<u>Therefore</u> and <u>consequently</u> show how one idea is the *result* or *consequence* of another. Other common transitions that show *result*: <u>Thus</u>, <u>As a consequence</u>, <u>As a result</u>
<u>First</u>, the mucus traps gas (*odor*) molecules; <u>next</u>, the cilia use the proteins in the mucus to recognize odors. This procedure was far from perfect. <u>Then</u>, over fifteen years ago, Dr. Trokel improved the eye surgery technique by inventing the Excimer Laser.	<u>First</u>, <u>next</u>, and <u>then</u> show *time* relationship between events. Other common transitions that show *time*: <u>Previously</u>, <u>Afterward</u>, <u>Later</u>
Some people experience problems after LASIK. <u>For example</u>, my friend Juan is now sensitive to bright light and is experiencing eye dryness. The average human being can memorize up to 10,000 different odors. <u>For instance</u>, most of us have smelled the aroma of freshly baked bread.	<u>For example</u> and <u>for instance</u> introduce *illustrations* (examples).

EXERCISE 15 Noticing punctuation

With two or three classmates, look again at the example sentences on the previous page and discuss the following questions:

1. Where is the transition found in the sentence?
2. What punctuation comes **before** the transition? Is there ever a comma before a transition?
3. What punctuation comes **after** the transition?
4. Write three punctuation rules that writers must follow when using transitions. Base your rules on your answers to questions 1 through 3:

   _____

   _____

   _____

5. Compare rules with another group of students. Are your rules the same? If not, why?

EXERCISE 16 Identifying transitions

With a classmate, read the following sentences and underline or highlight the transitions. Refer to the transitions listed in the Power Grammar box if you need help. <u>Remember</u>: *Dependent words* **are not** *transitions. An example has been completed for you.*

Example:

   My aunt lost some of her hearing because of a childhood illness. <u>Then</u>, her hearing got worse as she got older.

1. Most people do not realize the importance of smell sensation. However, for some food we cannot tell if it is good to eat just by looking at it.
2. A cold can cause temporary taste loss; in fact, a stuffy nose can prevent us from tasting the difference between a potato and an apple, because their texture is the same.
3. One of my father's friends used to be legally blind. Thus, he decided to have LASIK surgery and his eyesight improved dramatically.
4. Although many people rely on their sense of smell very often, they are not aware of doing so. On the contrary, they believe that they do not rely on smell at all when making important decisions.

EXERCISE 17 **Identifying errors**

In the sentences below, the writers made errors in the use of transitions and/or punctuation. With a classmate, identify and correct the errors. Then, compare your answers with those of two classmates. Two examples have been completed for you.

Examples:

                               Indeed

Most people rely on smell to choose a mate. ~~However,~~ recent studies have found that we tend to be attracted to people that have a different chemical composition and body odor than we do.

                ; however,

Smells surround us, ~~however~~ we rely on sight so much that we often ignore smell.

1. Digital hearing aids provide better sound quality than analogue hearing aids, nevertheless some people choose analogue aids because they are cheaper.

2. If a person cannot feel pain, she may hurt herself. However, my friend has no sensation in her left hand. One day she burnt her hand severely, but she did not know she was injured until she saw the burn.

3. Some people have more taste buds on their tongues than average therefore they are called "super tasters."

4. Skin sensation is very important, for example, we can tell if someone is running a fever just by touching the person's forehead.

5. Taste buds only recognize four flavors; in addition, we rely on our sense of smell to recognize all the other flavors.

6. First, the nose recognizes the smell of coffee, then the tongue tastes its bitterness.

EXERCISE 18 **Providing transitions**

With a classmate, read the sentences below and add transitions to show the logical relationship between the sentences. An example has been completed for you.

Example:

> *Therefore,*
> My father cannot hear well.^ We have to speak very loudly when we talk to him.

1. LASIK is usually a very safe procedure. Some people have experienced some problems after this laser surgery.

2. Digital hearing aids can be very small. Some hearing aids are small enough to fit inside the ear canal.

3. Cochlear implants are for severely deaf people and work extremely well. My brother, who is almost completely deaf in one ear, has a cochlear implant that allows him to hear like everyone else and even use a telephone without problems.

4. LASIK is not as invasive as traditional eye surgery. It is safer and has fewer complications than conventional surgery.

WEB POWER

For more practice with transitions and other cohesive devices, go to **http://esl.college.hmco.com/students**.

⭕ Focusing and Organizing

The focusing and organizing step of the writing process requires you to select and organize the ideas and supporting evidence for your report. You will write your "working" thesis statement, "working" topic sentences, and essay map as you did in Chapter 2. Analyzing student examples and doing peer reviews will help you in the decision-making process.

EXERCISE **19** **Evaluating a student essay**

Fernando wrote about an essay assignment that asked him to describe and compare two methods to treat or cure genetic eyesight disabilities. With a classmate, read Fernando's essay, but cover the notes in the left margin with a piece of paper or a ruler. Then, answer the questions that follow.

Fernando's Essay

CRT And LASIK

The Introduction includes interesting information about the topic.

The Thesis Statement lists the ideas that will control the essay.

The Background Paragraph defines *Myopia*, *Hyperopia*, and *Astigmatism* (information the reader needs in order to understand the essay topic).

Method of paragraph development: classification.

For some people to see things that are close is difficult. For others, on the other hand, to see far things is complicated. Those are two of many eye problems that cause vision impairment, the inability to see well. Why do people get vision problems? Sometimes loss of vision is caused by injuries or environmental factors, but the most common reason is *heredity* (genetics). People have eye problems because their parents or grandparents had these problems. Two popular methods for treating the three most common genetic vision impairments are *CRT* and *LASIK*.

Genetic eyesight disability has three common types: *Myopia*, *Hyperopia* and *Astigmatism*. *Myopia* is a refractive problem commonly called nearsightedness. It occurs when the eyeball is too long and the light is focused in front of the retina, which is at the back of the eye and reflects the light. With nearsightedness, distant objects are blurred, but the near objects are clear. The opposite occurs when a person has *Hyperopia*, or farsightedness. In this condition the eyeball is too short and the light is focused behind the retina (see Figure 1).

Figure 1

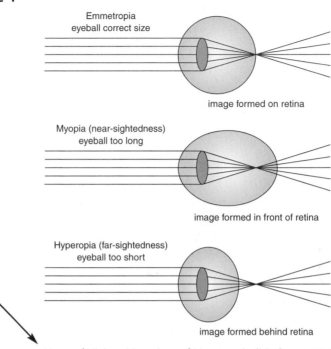

Normal Vision, Myopia and Hyperopia (McCourt, 2001)

The diagram is inserted below the words (see Figure 1). Below the diagram, a caption describes the diagram. Citation information is provided as for any other in-text source.

Reading glasses or lenses are required to have better sight. The third and the last of the most frequent vision problems is *Astigmatism*. This happens when the eye does not focus the light uniformly. In the normal eye, the cornea is curved like a baseball. In astigmatism, the cornea looks like a football ("Myopia, Hyperopia" 2003). Glasses and lenses are the most common remedy for these eye diseases, and without them people are disabled. For people that do not want to wear glasses or contacts and are approved by their doctors, two alternative methods are available: *CRT* and *LASIK*.

Body Paragraph 1 defines and explains *CRT*.

RGP is introduced and defined.

The pros and cons of *CRT* are explained.

Method of paragraph development: definition.

CRT, or *Corneal Refractive Therapy* is a way to treat myopia. It was approved by the FDA in June 2002. For clear vision, the eye's cornea and lens must refract, or bend, light rays properly, so that images are focused on the retina. *CRT* uses contact lenses made of breathable plastic called *RGP*, *Rigid Gas Permeable*. These lenses are similar to the old-fashioned hard lenses; however, the lenses have to be worn at night time when the person is sleeping instead of being used during the day (White, 2003). During the night, *RGP* lenses reshape the cornea so that people do not have to wear glasses or contacts during the day. *CRT* is different from other

Body Paragraph 2 defines and explains *LASIK*.

Cornea is defined for the reader.

Pros and cons of *LASIK* are explained.

Method of paragraph development: process.

nonsurgical methods because it has more lasting effects. However, *CRT* is still a temporary solution. A person has to wear the *RGP* lenses every night or his myopia will come back.

Another method that reshapes the cornea is *LASIK*: *Laser Assisted in Situ Keratomileusis*. *LASIK* is a permanent surgical procedure that changes the shape of the *cornea*, which is the transparent layer that covers the outside of the eyeball. The surgeon uses a laser to perform the surgery. Some eye drops are put in the eye to numb it, but the person is awake as the doctor performs *LASIK*. The outer layer of the cornea is cut on three sides so that it can be opened like the page of a book. Then, the surgeon reshapes the tissue exposed by removing the outer layer. Finally, he puts back the top layer without stitches. The cornea will heal by itself. LASIK does not take long, but it is irreversible ("Lasik Eye Surgery," 2003). Unfortunately, sometimes *LASIK* surgery does not work. My good friend Juan had *LASIK* surgery a few years ago. Recently he told me that he still has to wear eyeglasses because one of his eyes did not get better after surgery. Also, Juan's eyes are drier than they were before the surgery, and he has to use prescription eye drops regularly to keep his eyes moist.

The Conclusion recaps the essay's main points and adds a concluding comment (recommendation).

In conclusion, the three most common eye problems (*Myopia*, *Hyperopia* and *Astigmatism*) can be treated successfully with *CRT* or *LASIK*. The first method is only temporary, but at least people do not have to wear glasses or contacts during their daily activities. The second method is generally permanent, but it does not always work well. Therefore, people have to choose carefully what method to use and must seek the advice of a good eye doctor to help them make the best decision.

References

The end-of-text references are double-spaced, are listed in **alphabetical order**, and follow APA format.

LASIK eye surgery. (n.d.) *1 Up Health*. Retrieved October 20, 2003 from http://www.1uphealth.com/health/ lasik_eye_surgery.html

McCourt, M. E. (2001, September 22). Light as a stimulus for vision. Retrieved October 20, 2003 from North Dakota State University, Psychology Department website http://www.psychology.psych.ndsu.nodak.edu/mccourt/ website/nhtdocs/HomePage

Each entry is indented by 5–7 spaces after the first line.

Myopia, hyperopia, astigmatism, and presbyopia. (2003). *Bellevue LASIK*. Retrieved October 20, 2003 from http://www.bellevue-lasik.com/lasik-information/lasik-refractive.html

White, G., & Segre, L. (2003). Orthokeratology and corneal refractive therapy: Reshaping the eye with contact lenses. *All about Vision*. Retrieved October 21, 2003 from http://www.allaboutvision.com/contacts/orthok.htm

1. What is the thesis statement of the essay? What are its controlling ideas?
2. What does Fernando discuss in the background paragraph? Why?
3. What is the topic of each body paragraph? Does each body paragraph relate to one or more ideas in the thesis statement?
4. What method of development is used in each body paragraph? (Definition, classification, process, cause/effect, compare/contrast)
5. Where could Fernando add more supporting details and/or explanations?
6. What is the purpose of Figure 1?
7. What does Fernando say in the conclusion?
8. What transitions does Fernando use? Highlight or circle them.
9. Compare your answers to questions 1 through 4 to the notes in the margin. How are they different? Why?

EXERCISE 20   Evaluating thesis statements

Circle or underline the controlling ideas in each of the thesis statements on the next page as shown in the example. Then,

1. Predict what questions will be answered in the body paragraphs.
2. Answer these questions: Which of the thesis statements below would be easier for you to write about? Why?
3. Compare your answers with a classmate's.

Example:

Our <u>eye's ability</u> to <u>detect moving objects</u> is <u>crucial</u> to the <u>survival of the human species</u> for <u>three main reasons</u>.

Questions the writer will answer in the body paragraphs:

<u>How</u> does the human eye see objects?
<u>How</u> can it tell when something is moving?
<u>Why</u> is the ability to recognize motion important to people?
<u>What</u> are the three reasons?
<u>How</u> is this ability related to our survival?
<u>What</u> happens if a person loses this ability?
<u>What</u> can be done to restore the ability to see moving objects?

A. There are three main reasons why people lose their ability to taste: age, diseases, and mineral deficiencies.
Questions the writer will answer in the body paragraphs:

_____

_____

_____

_____

B. Some people lose their ability to feel pain in parts of their body when their nervous system is damaged because of accidents or diseases.
Questions the writer will answer in the body paragraphs:

_____

_____

_____

_____

C. Many people think that we taste flavors with the taste buds on our tongue, but our taste sensations also come from other parts of the mouth and even our nose.
Questions the writer will answer in the body paragraphs:

_____

_____

_____

_____

EXERCISE 21 Writing your working thesis

Reread your essay assignment and review the materials you have collected so far, especially your supporting evidence:

1. Write a **working thesis statement** for your essay. Base the statement on your materials. Make sure to address all aspects of the essay assignment.
2. Circle the controlling ideas in the thesis statement.
3. Review the list of questions you revised in Exercise 4. Do the questions relate to the controlling ideas in the thesis statement? Revise your thesis statement and/or your questions as needed.
4. Place your working thesis statement and questions in your writing folder.

EXERCISE 22 Writing your essay map

Review your working thesis statement, your questions, and all your notes.

1. On separate paper, write topic sentences for two or three body paragraphs. Leave half a page under each topic sentence (remember to use keywords and phrases from the thesis statement for the controlling ideas in your topic sentences).
2. Circle the controlling ideas in your topic sentences.
3. From your list of questions, decide which questions go with each topic sentence. List them under the corresponding topic sentence.
4. Answer each question and list the source(s) of your supporting evidence.

Here is Maya's essay map about the sense of smell. Maya put a definition in the thesis statement that she later moved to the background paragraph, where she thought it would be more appropriate.

Each of Maya's topic sentences develops one or more of the ideas in the thesis statement. Notice that Maya did not always use complete sentences to write her map.

Maya's Essay Map

<u>Thesis Statement:</u> The main causes of temporary hyposmia (reduction of smell sensation) are smoking, mucus and adaptation.

<u>Topic Sentence 1 (Background Paragraph):</u> The sense of smell is very important to human beings.

HOW do we smell? Describe neurons, smell cells and cilia (use information from Internet article 1)

WHY is smell important? Explain that we can tell if something has gone bad by its smell without ingesting it and risking poisoning ourselves (personal example) Survival of human beings depends in part on smell (historical information from article 3)

Topic Sentence 2: The sense of smell can be sometimes affected by smoking, mucus and adaptation.

HOW does smoke affect the sense of smell? Describe effects of cigarette smoke especially for the first 30 min. after smoking (summary of paragraph in article 1)

WHAT is mucus? Give dictionary definition

HOW does mucus affect smell? Describe how excess mucus stops cells from receiving odors (Internet article 2)

WHAT does adaptation mean? Give definition from article #2 (quotation)

WHAT are the effects of adaptation? Describe experience of working at McDonald's—drank sour milk without realizing it because the smell of cooked meat and fried foods was too strong

Topic Sentence #3: Smell sensation can be fully restored even after long exposure to smoking and other causes of sense loss.

WHAT makes it possible to restore smell sensation? Explain the unique ability of olfactory nerve cells to regenerate (paraphrase info from article #2)

HOW can hyposmia be avoided? Summarize options: quit smoking, see specialist about causes of mucus, wear a surgeon's mask to protect nose (summary, article 2)

Conclusion: Summarize importance of sense of smell, causes of hyposmia, possible solutions

EXERCISE 23 **Exchanging essay maps**

Exchange essay maps with a classmate. Then,

1. Read your classmate's working thesis statement and topic sentences.
2. Write two or three questions you expect will be answered in the body paragraphs that follow the topic sentences. As you read the evidence for each body paragraph, consider whether it answers your questions.
3. Suggest two or three ways your classmate can improve her or his essay map.

4. Put an asterisk (*) at the end of each piece of information that must be cited if the writer does not include in-text citations (for example: scientific information about a form of therapy or a surgical procedure must have in-text citations).

5. Carefully consider the order of the body paragraphs. If you think their order should be changed, write a suggestion at the end of your classmate's essay map.

6. Return the essay map to your classmate. Discuss your comments with your classmate, and ask questions about the comments your classmate wrote about your essay map.

7. Thank your classmate for the feedback.

8. Repeat steps 1 through 6 with a different classmate.

SPOTLIGHT ON WRITING SKILLS

Paraphrasing

Master Student Tips

You must cite any information that you did not know before you began gathering materials about your topic.

In Chapter 2, you learned that **plagiarism** means using another person's ideas or words without citing (giving credit to) that person. Therefore, when you use online or print sources in your essay, you must use an in-text citation and an end-of-text citation for each source as you learned in Chapter 2.

Paraphrasing means presenting the written information of another author by using the keywords of the original but restating the other ideas in your own words. That is, although you use the most important words, the key terms, of the author, you use synonyms and your own sentences to describe the rest of the author's ideas.

Paraphrasing is not the same as summarizing. Both paraphrases and summaries often include keywords from the original text, and summaries often contain a few paraphrases. However, summaries are always much shorter than the original text; the paraphrase is as long as the original text, sometimes even longer. The paraphrase communicates the exact ideas as the original without quoting the original directly. On the other hand, a summary informs the reader only of the overall main ideas of the original.

When paraphrasing, you need to:

1. Change most words by using synonyms.
2. Use your own sentences.
3. Keep the same keywords of the original text.

Look at the excerpt below from the online article "Anosmia Means Loss of the Sense of Smell." Then, read the paraphrase that follows. Notice the following:

1. Some words and phrases have been changed in the paraphrase. Sometimes a different form of the same word is used in the paraphrase. For example, the words "stop noticing" in the original text have been changed to "do not notice."
2. *Keywords* have stayed the same. For example, the words *smell*, *odor*, and *olfactory* are keywords and have not been changed in the paraphrase.
3. The sentence structure is different. Notice the marked subjects (S) and verbs (V) in the clauses of the first sentences of both texts.
4. The paraphrase is followed by an in-text citation.

Original Text

      S   V   S   V

If you *smell* an *odor* for long enough, you eventually stop noticing it. This is because prolonged exposure to a *strong smell* is believed to saturate the *olfactory* epithelium *with odor molecules* to the point where information is no longer delivered *to the brain*. [44 words]

Paraphrase

      S   V   S   V

People do not notice a *strong odor* when they are exposed to it for a long period of time. The reason is that the *olfactory* tissue inside the nose gets filled up *with odor molecules* and stops transmitting the smell *information to the brain* ("Anosmia Means" 2001). [44 words]

Here is a summary of the same text. Notice the following:

1. The summary is much shorter than the original text and the paraphrase.
2. It states only the main ideas of the original.
3. Some *keywords* are used.
4. Synonyms are used for words that are not key terms.
5. An in-text citation is given at the end of the summarized information.

The human nose gets used to *strong* lingering *smells* ("Anosmia Means" 2001). [8 words]

EXERCISE 24 **Comparing texts**

With two or three classmates, read the following excerpt from J. S. Nevid's Psychology Concepts and Applications, *a textbook for introductory psychology courses. Then, read the summary and paraphrase below the original text. After you finish reading, answer the questions that follow.*

Original Text

Vocabulary:

Stimuli = signals from the world around us, such as odors, sounds, or lights.

Impinge = intrude, invade, enter by force.

Detect = notice, be aware of.

Notice that the text has three paragraphs.

Sensation is the process by which we receive, transform, and process stimuli that impinge on our sensory organs into neural impulses, or signals, that the brain uses to create experiences of vision, hearing, taste, smell, touch, and so on.

Each of our sense organs contains specialized cells, called **sensory receptors**, which detect stimuli from the outside world, such as light, sound, and odors. They are found throughout the body, in such organs as the eyes, ears, nose, and mouth, and in less obvious locations, such as the joints and muscles of the body and the entirety of the skin.

Our sensory receptors are remarkably sensitive to certain types of stimuli. On a clear, dark night we can detect a flickering candle thirty miles away. We can also detect about one drop of perfume spread through a small house. [138 words]

Source: Nevid, J.S., Psychology concepts and applications. Copyright © 2003 by Houghton Mifflin Company. Reprinted with Permission.

Summary

The author and title are mentioned at the beginning of the summary.

Only the main ideas are mentioned.

In Psychology Concepts and Applications, J. S. Nevid defines **sensation** as the ability to process external stimuli through sensory receptors. These specialized cells are found in the human body and can detect very weak signals (Nevid, 2003). [33 words]

Paraphrase

The paraphrase is the same length or longer than the original text. It includes all the ideas of the original.

The information is presented in the same order as in the original.

Each idea is given the same importance given by the author in the original text.

Keywords stay the same, but unimportant words are different.

Notice that the student used her own sentences.

The paraphrase is followed by an in-text citation.

Notice that the paraphrase has three paragraphs like the original.

   Our bodies rely on our sensory organs to collect, transform, and interpret outside stimuli. The sensory organs transmit information about the stimuli to the brain. The brain transforms these signals into neural impulses that allow us to see, hear, taste, smell, and touch the world around us. This whole process is called <u>sensation</u>.

   We sense external signals, such as light, sound, and smell, through our <u>sensory receptors</u>. These specialized cells are found everywhere in our bodies. Our eyes, ears, mouth, nose, and skin contain sensory receptors. However, even some unexpected areas in our bodies, such as our joints and muscles, have sensory receptors.

   Different sensory receptors specialize in detecting different external stimuli very efficiently. For example, our eyes can see the light of a candle at a distance of thirty miles on a clear, moonless night. Our noses can smell one drop of perfume spilled inside a small house (Nevid, 2003). [149 words]

1. What synonyms are used in the summary? Circle at least two.
2. What synonyms are used in the paraphrase? Circle at least four.
3. What keywords are used in the paraphrase? Highlight or underline at least six.
4. Look again at the in-text citations in the summary and paraphrase. Why are they different? What basic information must be included in the in-text citation?

EXERCISE 25 **Using synonyms**

With a small group of classmates, find synonyms for the words below. If you cannot think of a synonym, use a dictionary or ask your instructor for help.

Nouns:

Epithelium _____

Impairment _____

Reduction _____

Sensation _____

Adjectives:

Olfactory _____

Visual _____

Partial _____

Defective _____

EXERCISE 26 **Writing a summary**

With a classmate, read the excerpt below from Nevid's Psychology Concepts and Applications. *Then, complete the steps that follow.*

> People are noticeably more sensitive to changes in the pitch of a sound than to changes in volume. They will perceive the difference if you raise or lower the pitch of your voice by about one-third or 1 percent (1/333). Yet they will not perceive a difference in the loudness of a sound unless the sound is made louder or softer by about 10 percent. If you are going to sing, you had better be right on pitch (hit the note precisely), or people are going to groan. But you might be able to raise the volume on your stereo a little without the next-door neighbor noticing the difference. Then, too, your neighbor may not notice it if you lower the stereo by a notch.

Source: Nevid, J.S., Psychology concepts and applications. Copyright © 2003 by Houghton Mifflin Company. Reprinted with Permission.

1. Write a summary of the text. Use the strategies you learned in Chapter 2 about summarizing (read it once, reread and mark the text, read one more time, cover the text and retell the main ideas).

2. Paraphrase the first paragraph. Remember to follow this chapter's guidelines about paraphrasing (use keywords, use your own sentences and some synonyms).

3. Compare your summary and paraphrase with those written by another pair of students. Notice the similarities and differences. Why are they different?

POWER GRAMMAR

Paraphrase

To paraphrase correctly, you must follow specific punctuation rules as shown in the examples below.

Sentences	Explanations
According to Sophia P. Glezos, "patients who develop disease-induced taste deficiency typically add more salt to meals, simply because the foods are, to them, tasteless" (Glezos, 2003, p. 1).	As you learned in Chapter 2, **quoting** means reporting in your writing the **exact words** someone else said or wrote. When quoting, use quotation marks (" ") around the quoted phrase or sentence.
According to Sophia P. Glezos, people who lose their sense of taste because of illness tend to eat saltier foods in an attempt to add flavor (Glezos, 2003).	**Paraphrasing** means writing down what a person said by using **different words**. In a paraphrase, the meaning should stay the same as the original words.
Dr. James Brown, a famous eye specialist, maintains that although both LASIK and CRT may have some disadvantages, they mostly have beneficial effects (Brown, 2003).	When paraphrasing: 1. The report verb (*maintains*) is followed by *that*. 2. The paraphrase never begins with a capital letter (*both . . .*) 3. Quotation marks are not used.

(Continued)

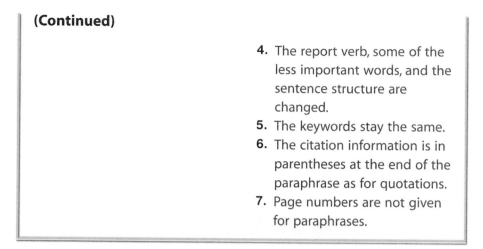

4. The report verb, some of the less important words, and the sentence structure are changed.
5. The keywords stay the same.
6. The citation information is in parentheses at the end of the paraphrase as for quotations.
7. Page numbers are not given for paraphrases.

EXERCISE 27 **Finding differences**

Read the quotations and paraphrases below. What differences do you notice between the quotations and paraphrases? Circle the differences in punctuation, and highlight or underline any words that differ. Two examples have been completed for you.

Examples:

Dr. Jameson, an experienced ophthalmologist, stated "Laser eye surgery is generally safer and less invasive than traditional eye surgery." (Quotation)

Dr. Jameson, an experienced ophthalmologist, stated that laser eye surgery is usually less traumatic and carries fewer risks than regular eye surgery. (Paraphrase)

1. **A:** As Glezos informs, "Self-help techniques for enhancing flavor are to chew well and to alternate bites of different foods in one meal."
   B: Glezos informs that chewing food well during meals and switching foods between bites is a good way to improve taste sensation.

2. **A:** Dr. Sara asserts, "Only 17% of hearing aids are returned nationwide by patients who are dissatisfied with them."
   B: Dr. Sara asserts that most patients are very happy with their hearing aids.

3. **A:** One patient admitted, "Since I quit smoking, my sense of smell has become much sharper."
   B: One patient admitted that her sense of smell improved considerably after she quit smoking.

EXERCISE 28 **Listing report verbs**

With a classmate, do the following:

1. On separate paper, list the report verbs used in the sentences above.
2. Change the report verb in each sentence.
3. Compare your sentences with those of two other classmates. Did you choose the same report verbs?
4. Keep your list of report verbs in your writing folder. You will need it when you draft your essay.

EXERCISE 29 **Noticing sentence structure**

Reread the sentences in Exercise 28 with two or three classmates. What differences in sentence structure do you notice between each quotation and paraphrase? Why is it necessary to use your own sentences when paraphrasing?

WEB POWER

For practice with quoting and paraphrasing and how to introduce them correctly, go to **http://esl.college.hmco.com/students**.

○ Writing, Revising, and Editing

As you put together your essay, keep in mind what you have learned about summarizing, paraphrasing, and quoting information. Use your sources wisely, and cite any information you did not know before you researched your topic.

EXERCISE 30 **Analyzing an introduction**

With two classmates, read Maya's introduction below. Then, answer the questions that follow.

Maya's Introduction Paragraph

Smell is the sense we most often take for granted. Most people rely on their eyes, their ears, and their hands for information, and they forget their noses unless some really powerful smell gets their attention. However, smell is part of our everyday lives, and we all have favorite smells. What is your favorite smell? I am sure most people can answer this question very quickly. My favorite smell is the scent of jasmine. Every spring, it blooms on the trellis outside my bedroom window and makes me think of India, where I was born. Smell can remind us of our favorite places or even our favorite foods. If I close my eyes, I can smell my grandmother's chicken curry even though her kitchen is on the other side of the world. Smell is in most of my memories, and most people would agree that they have many pleasant smell memories too. However, some people cannot smell very well because of disease or accidents, and they may never be able to completely regain their sense of smell.

1. Where is the general topic of the essay introduced?
2. How does Maya capture the attention of her readers?
3. Bracket the [thesis statement] and circle the controlling ideas.
4. Identify subjects (S) and verbs (V) in the first three sentences.
5. Which of these three sentences is a complex sentence? Underline the dependent clause, and circle the dependent word.

EXERCISE 31   Drafting your introduction

Write an introduction for your essay:

1. Introduce the topic right at the beginning of your introduction.
2. Use interesting information to capture the readers' attention. You may tell about a personal experience as Maya did, or you may choose some other method to make your introduction interesting (for example, a quote, an example, statistics).
3. Write your thesis statement.

EXERCISE 32   Evaluating introductions

Exchange introductions with a classmate. Read your classmate's introduction carefully, and then answer these questions:

1. Does the introduction contain interesting information that makes you want to read the rest of the essay?
2. Does the introduction contain a thesis statement?
3. Circle the controlling ideas in the thesis statement. Does the thesis answer the essay assignment? Can you predict what the essay will discuss?

4. Is the thesis statement a clear sentence? Identify the subject (S) and verb (V) in the thesis statement. If you are not sure, ask your instructor for assistance.

5. How can your classmate improve her or his introduction? Write one or two suggestions below the introduction.

EXERCISE 33 Analyzing background paragraphs

With two classmates, read Chien's and Maya's background paragraphs below. Then, answer the questions that follow.

Chien's Background Paragraph

Refractive eye surgery was established long before the invention of LASIK surgery. Refractive eye surgery is done to correct problems with the shape of the eyeball, such as nearsightedness and astigmatism. If the eyeball is not perfectly round, the eye cannot see images very well. The father of modern refractive eye surgery, Doctor José I. Barraquer of Bogotá, Colombia, performed the first refractive eye surgery almost sixty years ago. His technique was called *Keratomileusis* from the Greek *keratos,* cornea, and *mileusis,* carving. With Keratomileusis, Barraquer removed a small piece of *cornea* (the transparent outer layer that covers the eye), cut and reshaped it, and then sewed it back into place to allow the eye to focus better. This procedure was not very good, and patients often needed more than one operation to see real improvement in their vision ("History," 2003). Then, over fifteen years ago, Dr. Trokel improved the eye surgery technique by inventing the Excimer Laser that uses "ultraviolet light energy to reshape the corneal surface" ("The history of Lasik . . ."). This laser technique is more precise than Keratomileusis and is called *PRK (Photo Refractive Keratectomy).* However, PRK is performed to the top layer of the cornea and takes a long time to heal. Subsequently, in 1990, two Greek doctors combined Keratomileusis and PRK and invented *LASIK, Laser in-Situ Keratomileusis* ("History," 2003). LASIK surgery is done to the middle layer of the cornea, and it takes a lot less time to heal than PRK. In less than fifty years, eye surgeons were able to improve and perfect refractive eye surgery.

References

History of Lasik. (n.d.) *Laser Vision Professional Lasik Center*. Retrieved October 15, 2003 fromhttp://www.thailasikcenter.com/English/lasik.htm

The History of Lasik . . . (n.d.) *Ophthalmology Consultants of Fort Wayne*. Retrieved October 15, 2003 fromhttp://www.ophc.com/lasik_history.htm

Maya's Background Paragraph

The sense of smell is very important because it has helped humans survive. The way we identify smells involves smell cells and different types of nerve cells called *neurons*. The olfactory neurons really do most of the work. They are special nerves in the nose, mouth and throat that have tiny hairs (*cilia*) that are surrounded by mucus. First, the mucus traps gas (*odor*) molecules; next, the cilia use the proteins in the mucus to recognize odors. Then, the olfactory neurons transmit this smell information to the brain. Finally, the brain classifies and stores the smell in its memory. This complex process of identifying specific odors is called *chemosensation* ("Sense of Smell"). The brain is able to connect odor memories to specific events in our lives. The average human being can memorize up to 10,000 different odors ("Smell and Taste," 2002). For instance, most of us have smelled the aroma of freshly baked bread. We associate this smell to something good. Conversely, many of us have opened the milk carton only to find a sour smell to it. We associate this smell to something disgusting. While we would gladly taste the freshly baked bread, it would take a lot to convince us to drink sour milk unless we are on a reality TV show! This smell memory has, in part, preserved us as a species. Without a sense of smell, we would have probably poisoned ourselves to extinction long ago. As Dan Markiewicz reports, "smell was early humans' most important sense. It drew mates to each other, helped humans avoid predators, and allowed them to detect suitable food" (Markiewicz, 2000). Therefore, smell is one of our primitive senses and it is very important to our survival.

References

How our sense of smell works (n.d.). *Serene Aromatherapy*. Retrieved October 14, 2003 website http://www.angelfire.com/ms/OzConnection/How.html

Markiewicz, D. (2000, May 17). Sharpening the sense of smell. Retrieved October 16, 2003 from http://www.ishn.com/CDA/ArticleInformation/features/BNP_Features_Item/0,2162,3102,00.html

Smell and taste disorders (2003, December 24). *Ohio Health*. Retrieved October 14, 2003 from 12/24/2003 http://www.ohiohealth.com/healthreference/reference/561FAE4B-75EF-432E-AA30D60099AEC95B.htm

1. What questions are answered in each background paragraph? Write them on separate paper.
2. What key terms are defined in each paragraph? Circle them.
3. How many in-text citations does Chien's paragraph contain? How many does Maya's paragraph contain? Chien: —————— Maya: ——————
4. Why is the author information missing in some citations? What information is given instead? Why?
5. What information is quoted? What information is paraphrased or summarized? How can you tell?
6. Why is it important to cite your sources in academic writing?
7. What transitions do Chien and Maya use in their paragraphs? Highlight or circle them. Do they effectively connect ideas?

EXERCISE 34 **Drafting your background paragraph**

Reread your essay assignment. Then, review your essay map and the other materials in your writing folder. Begin writing your background paragraph. In your paragraph, provide the following:

1. A definition of the essay topic or key terms: how vision can be impaired; reason(s) for partial or permanent taste loss; how a person can become hard of hearing.
2. Additional information that you think will help the reader understand the essay's main idea, for example:
   a. A brief description of the topic (example: a description of the inner ear)

    b. Scientific information essential for reader understanding (example: categories of hearing impairment caused by extremely loud noises)

    c. Current relevant information and recent research about the topic from websites (in-text citations such as quotations, paraphrases, and/or brief summaries)

    d. Evidence that a problem exists (example: statistics about the side effects of taste loss).

EXERCISE 35 **Giving and receiving feedback**

Exchange background paragraphs and supporting materials with a classmate. Read your classmate's background paragraph. Then,

1. In the margin, identify two ways it prepares readers for the essay, and highlight each in the background paragraph.
2. Circle the controlling ideas in the topic sentence of the background paragraph.
3. If not all controlling ideas are explained in the paragraph, write one or two questions below the paragraph that your classmate should have answered in her or his background paragraph.
4. Read your classmate's comments about your paragraph, and ask her or him any questions you have about the comments.
5. Thank your classmate for the feedback.

EXERCISE 36 **Evaluating Chien's paragraph**

You already read Chien's background paragraph. Now, read her other body paragraphs about the disadvantages of LASIK surgery. Then, complete the steps that follow.

Chien's Body Paragraphs

    LASIK surgery is a form of refractive eye surgery that corrects nearsightedness, farsightedness and astigmatism. Nearsightedness is also called *myopia*. It occurs when the eye cannot focus on things that are far away. Farsightedness is also called *hyperopia*, and it means that people cannot see things that are close up. Older people get this type of problem, but it is called *presbyopia* when caused by age. Astigmatism affects the shape of the eye so the images seem distorted. People with myopia or hyperopia can also have astigmatism (LASIK). Laser surgery (LASIK) can correct all these problems. LASIK uses an excimer laser that produces a "computer controlled 'cool' ultraviolet beam of light" ("Basik Lasik," 2000). The laser changes the shape of the cornea by thinning it in specific areas. The eye doctor decides what areas need to be reshaped to improve vision. During LASIK, a thin layer of cornea is cut on three sides and then lifted so that after surgery it can be put back into place. Then, the eye doctor (ophthalmologist) "reshapes the curvature of the cornea and allows light to focus on the retina" (2000). Finally, the outer layer is put back in place. Because the two layers of cornea bond together very quickly, no stitches are necessary. Thus, LASIK is a quick, and generally safe technique.

However, some patients suffer some negative effects after LASIK surgery. A few patients lose some of their vision while others develop serious visual symptoms. According to the FDA, "some patients develop glare, halos, and/or double vision that can seriously affect nighttime vision" (LASIK, 2003). Some patients may not be able to see as well in situations of low light contrast, such as at night or on foggy days. Sometimes, patients develop severe eye syndrome. This syndrome causes eye dryness that can make vision blurry and unfocused. It can also cause pain and/or discomfort, and the patient may not be able to focus properly. Some negative consequences may be caused by the ophthalmologist that conducts the surgery. Dr. Marie Morre stated, "If he or she cuts too much or too little of the cornea, the patient may end up with worse sight than he had before" (personal communication, October 9, 2003). Also, Dr. Morre conceded that LASIK surgery does not always correct the vision problems completely. In fact, people with serious myopia or other refractive vision disabilities still need to wear glasses after LASIK because the operation cannot correct major vision problems (2003). Thus, it is a good idea to consider the possible disadvantages before choosing to have LASIK surgery.

1.   Bracket the topic sentence in each paragraph, and circle the controlling ideas.

2.   In each body paragraph, circle the words that relate to the controlling ideas in the topic sentence. Draw lines from the words to the controlling ideas.

3.   Chien defines the meaning of some words. What words does she define in her body paragraphs? Why does she provide this information?

4.   Highlight the in-text citations. Notice that the in-text citations do not always contain the same type or amount of information. Why? Discuss the reasons with a classmate.

5.   Underline the transitions Chien uses in her paragraphs. How do they help connect ideas?

Note: You will read Chien's References page later in this chapter.

EXERCISE 37   Writing your body paragraphs

Review the essay assignment, your essay map, supporting materials, introduction, and background paragraph. Type or write your introduction and background paragraph on another piece of paper. Compose your body paragraphs:

1.   Make sure your topic sentences refer to one or more of the controlling ideas in the thesis statement. If necessary, revise your thesis and/or topic sentences.

2.   Look carefully at the supporting details in each body paragraph. Make sure they support the controlling ideas in the body paragraph. If you need more information, go through your materials or return to the Internet for additional research.

3.   If some supporting evidence would be more effective in another paragraph, make the changes now. Eliminate any supporting details that do not seem to support the controlling ideas well.

4.   Check the method of development of each body paragraph (definition, process, comparison and/or contrast, classification, or cause and/or effect). Make sure you use the best method to communicate your ideas in each paragraph.

5.   Consider the overall sequence of your body paragraphs. Move them around if you think they would be more effective in a different order.

6. Check the citations of the supporting information in each of your body paragraphs. Remember that <u>any information you did not know when you began your assignment must be followed by an in-text citation</u>:

   a. If you **paraphrase** or **summarize** from a source (that is, write about the information in your own words), put an in-text citation right after the information (example: Nuttall, 2004).

   b. If you **quote directly** from a source, <u>add page numbers</u> to your in-text citation (example: Nuttall, 2004, p. 15).

7. Put your paragraphs and all your materials in your writing folder.

EXERCISE 38 **Completing a diagram**

Review your essay assignment. Look for the directions about the type of diagram you need to add to your essay.

1. Review your materials to find a diagram, or search the Internet. Choose the diagram you will add to your essay.

2. Print or draw the diagram on separate paper and put it in your writing folder.

EXERCISE 39 **Evaluating a conclusion**

You have already read Chien's background paragraph and body paragraphs. Now, read Chien's introduction and conclusion. After reading, answer the questions that follow.

1. In the introduction, underline the thesis statement and circle the controlling ideas.

2. Circle words in the conclusion that refer to the ideas in the introduction. Does Chien's conclusion match the topic of the introduction?

3. What concluding technique does Chien use in her conclusion? (examples: prediction, recommendation, solution, evaluation)

4. In what ways are the conclusion and introduction different? Why?

5. Compare answers with a classmate's.

Introduction

Nowadays, many people have to wear eyeglasses or contact lenses because their vision is not perfect. Some people start wearing glasses or contacts when they are very young and wear them for the rest of their lives. They never know what it is like not to wear glasses or contacts. These can be very expensive and need a lot of care. The glasses may break, so patients need to keep them in a case when they do not need to wear them. Glasses also need to be cleaned regularly and can get scratched. Contact lenses are a little better than glasses. People can forget they have them on. However, sometimes contacts can fall out, and then they are hard to find. Also, contacts can break and get scratched just like glasses. Today, a new technique called LASIK can help people say goodbye to their glasses forever. LASIK surgery is a safe, low-cost technique, but it has some risks and limitations.

Conclusion

In conclusion, LASIK is generally safe and patients heal quickly after it, but some people experience serious vision problems. In spite of these problems, LASIK has become the favorite choice of people who are tired of wearing eyeglasses or contact lenses everyday. Clearly, LASIK is still a surgical procedure and as such it includes some risks and may cause possible side effects. Therefore, patients should not rush to get LASIK just because they are tired of wearing glasses. People with refractive vision problems should research the topic extensively before they select to have LASIK. Also, they should consult an experienced doctor who will run various tests to make sure each patient is a good candidate for the surgery.

EXERCISE 40 **Writing your conclusion**

Reread your essay, especially the introduction and thesis statement. Then,

1. Begin your conclusion with a concluding word or phrase (see chart in Chapter 2, pp. 93–94).
2. Write a sentence that connects to the last sentence of the last body paragraph.
3. Add a brief summary (two or three sentences) of the essay's main idea and controlling ideas (thesis and topic sentences).
4. Use a concluding technique to leave the readers with a final message.

EXERCISE **41** **Listing your references**

Write a complete reference for every source you cite in your essay. Type your references on the last page of your essay. Follow Chien's example below:

Chien's References Page

Center heading. ————————————————————→ References

Give the date when you accessed the information.

LASIK Eye Surgery. (2003, June 6). Center for Devices and Radiological Health. *U.S. Food and Drug Administration.* Retrieved October 15, 2003 from http://www.fda.gov/ cdrh/lasik/risks.htm

Do not put a period at the end of the URL.

Double space and indent 1/2 inch after the first line (5–7 spaces).

Basik Lasik: Tips on Lasik eye surgery (2000). *Federal Trade Commission.* Retrieved October 15, 2003 from http://www.ftc.gov/bcp/conline/pubs/health/lasik.htm

If no author is given, begin with the title of the information.

History of Lasik. (n.d.) *Laser Vision Professional Lasik Center.* Retrieved October 15, 2003 from http://www.thailasikcenter.com/ English/lasik.htm

If no date is available, write (n.d.).

The history of Lasik . . . (n.d.) *Ophthalmology Consultants of Fort Wayne.* Retrieved October 15, 2003 from http://www.ophc. com/lasik_history.htm

 **EXERCISE** **42** **Using report verbs**

Reread your essay draft. Then,

1. Insert four or five report verbs in your essay.
2. Underline or circle each report verb you add.
3. Print your essay, and set it aside for a few hours.

EXERCISE 43 Revising your draft

As you reread your essay, answer the questions below, and make the appropriate changes to your draft.

1. What information should be added to make the essay stronger?
2. What details should be taken out?
3. What ideas and details offer the most convincing evidence?
4. Which ideas and details should go in another paragraph?
5. How well do the in-text citations follow APA format?

EXERCISE 44 Self-editing

Read your essay once again. Check off each item below as you complete it. When you are finished, <u>print four copies of your essay</u>—one for your writing folder and three for your classmates.

1. _____ Each sentence has a clear subject and verb (if a sentence is not very clear, rewrite it).

2. _____ Subjects and verbs agree. Plural subjects are followed by plural verbs (review subject-verb agreement in Chapter 1 if you are not sure).

3. _____ Complex sentences are punctuated correctly (review complex sentences in Chapter 1 if you are not sure).

4. _____ Sentences flow well together, and some sentences begin with a transition to show a logical connection with the preceding sentences.

5. _____ Quotations are introduced and punctuated correctly (review the grammar of quotations in Chapter 2 for help).

6. _____ The language is formal and appropriate for academic writing.

7. _____ The spelling has been checked twice for correctness.

EXERCISE 45   **Participating in read-around peer response**

Exchange essays with three classmates. Each one reads a different part of your essay. Use the "Read-around Peer Response" form (Appendix 6, p. 261) for your response.

EXERCISE 46   **Rewriting your essay**

Reread your essay carefully. Then,

1. Consider your classmates' responses:
    a. Which suggestions can you incorporate that will improve your essay?
    b. What did you learn from reading your classmates' essays that can be applied to your writing?
2. Type your essay.
3. Place your draft in your writing folder. Include your previous drafts, your essay map, your peer responses, and all the other materials you developed for Chapter 3 Essay Assignment.
4. Give the folder to your instructor.

EXERCISE 47   **Writing one more draft**

If your instructor requires to write a final draft, read your instructor's comments carefully. Then,

1. Answer these questions:
    a. What did your instructor like about your essay? List your essay's strengths on an index card or sheet of paper.
    b. What did you instructor say you need to improve? List your essay's weaknesses on the back of the index card or paper.
2. Keep the card or paper in your writing folder.
3. Revise your essay by following your instructor's suggestions.
4. Circle any instructor comments that confused you. Make an appointment with your instructor or go to her or his office during office hours to ask for help. Remember to bring your final draft and writing folder with you.

EXERCISE 48   **Reviewing chapter objectives**

Review the objectives at the beginning of this chapter and complete the checklist. Which objectives do you still need to work on? Discuss with a friend or a classmate how you will improve in these areas.

○ Additional Writing Assignments for More Practice and Assessment

Assignment 1: Summarize

Find a newspaper or magazine article about your essay topic. Write a one-paragraph summary of the article.

Assignment 2: Summarize and Paraphrase

Find an article on the Internet that describes how the brain processes information about the sense of touch. As you write a summary of the article, paraphrase one or two sentences that express the most important ideas.

Assignment 3: Write a Paragraph

Reread Marco's notes found earlier in this chapter (p. 112). Then, write the information in paragraph form by using formal language and sentence structure.

WEB POWER

You will find additional exercises related to the content in this chapter at **http://esl.college.hmco.com/students**.

Investigating College Stress

THERE ARE ONLY
TWO TIMES
I FEEL STRESS:

DAY AND NIGHT

Many college students experience high levels of stress because of the pressures and demands of college. In this chapter, you will investigate the impact of college stress on first-year students. You will be able to draw on your own experiences and observations as a college student. You will also interview an expert about college stress and will incorporate the interview in your research report.

Chapter Objectives

Return to this chart after completing the chapter, and check (✓) the appropriate box to the right.	I have learned this well.	I need to work on this.
Gather information about stress by		
Listing		
Evaluating other students' ideas		
Reading and analyzing a psychology textbook excerpt		
Discussing the topic with your classmates		
Freewriting about college stress		
Searching the WWW		
Interviewing an expert about college stress		
Evaluate conflicting information		
Summarize an interview		
Use a fishbone map to identify causes of stress		
Create a chart to identify and organize supporting materials		
Write a well-developed report about college stress		
Cite your sources, including the interview, according to APA format		
Give and receive peer feedback about your college stress essay		
Respond to your instructor's comments		
Revise and edit effectively before and after receiving peer and instructor feedback		
Identify count and noncount nouns and use them in definitions		
Understand the sentence structure of definitions		

Chapter Essay Assignments

Each of the four assignments below focuses on college students and stress. You will select one of these assignments to research and report about. You will also interview an expert, someone who has treated or experienced college stress. Read each assignment carefully.

1. Describe two or three psychological effects of stress on first-year college students. Interview an expert about the effects of college stress on college students' mental health. Include the results of the interview with your research report.

2. Describe two or three major physical symptoms of first-year college students' stress. Interview an expert about the physical symptoms of stress. Include the interview in your research report.

3. Describe two or three effective ways to treat severe college stress in first-year students. Interview an expert about the most helpful treatments of college stress, and report the results of the interview as part of your research for this paper.

4. Describe two or three strategies to prevent college stress in first-year students. Interview an expert about the most important steps college students can take to prevent stress. Report the results of the interview as part of your research for this paper.

Keep all the materials, drafts, and peer reviews for this essay assignment in your writing folder. You may use a new two-pocket folder for this assignment, or you may reuse the folder you used for Chapter 3's essay assignment. Ask your instructor for guidance.

To complete this assignment, you need to:

- Complete an Internet search
- Interview an expert
- Write a research-based report by following a three-step writing process

Your essay must include:

- An introductory paragraph in which you define *stress*
- A background paragraph in which you explain two or three *causes of stress*
- Two or three additional body paragraphs that focus on your essay topic (psychological effects, physical symptoms, treatments, or prevention strategies)

- Two to four in-text references
- A concluding paragraph
- A references page at the end of the paper
- A transcript of your interview (appendix)

EXERCISE 1   Analyzing the essay assignment

Reread the four choices for the essay assignment. Then, with three or four classmates, answer the following questions:

1. What is the **purpose** of the overall assignment? Why did your instructor give you this assignment? (*Hint*: Think about causes of college stress and how they affect students.)
2. Who will **read** your essay?
3. How much **knowledge** of the topic can you expect your readers to have? (Example: most students have a sense of what stress is, but they may not know an exact definition.)
4. Where can you find **information** about the topic? (Examples: the campus health center, the Internet.)
5. What level of **formality** is appropriate for this assignment? (*Hint*: Think about language and sentence structure.)
6. What questions will be answered in each assignment?

Here are some questions that could be applied to all the assignments.

What is stress?
Why is it a problem to experience too much stress?
Who experiences more stress—male or female college students?
What resources are available on this campus to students who are dealing with severe stress?
Who did the first study on stress and college students?

Essay Assignment Choice 1

What does "psychological effects" mean?

_____

_____

_____

Essay Assignment Choice 2

What is a "symptom"?

_____

_____

Essay Assignment Choice 3

Who treats stress?

_____

_____

_____

Essay Assignment Choice 4

What does "prevent" mean?

_____

_____

_____

○ Gathering Information

The topic of college stress has been studied extensively, and you will find a great quantity of material online and in print. Therefore, you will have to be very selective about the sources you choose for your essay. As you gather information and do the exercises in this section of the book, always keep in mind the topic of your essay assignment.

EXERCISE 2 **Recalling what you know**

On separate paper, answer the questions that follow:

1. What is stress?
2. As a first-year college student, what stresses (or stressed) you the most?
3. How does stress affect you mentally?
4. How does stress affect you physically?
5. Look at the cartoon on the first page of this chapter. Do you think that humor helps avoid or reduce stress? How? Why?

6. What other strategies do you know or have you used to avoid or
   reduce stress?
7. Discuss your answers with four or five classmates. Add new
   information shared by your classmates to the paper with your list
   of answers.
8. Place the paper in your writing folder.

EXERCISE 3 **Listing ideas**

*Review the four essay assignment choices for this chapter, the questions you
listed in Exercise 1, and your answers in Exercise 2. Then, do the following
with a classmate:*

1. On separate paper, create four columns, one for each of the four
   topic choices in the essay assignment.
2. In the columns, list what you know about each topic.
3. Put your list in your writing folder.

EXERCISE 4 **Analyzing two lists**

Read Lani's and Hung's lists below. Then, answer the questions that follow.

Lani's Lists

1. Mental Effects	2. Physical Symptoms	3. Treatment	4. Prevention
1) anxiety	1) headaches	1) medication	1) money management
2) depression	2) digestive problems	2) time management	2) study plan
3) anger	3) weight loss		3) time management
4) forgetfulness	4) weight gain		
5) irritability	5) heart conditions		
6) fear	6) irregular heart rhythm		
	7) sleeplessness		

Hung's Lists

1. Psychological Effects

1) Feeling sad
2) Being mad all the time

2. Physical Symptoms

1) Stomachache
2) Insomnia

3. Ways to Treat Stress

1) Go to the gym
2) Spend quality time with friends
3) Watch a really funny comedy
4) Make time for things you like
5) Take yoga or Tai Chi
6) Get a massage once a month

4. Ways to Prevent Stress

1) Take it easy— it's only school
2) Don't take too many classes
3) Stick to your budget
4) Exercise regularly
5) Make time for friends
6) Breathe deeply every time you feel some stress coming on
7) Don't be friends with negative people
8) Study regularly— don't cram!

1. Lani chose to write about the physical symptoms of stress (List 2). Why do you think she made this choice? Also, she decided to focus on symptoms 1, 6, and 7 ("headaches," "irregular heart rhythm" and "sleeplessness"). Why do you think she chose these symptoms? What do you think about her choice?

2. Hung chose to write about ways to prevent stress (List 4). Why do you think he chose this topic? After reviewing his list, he decided to find supporting evidence for ideas 5 and 6 ("make time for friends," and "don't be friends with negative people"). Why do you think he chose these two ideas? What do they have in common?

3. Which topic would be easier for you to write about, Lani's or Hung's? Why?

4. Add interesting ideas from Hung's and Lani's lists to your lists for this chapter's essay assignment. Put your revised lists in your writing folder.

EXERCISE 5 Choosing your topic

Review this chapter's essay assignment choices and the four lists you wrote. Choose the topic for your essay, and put an asterisk (*) next to the list of ideas for your essay topic.

SPOTLIGHT ON WRITING SKILLS

Information about Stress

The following excerpt is from a chapter about stress found in *Psychology Concepts and Applications*, a textbook for introductory psychology courses. In the excerpt, the author, Jeffrey S. Nevid, defines the meaning of stress, gives examples of stress-related problems, and then defines some sources of stress.

As you read, try to guess the meaning of unfamiliar words by looking at the *context* (the words and sentences near the unfamiliar words). The exercises that follow the excerpt will help you analyze the text.

Stress: What It Is and What It Does to Your Body

1. The study of interrelationships between psychology and physical health is called *health psychology*. Health psychologists use the term *stress* to describe pressures or demands placed upon an organism to adjust or adapt to its environment. Stress is a fact of life. We may even need a certain amount of stress to remain active, alert, and energized. But when the stress we face in our lives increases to a level that taxes our ability to cope, we may experience *distress*, which is an internal state of physical or mental pain or suffering. Distress may take the form of psychological problems, especially anxiety and depression, or physical health problems, including headaches, digestive problems, even heart conditions such as irregular heart rhythms (Cohen, Tyrell & Smith, 1993; see Table 4.1). Though most people are remarkably resilient to stress, we all have our limits.

Table 4.1

Examples of Stress-Related Health Problems

Biological Problems	
Tension or migraine headaches	Allergic reactions
Back pain, especially low back pain	High blood pressure
Skin inflammations (such as hives and acne)	Rheumatoid arthritis (painful inflammation of the joints)
Regional enteritis (inflammation of the intestine, especially the small intestine)	Ulcerative colitis (inflammation and open sores of the colon, or large intestine)
Heart disease and cardiac irregularities such as arrhythmias (irregularities in the rhythm of the heart)	Sleep Problems
Nausea and vomiting	Upset stomach or indigestion
Ulcers	Frequent urination or diarrhea
Skin rashes	Asthma
Fatigue	

Psychological Problems	
Depression	Anger
Irritability	Anxiety
Difficulty concentrating	Feeling overwhelmed
Alcohol or substance abuse	

Source: Adapted from Nevid, Rathus, & Rubenstein, 1998.

Sources of Stress

2. If you had to identify the sources of stress in your life, what would you list? School or work demands, relationship problems, traffic jams, or such daily sources of stress as preparing meals, shopping, and doing household chores? Sources of stress are called *stressors*. We face many stressors in our lives, including daily hassles, life events or life changes, frustration, conflict, Type A behavior pattern, and pressure to adjust to a new culture, which is a stressor faced by immigrant groups.

3. Positive as well as negative experiences can be sources of stress. Happy or joyous events, such as having a baby, getting married, or graduating from college, are stressors because they impose demands on us to adjust or adapt. Positive changes in our lives, like negative ones, can tax our ability to cope, as any new parent will attest. How well we are able to cope with the stress we experience in our daily lives plays a key part in determining our mental and physical well-being.

4. **Hassles**   Hassles are annoyances we commonly experience in our daily lives. Examples include traffic jams, household chores, coping with inclement weather, and balancing job demands and social relationships. Few, if any, of us are immune from daily hassles. Table 4.2 lists the ten most common hassles reported by a sample of college students.

5. We may experience some hassles on a daily basis, such as hunting for a parking spot in overcrowded parking lots. Others occur irregularly or unexpectedly, such as getting caught in a downpour without an umbrella. A single hassle may not amount to much in itself. But the accumulation of daily hassles can contribute to the general level of **chronic stress** in our lives. Chronic stress is a state of persistent tension or pressure that can lead us to feel exhausted, irritable, and depressed. Other contributors to chronic stress include ongoing financial problems, job-related problems, marital or relationship conflicts, and persistent or recurrent pain or other chronic medical conditions.

Table 4.2

The Ten Most Common Hassles Reported by College Students

Hassle	Students Reporting (%)
1. Troubling thoughts about the future	77
2. Not getting enough sleep	72.5
3. Wasting time	71
4. Inconsiderate smokers	71
5. Physical appearance	70
6. Too many things to do	69
7. Misplacing or losing things	67
8. Not enough time to do the things you need to do	66
9. Concerns about meeting high standards	64
10. Being lonely	61

Source: Kanner et al., 1981.

6. **Life Events** Stress can also result from major changes in life circumstances, which psychologists call life events. These may be negative events, such as the loss of a loved one or a job termination, or positive events, such as getting married, receiving a promotion, or having a baby. In other words, changes for better or for worse can impose stressful burdens that require adjustment. Unlike daily hassles, life events occur irregularly and sometimes unexpectedly.

7. The ways in which we appraise or evaluate a life event also have an important bearing on how stressful it becomes for us. The same event may hold different meanings for different people. A life event like a pregnancy is probably less stressful to people who welcome the pregnancy and believe they can cope with the changes the birth of a child will bring. Similarly, whether or not you find work

demands to be stressful may depend on whether or not you like your job and feel in control of how and when you do your work.

8. **Frustration**   Another major source of stress is frustration, the negative emotional state that occurs when our efforts to pursue our goals are blocked or thwarted. Adolescents may feel frustrated when they want to drive, date or drink alcoholic beverages but are told they are too young. People desiring higher education may be frustrated when they lack the financial resources to attend the college of their choice. We may frustrate ourselves when we set unrealistically high goals that we are unable to achieve.

9. **Conflict**   Conflict is a state of tension resulting from the presence of two or more competing goals that demand resolution. People in conflict often vacillate, or shift back and forth, between competing goals, such as pursuing a graduate degree or getting started in a career. The longer people remain in conflict, the more stressed and frustrated they feel. Conflicts are most easily resolved and least stressful when one goal is decidedly more attractive than another, or when the positive qualities of a goal outweigh the negative. But when two goals pull you in opposite directions, such as choosing between two attractive job offers, or when the same goal both strongly attracts and repels you (you may want to attend graduate school, but fear incurring heavy loans), you may experience high levels of stress and confusion about which course of action to pursue.

10. **Type A Behavior Pattern**   People with Type A behavior pattern are impatient, competitive, and aggressive. They are constantly in a rush and have a strong sense of time urgency. They feel pressured to get the maximum amount done in the shortest possible amount of time. They quickly lose patience with others, especially those who move or work more slowly than they would like. They may become hostile and prone to anger when others fail to meet their expectations. Hostile people are angry much of the time, and strong negative emotions such as anger, anxiety, and depression are associated with an increased risk of cardiovascular problems.

11. **Acculturative Stress**   For immigrants, the demands of adjusting to a new culture can be a significant source of stress. Establishing a new life in one's adopted country can be a difficult adjustment, especially when there are differences in language and culture and few available job or training opportunities. One significant source of stress is pressure to become *acculturated*—to adapt to the values, linguistic preferences, and customs of the host or dominant culture.

12. The process of adjusting successfully to a new society depends on a number of factors. For example, stress associated with economic hardship is a major contributor to adjustment problems in immigrant groups, as it is for members of the host culture.

13. All in all, factors such as economic opportunity, language proficiency, and connections to a social network of people whom one can identify with and draw support from may underlie the psychological adjustment of immigrant groups.

References

Cohen, S., Tyrell, D. A. J., & Smith, A. P. (1993). Negative life events, perceived stress, negative affect, and susceptibility to the common cold in healthy adults. *Journal of Personality and Social Psychology, 64*, 131–140.

Kanner, A. D., Coyne, J. C., & Lazarus, R. S. (1981). Comparison of two modes of stress measurement: Daily hassles and uplifts versus major life events. *Journal of Behavioral Medicine, 4*, 1–39.

Nevid, J. S., Rathus, S. A., & Rubenstein, H. R. (1998). *Health in the new millennium*. New York: Worth.

EXERCISE 6 **Discussing vocabulary**

With three or four classmates, discuss unfamiliar words. Ask the instructor about words your group does not know or cannot guess from the context. Write the definitions of difficult words in the margins of the text.

EXERCISE 7 **Marking the text**

Reread the text and do the following:

1. Underline the definitions of *stress* and *distress* in paragraph 1.
2. Bracket one example of distress in paragraph 1.
3. Underline the definition of the word *stressors* (¶ 2).
4. Bracket one example of a stressor. In the margin, write whether the stressor is positive or negative.
5. Underline the definition of *hassles* (¶ 4).
6. In Table 4.2, check (✓) two hassles that you have experienced most recently.

7. Underline the definition of *life events* (¶ 6).
8. Bracket an example of a life event.
9. Underline the definition of *frustration* (¶ 8).
10. Bracket one example of frustration that affects college students.
11. Underline the definition of *conflict* (¶ 9).
12. Bracket one example of conflict.
13. Underline the definition of *type A behavior* (¶ 10).
14. Underline the definition of *acculturative stress* (¶ 11).

EXERCISE 8 **Discussing and taking notes**

With two students who chose the same essay assignment as you did, do the following:

1. Discuss the definition of each stressor listed by Nevid without reading it from the text. If you cannot remember the meaning of one of the stressors, read the definition in the text and then try to restate it in your own words. Take notes on separate paper.
2. With the same two students, identify information that can help you with your essay topic and write it on your paper. For example, depression and anger are mentioned in the paragraph about Type A behavior pattern. Therefore, a student writing about the psychological effects of college stress could use this information in her or his background paragraph or as the basis for an Internet search.
3. Put an asterisk (*) next to other useful information in "Stress: What It Is and What It Does to Your Body" that you can use in your essay.

EXERCISE 9 **Freewriting**

For each idea in the list you chose in Exercise 5, write two or three questions that can be answered in a body paragraph. As you write, leave a half page below each question. Then,

1. Go back and try to answer each of your questions. Write quickly, without worrying about spelling, sentence structure, or grammar errors.
2. Discuss the ideas in your freewriting with one of your classmates who chose the same essay assignment. Put an asterisk (*) next to the information your classmate finds most interesting. Write two questions that your classmate thinks you should answer in your essay about this information.
3. Add your classmate's most interesting ideas to your freewriting if they are different from yours.

SPOTLIGHT ON WRITING SKILLS

Website Evaluation

In Chapter 3, you learned about different website domains (.*com*, .*org*, .*edu*, .*gov*). In this chapter, you will search the WWW for sites that contain information about *college stress* and its *psychological effects*, *physical symptoms*, *treatment options*, and/or *preventive measures*. It is important that you evaluate the information carefully. If you select websites that have inaccurate or limited information, your essay will not be well supported and you may not receive a good grade on your paper.

Here are some questions that can guide your Internet search:

1. Who is the **author** of the website? Is it a person, an institution, an organization? What are the author's **credentials**? Does the website provide contact information for the author? Is the author a psychologist, health professional, or some other **reliable source**?

2. Does the website provide **accurate information**? Is the information supported with statistics, research results, and/or expert opinions? Does the website provide **enough information**? Is advertising kept to a minimum?

3. Is the website **current**? Is it updated regularly (as stated on the main page)? Are the **links up to date**? Is the information easy to access?

WEB POWER

You will find additional information about evaluating websites at http://esl.college.hmco.com/students.

EXERCISE 10 Searching the Internet

Go on the Internet and find information about the essay topic you selected. Consider your freewriting and your list of ideas and questions to help you decide what information to search for and select. Here are examples of actual search words used by students in this course:

- college students stress psychological effects
- stress college students physical symptoms
- college freshmen conflict stress
- ways reduce college stress

1. Select at least six potential sources for your essay. Print the first page and the URL (Web address) of each site.
2. Review your sources, and choose three or four of the most valuable to print completely.
3. Place the printed webpages in your writing folder.

EXERCISE 11 Evaluating materials

Bring to class the materials you collected on the Web. Exchange materials with one of your classmates, preferably someone who chose a different topic. Review your classmate's materials carefully; then, follow the instructions in "Peer Review of Sources" (Appendix 7, p. 263).

SPOTLIGHT ON WRITING SKILLS

The Interview

Interviewing experts about a topic can add valuable information to your academic papers. For this chapter's writing assignment, you will interview a stress "expert," such as a student who experienced distress in her or his freshman year, or a health or mental care professional who has experience treating college student stress. You may want to interview one of the doctors or psychologists at the campus health center, your family physician, or someone you know who experienced stress in her or his first year of college.

Interviews can be conducted face-to-face or by telephone or e-mail. For this assignment, it is preferable that you meet with an expert face-to-face. However, if the expert lives far away or cannot meet with you for some other reason, you may interview her or him by telephone or e-mail.

Your interview questions will depend on the topic you chose for your essay and the expert you interview.

For successful interviews, follow these steps:

1. If the person you wish to interview is someone you do not already know, introduce yourself and explain why you wish to interview her or him.
2. Set a date and time for your interview. Be on time!
3. Bring a notebook and two or three pens or pencils. If the expert agrees, you may also bring a tape recorder. Even if you bring a tape recorder, take accurate notes during the interview (review note-taking in Chapter 3 if you feel unsure about this).
4. Before you begin, thank the expert for agreeing to the interview.
5. If you do not understand a point the expert makes during the interview, interrupt the expert politely and ask for clarification immediately. Here are two polite ways to begin your questions:

    "Could you repeat your answer, please?"
    "Did you say that . . .?"

6. Follow your list of questions. Do not ask questions unrelated to your essay topic.
7. Try to keep the interview short (ten to fifteen minutes).
8. At the end of the interview, thank the expert for her or his help.
9. After the interview, write a note of thanks and mail it to the person you interviewed.

Below are some questions you can ask during the interview. Develop other questions based on your essay topic.

For example, you could ask a specialist who treats stress on a regular basis the following questions:

-   How many cases of stress do you treat every year?
-   What stress treatment do you find most effective? Why?
-   Does this treatment have any drawbacks? (If the answer is yes) What are they?
-   Do you think _____ (type of treatment) is also effective? Why?
-   In your opinion, what are the disadvantages of _____ (type of treatment)?
-   Does this hospital/health center offer stress management classes?
-   How do patients find out about these classes?

- Do you think these classes are helpful? Why?
- What prevention techniques do you find most successful? Why?

Many campuses offer psychological services, counseling, or support groups as part of student health services. If you choose to interview someone who works at the campus health center, you could ask:

- How many students at this campus seek help for stress?
- What resources are available to them on campus?
- Which of these services are free? How much do the other services cost?
- Where can students get information about these services?
- Whom can students contact if they need help dealing with stress?

Below are some questions you can choose from when interviewing college students who experienced severe stress in their first year of college:

- When did you experience too much college stress?
- What symptoms and effects did you experience?
- Why were you feeling stressed?
- How did you deal with your stress?
- Did you seek help from a professional? If yes, how did you arrange that?
- What did you learn about stress?
- What did you learn about coping with stress?
- What helped you get over the stress?
- Do you think this method is a good way of dealing with stress? Why?
- What are you doing this semester to avoid too much stress?
- What advice can you give to college students who suffer from severe stress?

EXERCISE 12 Preparing the interview

After reviewing the steps to a successful interview (above), do the following with a classmate who has chosen the same essay topic:

1. Identify the person you want to interview, and set an appointment for the interview. Remember that the total time of your interview should not exceed twenty minutes.

2. Select the questions you want to ask during the interview from the ones listed above. Be sure to choose questions that fit your essay topic (symptoms, effects, treatment, <u>or</u> prevention).

3. Write them in your notebook.

4. Add some questions of your own. Remember that you should ask about information you cannot find on the Internet (for example: what specific stress symptoms your expert has treated or experienced, if he or she recommends yoga classes, where the students can find information about these classes).

5. Review your list of questions. You should have at least ten questions.

6. Practice the interview with your classmate. Decide who will ask the questions and who will take notes. Will you both take notes? Will one of you bring a tape recorder? Decide on these issues <u>before</u> your interview.

EXERCISE 13 **Summarizing the interview**

Review your interview notes. If your interview partner took the notes, ask her or him for help to make sure you understand the notes well. If you used a tape recorder, listen to the interview as you follow along in your notes. Add or change any information to make sure the notes are as accurate as possible. Then,

1. Read your notes and mark the most important information you could use in your essay.

2. Review your notes one more time.

3. Write a one-paragraph summary of the interview.

4. Read your summary, and compare it to the interview to make sure you did not leave out any important information. Revise your summary as needed.

5. Edit your summary for sentence structure, informal language, spelling, and grammar errors.

6. Compare your summary to your classmate's summary. Did you forget any important details? If you did, add them to your summary.

7. Put your summary in your writing folder.

W E B   P O W E R

You will find additional information about
conducting and summarizing interviews at
http://esl.college.hmco.com/students.

P O W E R   G R A M M A R

Count and Noncount Nouns in Definitions

As you write your research report, you will define some important terms (nouns) related to the topic. Some of these nouns will be count, and some noncount. To learn more about these noun categories, study the examples and guidelines below.

Examples	Explanations
<u>A</u> *computer* **is** a machine . . .	The subject is a singular noun (*computer*), so the verb is singular too (**is**). We know it is singular because it is preceded by the article <u>a</u>, which means "one." Dictionary definitions often use the singular form.
Computers **are** machine<u>s</u> . . .	Generalizations about the whole category are often made with plural nouns (*computers*). The verb must be plural too (**are**). Generalizations with plural nouns are the most commonly used in writing. **Count nouns** have a plural form. You can add an *-s* to most of these countable nouns: *one student, two student<u>s</u>, three student<u>s</u>, many student<u>s</u>.*
Money **is** a medium that can be exchanged for goods and services and that can be used to measure those goods and services.	*Money* is a **noncount noun**. **Noncount nouns** are nouns that do not have a singular or a plural form. You cannot say "one money, two moneys" or "one homework, two homeworks. " Instead, you can say "a lot of money" or "not much homework."

Continued

1. I like **coffee**.
2. I bought a *coffee* before class.
3. Brazil produces several coffees.
4. **Stress** is a feeling.
5. Students experience the stresses and strains of academic life.

Many words can be either count or noncount with a change in meaning. For example, in the first sentence **coffee** refers to the general substance just as **stress** in the fourth sentence refers to a general feeling.

In the second sentence, *coffee* refers to "a cup of coffee."

In the third sentence, coffees refers to the "types of coffee" produced in Brazil.

In sentence 5, stresses refers to the many kinds of stress students can experience.

---

1. Students should do their **homework** every day.
2. A student stopped by my office yesterday.
3. I need some **information** about this course.
4. My **grammar** *needs* to improve.

Some common words are always used as count nouns (students, a student); others are always used as noncount nouns (**homework, information**).

Notice that noncount nouns such as **grammar** take a singular verb (*needs*).

Stress *n.* [C; U] **1.** force or pressure caused by difficulties in life: *He's under stress because he has too much work to do.* **2.** force of weight caused by something heavy: *The heavy trucks put stress on the bridge.* **3.** the degree of force put on a part of a word: *In "under," the main stress is on "un."*

The best way to find out whether a noun is count or noncount is to look up the word in a dictionary like *The Longman Dictionary of American English*. This dictionary tells you if a noun is count [C], noncount [U], or both, and it also gives examples of sentences that use the noun as count or noncount.

EXERCISE 14 Correcting noun errors

Read the sentences below with two or three classmates. Then, correct the noun errors (one error per sentence). An example has been completed for you.

Example:

College students sometimes experience an overwhelming
feeling of ~~stresses~~. *stress*

1. Some college students feel stressed because of their many financial responsibility.

2. Last night I did not finish all my homeworks.

3. One of the student in my French class has trouble learning new vocabulary.

4. The Admissions office did not give me clear informations about adding classes late.

5. I ordered two coffee to go.

6. It is hard for college student to deal with high levels of stress in their first year.

7. Some students experience severe depressions in their first year of college.

8. Computer are used by every bank in America.

EXERCISE 15 Practicing with nouns

Write a sentence with each of the words listed below. Some of the words are from the excerpt you read earlier ("Stress: What It Is and What It Does to Your Body"). After you write your sentences, compare them with a classmate's.

1. *money:*

_____

_____

2. *stress*:

_____

_____

3. *grammar*:

_____

_____

4. *stressor*:

_____

_____

5. *information*:

_____

_____

6. *behavior*:

_____

_____

7. *tension*:

_____

_____

8. *coffee*:

_____

_____

WEB POWER

For more practice with count and noncount nouns,
go to **http://esl.college.hmco.com/students**.

○ Focusing and Organizing

Now that you have collected your information, it is time to select ideas and plan your essay. You will use a fishbone map to plan your background paragraph and a chart to organize your supporting details.

EXERCISE 16 Evaluating a student essay

Nancy wrote about Essay Assignment 4 (ways to prevent college stress) and used a survey, not an interview, as one way to gather information. Read Nancy's essay but cover the notes in the right margin. Then, with two or three classmates, complete the steps that follow.

College Stress: Prevention and Treatment

The introduction begins with a general statement about stress, gives a definition of stress, and then becomes more specific. The thesis statement is the most specific sentence in the introduction.

The background paragraph gives information about causes and effects of stress (background of the problem).

Definition of conflict is quoted. The page number (if available) is given in the in-text citation.

Stress is a fact of life, and even animals experience it when they are faced with difficult situations. In fact, stress is the "pressures or demands placed upon an organism to adjust or adapt to its environment" (Nevid, 2003, p. 94). First-year college students have to adapt to their new environment, college, and this creates a lot of stress. Some freshmen experience a high degree of stress, called "distress," which can lead to serious health problems. However, college freshmen can prevent distress by managing time wisely and exercising regularly, and they can lower stress successfully with anger management and meditation.

Stress has many **causes**, but two of them, **conflict** and **procrastination**, are **closely related** in **first-year college students** and can have **serious consequences**. First-year college students have to learn to juggle many activities: attend classes, study for tests, write papers, work, maintain meaningful relationships, and still find time to enjoy themselves. Trying to do all these activities is practically impossible, so students learn to compromise. But having to choose one activity over another creates conflict and therefore stress. As stated by Jeffrey S. Nevid, "Conflict is a state of tension resulting from the presence of two or more competing goals that demand resolution" (Nevid, 2003, p. 94). Sometimes students deal with conflict by just procrastinating, relaxing, and putting off making a decision (Williams, 2001). By procrastinating, freshmen cause more stress for themselves because they end up cramming for tests and not sleeping. Lack of sleep can weaken the immune system, and students get sick more easily (Fusfield, 2002). Thus, conflict and procrastination can make freshmen feel really stressed out.

This body paragraph describes **two ways** to prevent stress: setting goals and exercising.

A good way to prevent stress is to prioritize goals and to schedule time for regular exercise. Freshmen are not used to the demands of college. They think that college is going to be just like high school, where the teacher reminds the students of due dates and project deadlines. However, in college it is the students' responsibility to remember when an assignment is due or when a midterm exam will take place. Also, students must learn to separate tasks that need immediate attention from tasks that can be done later. Joe Hamilton, a counselor at Truman State University's Counseling Services, says that a good way to prioritize goals is to use a planner (Heavin, 1998). He advises students to set aside time for studying and doing homework but also for relaxation. He says, "Highlight fun upcoming activities that you can look forward to" (Heavin, 1998). That is a great idea and can motivate students to work hard so that they will have time to go to fun events. In addition, students should exercise more in order to keep stress away. In fact, exercise makes the brain release endorphins, chemicals found in the brain that ease pain and make people feel better (Beck, 2003). Most health experts suggest that people exercise 30–60 minutes every day, 3–5 days a week. Even though aerobic exercise is ideal, one study suggests that even weight training can have positive effects and help students prevent stress ("Weight Training," 2003). Thus, by exercising and planning their daily activities, students can avoid too much stress.

When there is no author, use the title in your in-text citations. If the title is too long, use part of it.

The topic sentence connects to the previous paragraph and introduces two solutions (anger management, meditation) to the problem (stress).

Two more ways to lower stress are anger management classes and meditation exercises. Not many people would associate stress and anger, but according to a survey done by Pamela Jackson at Indiana University, many freshmen react with anger when they feel stressed out. Anger can be a positive motivator if a student reacts by taking constructive action, such as protesting against unfair grades by writing a letter to the department chair. On the other hand, anger can be very negative. As Jackson stated, "anger . . . can be quite perilous. Anger has both physiological and cognitive components. Being angry can result in physical health problems" (Williams, 2001). If the students do not know how to deal with stress and anger, they may get physical problems such as stomach ulcers, headaches, sleeplessness, and inability to concentrate. Freshmen can avoid

Relevant survey information is summarized in the essay, and it is used as supporting evidence. Survey information is included in the text but **not** on the reference list.

Conclusion recaps the essay's main points and suggests measures that colleges can take to help prevent freshmen's stress.

these problems if they take anger management classes that teach ways to express feelings without lashing out at other people. Also, meditation is a powerful tool to avoid stress build-up. Meditation is a way to slow down your breathing and emptying your mind from stressful thoughts. In a recent survey, I asked 15 students who were taking meditation classes at the campus health center whether their ability to cope with stress had improved since they had begun meditation exercises. All of the respondents agreed that they felt calmer, more able to deal with stress, more sure of themselves, and more in control of their lives since beginning meditation exercises. Therefore, meditation and anger management can help freshmen prevent and control stress more successfully.

In conclusion, stress is a factor in everyday life, and college students have to learn to deal with it so that it does not become too overwhelming. Too much stress can affect a student's health and may lead to anger management problems. By exercising regularly and prioritizing tasks, students can prevent and cope with stress. However, taking anger management classes and doing meditation can help freshmen who feel overwhelmed and frustrated because of the amount of stress they experience. Colleges and universities should make sure incoming freshmen know about campus resources that can help them deal with stress and prevent distress.

References are listed in alphabetical order.

Remember to include the date you retrieved the Internet information.

Indent each entry 5–7 spaces after the first line.

References

Beck, M. (2003, April 24). Relieving stress through exercise. *The Tufts Daily*. Retrieved November 10, 2003 from http://nutrition.tufts.edu/ consumer/balance/2003-04/stress.html

Dealing with stress: Meditation. (n.d.) Retrieved November 10, 2003 from Brooklyn College Personal Counseling website http://depthome.brooklyn.cuny.edu/career/MED.htm

Fusfield, J. (2002, December 6). Study finds perceptions of stress may weaken immune system. *Diamondback*. Retrieved November 10, 2003 from http://www.inform.umd.edu/News/ Diamondback/archives/2002/12/06/news7.html

Remember to
italicize:
1. titles of Internet
   sources
2. book titles
3. journal, magazine
   and newspaper
   titles

Heavin, J. (1998, February 19). Students find stress relief by
        acknowledging symptoms. *New Media Index News*.
        Retrieved November 10, 2003 from http://index.truman.edu/
        issues/980219/News/intune19.asp

Nevid, J. S. (2003). *Psychology concepts and applications*. Boston:
        Houghton Mifflin.

Regular weight training reduces stress in college students. (2003,
        March 13). *NewsRx*. Retrieved October 31, 2003 from http://
        thestressoflife.com/regular_weight_training_reduces_.htm

Williams, Susan. (2001, October 12). College students and stress: New
        survey explores effects of negative life events. Retrieved
        October 31, 2003 from Indiana University, homepages
        http://www.homepages.indiana.edu/101201/text/stress.html

1. Circle the controlling ideas in Nancy's thesis statement.
2. Circle the controlling ideas in the topic sentences. (Paragraph 2 has
   already been completed for you.) Do the controlling ideas match
   those in the thesis statement?
3. In the background paragraph, notice how Nancy repeats keywords
   that refer to the **controlling ideas** in the topic sentence. The other
   information in the paragraph explains and adds information about
   the keywords. In each body paragraph, underline keywords that
   relate to the controlling ideas you circled in the topic sentence.
4. Highlight the transitions Nancy uses to connect sentences.
5. Read the notes in the right margin of the essay. What important
   information do they provide?
6. Which of Nancy's paragraphs do you find most interesting? Why?
7. Read Nancy's References. Why do some entries begin with the
   author and some with the title of the article?
8. What does "n.d." mean? When is it used?
9. Why are two different dates provided for most Internet sources?

EXERCISE 17 Evaluating thesis statements

Read the thesis statements below with a classmate. Each thesis statement focuses on a different essay assignment. Circle or underline the main ideas in each thesis statement, and list four or five questions that can be answered in the body paragraphs. An example has been completed for you.

Example:

The two main causes of stress in college freshmen are homesickness and academic expectations.

Questions readers expect will be answered in the essay:

- *What* is stress?
- *Why* does homesickness cause stress?
- *What* are some of the stress signs of homesickness freshmen need to look for?
- *How* are academic expectations different from high school expectations?
- *Why* do academic expectations cause stress?
- *What* can freshmen do to reduce or cope with these causes of stress?

Thesis Statement 1:
Freshmen in college can prevent stress by taking charge of their time, seeking help early, and not procrastinating.

Questions:

_____

_____

_____

_____

Thesis Statement 2:
First-year college students can treat stress by practicing self-control, doing relaxation, and having good time management.

Questions:

_____

_____

_____

_____

Thesis Statement 3:
Loss of appetite, insomnia, and inability to concentrate are the most serious effects of college stress on first-year students.

Questions:

_____

_____

_____

_____

EXERCISE 18 **Writing a "working" thesis**

Reread your essay assignment and the questions you need to answer in your essay (Exercise 2). Review your notes and the materials you found on the Internet and at the library. Also review your summary of the interview. Highlight information that seems closely related to your essay assignment. Then,

1. Using your materials, write a _working thesis statement_ for your essay that answers the essay assignment. This thesis is a "work in progress," and you may modify it later if necessary.
2. Circle the controlling ideas in the thesis statement.
3. For each controlling idea, write three to five questions you plan to answer in the body paragraphs.
4. Place your working thesis statement and questions in your writing folder.

EXERCISE 19 **Participating in a read-around peer review**

Form a group with three or four classmates. Review each other's thesis statement by following the steps below. Review all the steps before you begin your peer reviews.

1. Read one classmate's thesis statement and the questions he or she wrote in Exercise 2. Then, answer the questions below:
   a. Does the thesis statement answer the essay question chosen by your classmate?
   b. What other questions should your classmate answer in her or his essay to develop the thesis statement's controlling ideas? Add them to your classmate's list of questions. Sign your name below your comments. If you do not have any questions, write your name in the margin, next to the three questions you find most interesting.
2. Pass your classmate's thesis statement to the student sitting at your left. Take the thesis statement from the student sitting at your right.
3. Answer questions 1 and 2 for the next thesis statement. When you are done, pass the thesis statement to your left and take one from the student at your right. Keep going until your have read all the thesis statements.
4. Collect your own thesis statement. Read your classmates' comments, and ask questions if you are confused. Thank your classmates for their feedback, and put your working thesis statement and questions in your writing folder.

EXERCISE 20 **Identifying stressors**

*Reread the essay topic you chose and your list of ideas (effects, symptoms, treatments, or preventive strategies). Then, reread the excerpt from Nevid's book (pp. 159–164), and look for the causes of stress that match your essay topic. List these causes on separate paper, and put it in your writing folder. For example, Julie decided that people coping with difficult **life events** and people with **Type A behavior pattern** would benefit the most from the coping strategies she had listed in Exercise 3. Therefore, she listed "life events" and "Type A behavior pattern" as the causes she would discuss in her background paragraph.*

SPOTLIGHT ON WRITING SKILLS

The Fishbone Map

The purpose of the background paragraph in Essay Assignment 4 is to discuss causes of college stress. The causes you select for your background paragraph must be <u>directly related</u> to the effects, symptoms, treatment options, or prevention techniques you discuss in the rest of the essay.

A good way to identify the causes of stress that best fit your essay is to use a fishbone map. This mapping method will help you create a visual correlation between ideas so that you can decide more easily whether they are truly connected.

To create a fishbone map, draw a line in the middle of the page. Write one effect, symptom, treatment method, or preventive technique above the line. Then, write in the causes and draw lines to show the relationship between ideas as in the example below, which is about Essay Assignment 2:

> cause #3: lack of sleep
> support: information from article #2 about the relationship between hours of sleep and alertness/concentration
>
> psychological effect: inability to concentrate
>
> cause #1: anxiety
> support: information from psychology textbook (test anxiety makes students lose concentration- can't recall what they know)
>
> cause #2: fear
> support: personal experience about Chemistry 4 midterm exam

The example below was written by a student about Essay Assignment 4 (treatment of stress). Notice that one of the causes, financial problems, does not relate to the treatment method:

> cause #1: financial problems
> support: Internet article about the stress college students feel about school loans
>
> treatment: stress management classes
>
> cause #2: test anxiety
> support: survey results about tests and stress levels

Taking a stress management class may help students deal successfully with test anxiety, but it will not help with the stress caused by financial problems. Getting a part-time job or a better student loan would be a more appropriate way of dealing with financial stress.

EXERCISE 21 Creating a fishbone map

Reread the causes (stressors) you listed in Exercise 20. Then,

1. Follow the examples above to create a fishbone map of your background paragraph.
2. Be sure to state at least two causes of stress.
3. Provide supporting evidence from the materials you have gathered so far.
4. If you do not have enough evidence or the materials do not seem to support your ideas well, reread your materials for more support or go back to the Internet to search for more information. Place your fishbone map in your writing folder.

EXERCISE 22 Reviewing a fishbone map

Exchange fishbone maps with one of your classmates, and answer the following questions:

1. Does your classmate's map show at least two causes related to the topic of the essay?
2. What type of supporting evidence is listed below each cause? (Examples: personal experience, interview, Internet article)
3. How might reviewing your classmate's fishbone map help you improve yours?

EXERCISE 23   **Writing your topic sentences**

Review the essay assignment, working thesis, and list of questions reviewed by your classmates (Exercise 19). Make sure that your thesis statement answers the essay assignment. Then, on separate paper,

1. Write two or three topic sentences for the controlling ideas in your thesis statement.
2. Circle the controlling ideas in each topic sentence.
3. Place your topic sentences in your writing folder.

SPOTLIGHT ON WRITING SKILLS

Supporting Materials

Many students have difficulty organizing their ideas in an essay because they are visual learners and need to use graphic organizers such as charts and tables to see how their ideas fit together.

A chart can help you evaluate your controlling ideas and supporting materials more clearly than an essay map. Use labels to identify your evidence:

fact (F)	statistics (S)
example (EX)	personal experience (PE)
paraphrase (P)	quotation (Q)
interview information (II)	other (O)

Here is Estela's chart for body paragraph 1 about the causes of stress. Estela changed "financial difficulties" and added "poor time management," which fits better with the causes and symptoms she chose for her essay. In addition, she added a personal experience to support Controlling Idea #2. Her personal experience shows the connection between moving away from home and time management, which may not have been clear otherwise. Notice that Estela listed her sources in parentheses in the column "Supporting Materials."

Estela's Chart for Body Paragraph 1

Controlling Idea #1	Supporting Material	Type of Evidence
moving away from home	This is the first time I'm away from my family. "No supportive family is around to share the the triumphs and the miseries" (The Big Five).	(PE) (Q) (f)
Controlling Idea #2	Supporting Material	Type of Evidence
lack of time	College students have so many demands on their time: school, work, study time, fun activities. They just run out of time ("Stress"). My mom is not around to wake me up in the morning or to remind me to do my homework.	(P) (EX) (PE)
Controlling Idea #3	Supporting Material	Type of Evidence
poor time management	Students do not know how to manage their time better ("The Big Five"). My roommates are very stressed out because they do not know how to schedule their time and prioritize.	(P) (f) (PE)

EXERCISE 24   **Selecting supporting materials**

Review your thesis statement and topic sentences. Then,

1. On separate paper, make a chart to list your supporting materials for each body paragraph. Label the supporting evidence for each controlling idea as shown in Estela's example.
2. If you do not have enough supporting details for one or more of your ideas, look for more details in your writing folder, or return to the Internet for additional research.
3. If some supporting material would "fit" better in your background paragraph or in another body paragraph, make the changes now.
4. Take out any material that is no longer relevant to your essay.
5. Place your charts in your writing folder.

POWER GRAMMAR

The Sentence Structure of Definitions

In this chapter, you will give some definitions; that is, you will describe or explain some keywords.

To learn about your choices for grammar in definitions, analyze the following definitions. Most of them are from the reading "Stress: What It Is and What It Does to Your Body" from Nevid's psychology textbook.

Examples of Definitions	Explanations
Hassles **are** <u>annoyances we commonly experience in our daily lives.</u>	This is the most common pattern for definitions: *Noun* to be defined + **be** verb + <u>category</u> the noun belongs to. In this example, the word *hassles* is a plural count noun, so the verb must also be plural (**are**).

Chronic *stress* **is** a state of persistent tension or pressure that can lead us to feel exhausted, irritable, and depressed.

The definition of *chronic stress* is also introduced by the verb **be**. In this case, the verb is singular (**is**) because *stress* is noncount.

But when the stress we face in our lives increases to a level that taxes our ability to cope, we may experience distress, **which is** an internal state of physical or mental pain or suffering.

The definition of *distress* is introduced by the words **which is**. Notice that the word **which** comes right after the word *distress*. *Which* is a pronoun taking the place of the word *distress*, so the verb (**is**) must agree with *distress*.

Health psychologists use the term *stress* **to describe** pressures or demands placed upon an organism to adjust or adapt to its environment.

The definition of *stress* is introduced by "to." Notice the structure of the sentence: Subject (Health psychologists) + verb (use) + object/word to be defined (*stress*) + infinitive (**to describe**) + definition (pressures or demands . . .).

Another major source of stress is *frustration*, the negative emotional state that occurs when our efforts to pursue out goals are blocked or thwarted.

Here's a challenging example. The writer has combined two sentences and then dropped some words in the middle. Read it carefully. What is the definition of *frustration*?

In this case, the definition comes after the word itself (*frustration*). Notice the comma (,) that separates *frustration* from its definition.

EXERCISE 25 **Analyzing student sentences**

The sentences below contain different definitions that are similar to the examples listed in the chart on the previous pages. With the help of two classmates, circle the word being (defined) and underline each definition. Ask your instructor for help if you are confused. An example has been completed for you.

> **Example:**
>
> A common effect of stress is (sleeplessness), the inability to fall asleep or to stay asleep.

1. Some freshmen experience distress, which is a high degree of stress.

2. Conflict is a state of tension resulting from the presence of two or more competing goals that demand resolution.

3. The word *stress* is generally used to indicate the many pressures people cope with as they adapt to the world around them.

4. Hassles are everyday annoyances that can cause stress.

EXERCISE 26 **Paraphrasing definitions**

With another classmate, rewrite the definitions from Exercise 25 so that each definition is structured differently from the original. You may change or eliminate some of the original words, but the meaning must remain the same as the original definition. The example definition has been rewritten for you.

1. *Sleeplessness is the inability to sleep regularly, and it is caused by stress.*

2. _____

_____

3. _____

_____

4. _____

_____

5. _____

_____

EXERCISE 27 Writing your definitions

Review your working thesis, topic sentences, fishbone map, and supporting materials. Then, on separate paper,

1. Write the definition of stress you will use in your introduction.
2. Write the definitions of other words that will go in your introduction, background paragraph, and body paragraphs.
3. Keep these definitions in your writing folder.

⭕ Writing, Revising, and Editing

You have organized your ideas and supporting materials, and you have planned for your essay. Now, you are ready to put your essay together. You will follow the steps you learned in the previous chapters to write your introduction, background paragraph, body paragraphs, conclusion, and references.

EXERCISE 28 Comparing two introductions

Read Estela's and Julie's introductions. Then, with two or three classmates, answer the questions that follow.

Estela's Introduction

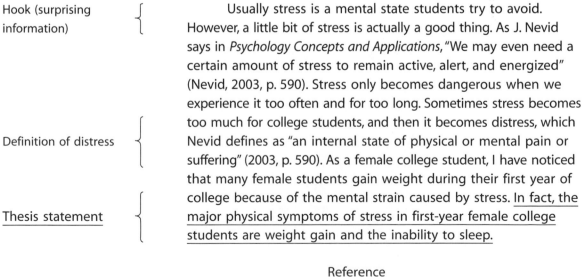

Hook (surprising information)

  Usually stress is a mental state students try to avoid. However, a little bit of stress is actually a good thing. As J. Nevid says in *Psychology Concepts and Applications*, "We may even need a certain amount of stress to remain active, alert, and energized" (Nevid, 2003, p. 590). Stress only becomes dangerous when we experience it too often and for too long. Sometimes stress becomes too much for college students, and then it becomes distress, which

Definition of distress

Nevid defines as "an internal state of physical or mental pain or suffering" (2003, p. 590). As a female college student, I have noticed that many female students gain weight during their first year of college because of the mental strain caused by stress. In fact, the

Thesis statement

major physical symptoms of stress in first-year female college students are weight gain and the inability to sleep.

Reference

First letter of title is capitalized

Nevid, J. S. (2003). *Psychology concepts and applications*. Boston: Houghton Mifflin.

Julie's Introduction

General statement
about stress {

Definition of stress {

Hook (interesting
statistics) {

Thesis statement {

Titles of books and
names of websites
are italicized. {

> Stress is a normal part of life, and without stress we would lead a rather boring existence (Nist & Holschuh, 2003). However, when a person experiences high stress levels, that it something to worry about. This type of stress is "a state of extreme difficulty, pressure, or strain" (*Dictionary.com, 2003*). College life is very stressful especially for freshmen. In fact, a study done at UCLA showed that 30.2 percent of the freshmen surveyed reported that when they thought about everything they had to deal with, the feeling of stress was overwhelming (Nist & Holschuh, 2003). <u>Freshmen have a lot of stress due to their financial burdens and problems adapting to college life, yet money and time management workshops can help freshmen learn how to deal with these most serious stressors.</u>

References

Nist, S. & Holschuh, J. (2003). *College success strategies*. New York: Pearson Education.

Stress. (n.d.) *Dictionary.com*. Retrieved October 23, 2003 from http://dictionary.reference. com/search?q=stress

1. How does each introduction capture the reader's attention?
2. Are outside sources cited in each introduction?
3. Is the author's name mentioned with each citation? Why not?
4. Are page numbers given for each citation? Why not?
5. In each thesis statement, underline and label each subject (S) and verb (V).
6. Underline the IC's and circle the DC's in the last two sentences of each introduction.
7. Which introduction do you find more interesting? Why?
8. If you have difficulty answering any of these questions, ask your instructor for help.

EXERCISE 29 Writing your introduction

Review your essay map, thesis statement, and background paragraph. Then, write an introduction for your essay. Be sure to:

1. Introduce the topic of college stress to your readers.
2. Define the meaning of stress.
3. Capture the readers' attention with a "hook": some interesting or surprising information, a question, or a personal experience.
4. Write your thesis statement. Revise the working thesis statement from your essay map if necessary so that it will "flow" with the rest of the introduction.
5. Place your introduction in your writing folder.

EXERCISE 30 Responding to an introduction

Exchange introductions with a classmate, and answer the following questions:

1. Does the introduction begin with a general statement that introduces the topic of college stress?
2. Does the introduction contain a "hook" that makes the reader want to continue reading?
3. Review the essay question chosen by your classmate. Does the thesis statement answer the essay question?
4. How can your classmate's introduction be improved? Write one or two suggestions at the end of your classmate's introduction. Sign your name and give the introduction back to your classmate.

EXERCISE 31   Analyzing background paragraphs

With a classmate, read the background paragraphs below. Then, answer the questions that follow.

Adrjana's Background Paragraph

Controlling ideas {

      Two major causes of **first-year college students'** stress are **time management** and **financial difficulties**. Time management is "the ability to program a schedule where the amount of time spent on one thing is not too much or too little but just enough"

In-text citation of direct quotation (last name of the author, date, and page number) →

(Abela & Renfro, 2003, p. 6). It is knowing when to study, when to rest, and when to have fun while having many other things that have to be done at the same time. Many students are not used to juggling so many activities, and they are not used to the amount of homework they have to do in college, especially

In-text citation (date only because it is the same source again) →

reading (2003). Therefore, freshmen become stressed out by the fact that they do not know how to manage their time wisely and sometimes spend too much time studying for one class and forget to set time aside to do other homework. In addition to this stressor, students also have financial difficulties. These are the crises that students face when they do not have enough money for important things such as books, rent, and even food. It is very hard to go through the day, pay attention in class, do the homework, and study for tests when a student is worried about

Concluding sentence {

not having enough money for rent or food. These problems are the main stressors students have to deal with in college.

Reference

Abela, C., M.Ed. & Renfro, T. (2001). Time management for college
    students. On-line workshop. Retrieved October 19, 2003
    from http://www.selu.edu/Academics/BasicStudies/
    DSES/TimeManagementIntro.html

Taras's Background Paragraph

Topic sentence {

In-text citation: because there is no author, the title is given instead and the date. The online article does not have page numbers.

      Lifestyle, time management, and expectations are the most common stress factors of first-year college students. There are two types of college students: those who study and those who party. According to a CNN.com article, many first-year college students have difficulty transitioning into a more independent lifestyle, which obligates them to take responsibility for their education and future ("Student Body Healthy," 2002). First-year college students have to learn to organize many activities: attend classes, study for tests, write papers, and have time to go out with their friends. However, they are not ready for the responsibility and end up choosing a carefree lifestyle and going to too many parties. These students do not know how to manage their life and time, so they set up unrealistic expectations, such as "I will be able to party a lot but also do all my studying." Without making the right lifestyle choices and managing their time well, the students get really stressed out and set themselves up for failure. The majority of freshmen enter college with the same mind frame that they left high school with and do not realize that college is a big step and requires commitment, time management and realistic goals.

References

No author: begin with source title. {

Keeping your student body healthy. (2002, January 11). *CNN.com.* Retrieved October 20 from http://robots.cnn.com/ HEALTH/library/HQ/00965.html

1. In Adrjana's paragraph about Essay Assignment 3, main keywords are underlined. Do they refer directly to the **controlling ideas** in the topic sentence? Draw lines between the controlling ideas and the corresponding keywords in the paragraph.
2. Bracket the definitions of keywords. Are the definitions clear?
3. Circle the controlling ideas in Taras's paragraph about Assignment 4.
4. Underline keywords that refer to the controlling idea. Draw lines between the ideas and the keywords related to them.
5. Compare your marked paragraph with two classmates'. Did you circle the same controlling ideas and identify the same keywords? Did you identify the definitions correctly? Ask your instructor if you are not sure.

6. Which paragraph do you like best? Why?

7. What have you learned by reading these two background paragraphs that you can apply to your writing? Write your answer on separate paper, and place it in your writing folder.

EXERCISE 32 **Analyzing citations**

With a classmate, look again at the in-text citations and end-of-text references in Adrjana's and Taras's paragraphs. Then, answer the following:

1. How many sources does Adrjana cite in her paragraph? How many does Taras cite?

2. Why do you think they cite these sources?

3. What information do they provide in parentheses for the in-text sources?

4. How do the end-of-text references differ from the in-text citations?

EXERCISE 33 **Writing your background paragraph**

Reread your essay assignment. Then, review your fishbone map, essay map, and other materials in your writing folder. Begin writing your background paragraph. Be sure to provide the following:

1. A definition of the causes of stress that relate to the symptoms, effects, treatment, or prevention stated in your thesis statement

2. Current information about these causes of stress, such as data from a university or college website

3. Evidence that these are serious causes, such as statistical information from a recent study, interview, or survey

4. Additional information that you think will help the reader understand the essay's main idea.

EXERCISE 34 **Responding to a paragraph**

Exchange essay maps, background paragraphs, and supporting materials with a classmate who chose the same essay assignment you are writing about. After reading the essay map carefully, do the following:

1. Circle the controlling ideas in the topic sentence of the background paragraph.

2. In the margin, identify the causes of stress that are explained in the background paragraph. Put a star next to the information that best prepares readers for the essay.

3. At the end of the background paragraph, write one question that your classmate might also answer in her or his background paragraph.
4. Return the materials to your classmate.
5. Read your classmate's comments, and ask her or him any questions you have about her or his observations.
6. Thank your classmate for the feedback, and place your background paragraph with your classmate's comments in your writing folder.

EXERCISE 35 Evaluating Julie's paragraphs

You have already read Julie's introduction earlier in this chapter (p. 190). Now, read her background paragraph and body paragraphs. Notice how, in Julie's paragraphs, the **controlling ideas** *in the topic sentence relate closely to the* keywords *in the body paragraph. After you finish reading, complete the steps that follow.*

Julie's Background Paragraph and Body Paragraphs

Topic sentence (controlling ideas)

Keywords related to financial burdens

Keywords related to stress

Keywords related to adapting to college life

Main point (self-control)

Financial burdens and **adapting to college life** are the **major causes of stress** for **freshmen in college**. Students usually take out loans, get jobs, or get their own credit card to pay for college. Usually, many freshmen are stressed out about the new financial responsibility of paying their bills and supporting themselves through school (Nist & Holschuh, 2003). Especially, working and going to school at the same time is really hard to do for many students. They usually get worn out after long hours at work, cram through their homework when they get home, and do not sleep enough. These are all new problems that college students did not have in high school. Also, many students go to college far away from home, and they do not know how to keep track of deadlines and important events. All these changes make it tough to adapt to the hectic pace of college life, and freshmen get stressed out trying to pay for college and get used to the demands of college life at the same time.

College freshmen can reduce financial stress by managing their money better. They need to learn self-control to avoid using their credit cards to pay for clothes and outings with friends (2003). In "Psychology of Time Management," Richard Boyum gives

Supporting detail
(quotation)

Main point
(financial counseling)

Supporting detail
(Information about
the Student Financial
Service Center)

Summary
of the interview:
Notice how Julie did
not summarize
interview questions.
She only
summarized the
most important
interview.

In parentheses:
month, day, and
year the interview
took place. Because
the interview is
unpublished, it is not
listed in the end-of-
text references.

this important piece of advice to college students, "Differentiate between what you want and what you truly need" (Boyum, 2002). Since many freshmen are in charge of their finances for the first time,they do not know how to budget their money wisely. To help with this problem, many colleges and universities offer financial counseling to students. At California State University, Sacramento (CSUS), students can receive financial advising at the Student Financial Service Center. Each semester, the Center offers workshops and individual appointments to students who need help. The counselors can teach students how to prioritize their bills, how to avoid credit card debt, and how to access scholarships and grants ("Advisors," 2003). Also, students can contact the Center if they are having problems paying their tuition. The Center can help the students discuss alternatives to help pay for college. By getting help and learning money management, freshmen can reduce their financial stress.

Students can also reduce the stress of adapting to college life by taking time management workshops where they can learn how to use planners and calendars efficiently. According to one of the counselors at CSUS Psychological Counseling Services, the best way students can manage their time is by using a monthly planner and a weekly planner. The monthly planner goes on the wall in the student's room, where he or she can see it on a daily basis. On this calendar, the student can keep track of major assignments and important social events. The weekly planner should be used for daily and weekly deadlines. Freshmen should write all their responsibilities and tasks in their weekly planner and check off everything as it is accomplished. By doing that, students will be able to know exactly what they have to do on what day and what time. They can learn how to manage their time wisely by fulfilling the important and urgent tasks first and then worrying about the unimportant ones later. Also, because stress causes forgetfulness, a planner may be the only reliable method to keep track of important due dates and appointments (personal communication, October 22, 2003). By adopting a monthly calendar and a weekly planner, freshmen can avoid time management problems and unnecessary stress.

References

Advisors. (2003, November 13). Retrieved October 23, 2003 from California State University, Sacramento, Student Financial Services Center website: http://www.csus.edu/sfsc/ #ADVISORS

Boyum, R. (2002). Psychology of money management. Retrieved from University of Wisconsin-Eau Claire, Counseling Services website: http://www.campusblues.com/mgemoney.asp

Nist, S., & Holschuh, J. (2003). *College success strategies*. New York: Pearson Education.

1. Circle the controlling ideas in the second and third paragraphs (the first paragraph has been completed for you).
2. Underline keywords in the second and third paragraphs (the first paragraph has been completed for you).
3. Compare your marked paragraphs with a classmate's. Discuss any differences in the way you marked the paragraphs. Ask your instructor for help if you disagree with your classmate.

EXERCISE **36** **Evaluating in-text citations**

With two classmates, highlight the in-text citations in Julie's paragraphs (pp. 195–196). Then,

1. Write P above each paraphrase or summary, and Q above each quotation.
2. Which in-text citation do you find most interesting? Why?
3. What information does Julie provide in parentheses for each in-text citation?
4. Why does this information vary? (For example, sometimes she gives the name of the author and sometimes she does not.)
5. If you have trouble answering any of these questions, ask your instructor for help.

EXERCISE 37 Drafting your body paragraphs

Review your essay map, supporting materials, introduction, and background paragraph. Then,

1. Write or type your introduction and background paragraphs on a new page.
2. Circle the controlling ideas in the thesis and background paragraph.
3. Compose your body paragraphs.
4. Circle the controlling ideas in each body paragraph.
5. Make sure the controlling ideas in the paragraphs match the controlling ideas in the thesis statement.
6. Make sure the supporting evidence in each body paragraph matches controlling ideas in the topic sentence.
7. Check the citations of the supporting information in each of your body paragraphs. Remember that any information you did not know when you began your assignment must be followed by an in-text citation:
   a. If you **summarize** from a source (that is, write a shorter version of the original information in your own words), put an in-text citation right after the information. Example: (Nuttall, 2004)
   b. If you **paraphrase** from a source (that is, write about the information in your own words), put an in-text citation right after the information. Example: (Nuttall, 2004)
   c. If you **quote directly** from a source, add the page number(s) to your in-text citation. Example: (Nuttall, 2004, p. 15)
   d. When you cite from your interview, add: (personal communication, October 22, 2003).
8. Put your introduction, background paragraph, and body paragraphs in your writing folder.

EXERCISE 38 Evaluating Julie's conclusion

You have read Julie's introduction (Exercise 28) and body paragraphs (Exercise 35). Now read Julie's conclusion below with two classmates. Then, answer the questions that follow.

Notice how Julie's conclusion begins with a sentence that connects to the last sentence of the last body paragraph.

Julie's Conclusion

Transitions and repetition of keywords and ideas help connect the sentences together and create coherence.

To conclude, stress is a common part of life. **However**, financial burdens and problems adapting to college life can become major causes of too much stress for college freshmen. These students need to learn how to prevent and cope with stress. Freshmen can prevent and eliminate excessive stress from the beginning by taking control of their finances and managing their time better. **Therefore**, I recommend that all colleges encourage freshmen to take money- and time-management workshops so that they can be successful in college and avoid major stress.

1. What idea(s) does Julie mention in the conclusion that she had stated in her introduction?
2. Does Julie summarize the essay's main ideas? If she does, underline or highlight them in the conclusion.
3. What concluding technique(s) does Julie use? (Examples: prediction, recommendation, solution, evaluation)
4. Do you find Julie's conclusion effective? Why or why not?

EXERCISE 39 Writing your conclusion

Reread your essay, especially your introduction and thesis statement. Then,

1. Begin your conclusion with a concluding word or phrase
2. Write a sentence that connects with the last sentence of the last body paragraph
3. Add a brief summary (two or three sentences) of the essay's main idea and controlling ideas (thesis and topic sentences)
4. Use a concluding technique to leave the readers with a final message (a final recommendation, prediction, solution or evaluation).

EXERCISE 40 Writing your References page

In this chapter, you are given many examples of end-of-text references. Review some of these examples before you write your References page. Remember to do the following:

1. Double-space your references.
2. List your references in alphabetical order.
3. Indent each reference five to seven spaces after the first line.
4. Begin each reference with the author's name, or the title of the source if the author is not given.
5. Give date of publication, title, and other pertinent information.
6. Remember to add page numbers for journal, magazine, and newspaper articles.
7. Give the URL for website and the retrieval date.
8. Put your References page in your writing folder. Set your essay aside for a day or two if possible before you revise it.

EXERCISE 41 Revising your essay

Reread your essay carefully. Use this checklist:

1. _____ Your introduction defines the meaning of stress and gradually leads to your thesis statement.

2. _____ Your thesis statement has a clear main idea about the effects, symptoms, treatment, or prevention of stress and controls the rest of the essay.

3. _____ Your background paragraph explains two or three causes of stress that are directly related to your essay topic.

4. _____ Your body paragraphs have clear topic sentences that relate to the thesis statement.

5. _____ The main points and supporting details in each of your body paragraphs explain the controlling ideas in the topic sentence.

6. _____ Your essay includes at least two in-text citations.

7. _____ Your essay includes a brief summary of your interview.

8. _____ Your conclusion restates the essay's main idea and provides a final comment about the topic.

9. _____ Your References page lists all the sources in your essay and follows APA style.

10. _____ You have included a transcript of your interview.

EXERCISE 42 Self-editing your essay

Read your essay and focus on the grammar and sentence structure:

1. Underline all the definitions you give in the essay. Identify the subject (S) and verb (V) in each definition. Does the subject in each definition agree with the verb? Remember that noncount nouns and singular count nouns need a singular verb. Plural nouns need a plural verb (examples: "Stress is . . ." "A conflict indicates . . ." "Hassles cause . . .")

2. Check the beginning of each body paragraph. Do you need to add a transition word or phrase?

3. Check your conclusion. Do you need to add a concluding word or phrase?

4. Spell check and proofread your essay before you print three copies—one for your writing folder and two for peer responses.

EXERCISE 43 Responding to an essay

Exchange essays with two classmates. Use "Two-Part Peer Review" (Appendix 8, pp. 264–265) to respond to your classmates' essays. You will be Reviewer #1 for one classmate, and Reviewer #2 for the other classmate.

EXERCISE 44 Rewriting your essay

Reread your essay carefully. Then,

1. Consider your classmates' responses:
   a. Which suggestions can you incorporate that will improve your essay?
   b. What did you learn from reading your classmates' essays that can be applied to your writing?

2. Type your essay.

3. Place your draft in your writing folder. Include your previous drafts with peer responses, your essay map, and all the other materials you developed for Essay Assignment 4. Do not forget the notes you took during the interview! They need to be at the end of your essay.

4. Give the folder to your instructor.

EXERCISE 45 **Analyzing the instructor's response**

When you receive your essay back, read your instructor's comments carefully. Then,

1. List your essay's strengths on an index card or separate paper.
2. List your essay's weaknesses on the back of the index card or paper.
3. Keep the card or paper in your writing folder.
4. Circle or highlight any instructor comments that confused you. Make an appointment with your instructor or go to her or his office during office hours to ask for help. Remember to bring your writing folder with you.

EXERCISE 46 **Writing one more draft**

If your instructor requires a final draft, reread your instructor's comments carefully. Make the necessary changes to your essay. Put your final draft with all the other materials related to this essay assignment in your writing folder. Give your writing folder to your instructor.

○ Additional Assignments for More Practice and Assessment

Assignment 1: Review Chapter 4 Objectives

Review the list of objectives at the beginning of the chapter and complete the checklist. Then, write one or two paragraphs in response to the following questions:

1. Which of the three writing steps (gathering information; focusing and organizing; writing, revising, and editing) was the most difficult for you? Why?
2. Which step was the easiest? Why?

Assignment 2: Summarize the Reading about Stress

Reread the excerpt found earlier in this chapter, "Stress: What It Is and What It Does to Your Body" (pp. 159–164). Review your answers to Exercises 6 through 8. Then, write a summary of the excerpt. Follow the summarizing strategies you learned in Chapters 2 and 3. In your summary, **paraphrase** the author's definitions of *stress* and *hassles*.

Assignment 3: Learn More about the Topic

Find an article or a research study on the World Wide Web about the effects of college stress on seniors (graduating students). Write a summary of the article in fifty words or less.

Then, write a short paragraph explaining why you chose this article. What did you learn about seniors and stress? What can you learn from this article that can help you succeed in college?

WEB POWER

You will find additional exercises related to the content in this chapter at http://esl.college.hmco.com/students.

Explaining Ancient Mysteries

In previous chapters, you learned how to write explaining essays and reports by following a three-step writing process. In this chapter, you will summarize and blend together information from different print and online sources. You will also demonstrate the writing skills you have learned in this course by writing an explaining essay about an important archeological or anthropological discovery.

Chapter Objectives

Review this chapter's objectives before you start. Return to this chart after completing the chapter, and check (✓) the appropriate box to the right.	I have learned this well.	I need to work on this.
Review methods of gathering and organizing ideas from previous chapters and select the most appropriate for your essay		
Apply the critical reading skills you learned in this book to select appropriate sources for your essay on the Internet and at the library		
Prepare and give an oral report about your Internet and library searches		

Avoid plagiarism by:
    Using synonyms
    Changing report verbs
    Changing sentence structure		

Write a well-developed research report about an archeological mystery		
Develop specific questions for peer reviews		
Use and cite figures in your essay by using correct APA format		
Use parallel structure to write a thesis statement		
Use modals of possibility to convey uncertainty about archeological discoveries		
Use past tenses appropriately to write about ancient mysteries		

Chapter Essay Assignment

Human history is full of mysteries that archeologists, anthropologists, and other scientists have been trying to solve or have solved through the years. In this chapter, you will write a three- to four-page (double-spaced) explaining essay about one of the mysteries listed below:

- The Lascaux Cave
- Otzi the Iceman
- Copan
- Orrorin Man
- The Pyramids of Sudan

This essay will demonstrate all the writing skills you have learned in this course.

To complete this assignment you need to:

- Complete an Internet search and/or a library search
- Write a research-based report by following a three-step writing process

Your essay must include:

- An introductory paragraph in which you engage the reader with interesting information about the topic
- A background paragraph in which you explain *what* your topic is (e.g., give history about the topic, define some terms associated with the topic, describe the topic)
- One body paragraph to explain *how* your mystery was discovered, investigated, and/or solved
- One or two body paragraphs to explain *why* your topic is important (e.g., for historical, anthropological, archeological reasons)
- A concluding paragraph

   In addition to your three- to four-page essay, you will include:

- A cover page
- Six to eight in-text citations
- Four to six end-of-text references (on a separate page)

- One or two charts or illustrations (nontext materials) that are appropriately cited. Include these materials in your essay (do not put them at the back of your essay). You may leave space in your essay and tape the charts and/or illustrations into the text.

Note: Keep all the materials, drafts, and peer reviews for this essay assignment in your writing folder.

EXERCISE **1** Analyzing the essay assignment

Reread the essay assignment carefully. Then, with three or four classmates, answer the following questions. Write your answers on the lines below.

1. What is the **purpose** of this chapter's essay assignment? Why did your instructor give you this assignment?

   _____

   _____

2. How much **knowledge** of the topic can you expect your readers to have?

   _____

   _____

3. Where can you find **information** about the topic?

   _____

   _____

○ Gathering Information

EXERCISE **2** Doing a Web search

*On your own or with a classmate, visit **each** website listed on the next page. The purpose of this assignment is to help you learn some general information about the topic. Therefore, spend less than five minutes viewing each website. Then, on separate paper, answer the questions that follow.*

Master Student Tip

Ask your instructor for help if you have trouble doing one of the exercises in this chapter.

1. The Cave of Lascaux
   http://www.culture.gouv.fr/culture/arcnat/lascaux/en/

   a. *Where* is the Cave?
   b. *When* was it discovered?
   c. *Who* discovered it?
   d. *What* was found in it?

2. Otzi the Iceman
   http://www.athropolis.com/news/iceman.htm

   a. *Who* is Otzi?
   b. *Who* found him?
   c. *Where* was he found?
   d. *How* did he die?

3. Copan
   http://www.learner.org/exhibits/collapse/copan/index.php

   a. *What* is Copan?
   b. *Where* is it?
   c. *Who* lived there?
   d. *What* happened to them?

4. Orrorin Man
   http://www.pbs.org/wnet/secrets/case_firsthuman/clues.html

   a. *Who* is Orrorin Man?
   b. *Where* was he found?
   c. *Who* found him?
   d. *How* old are his remains?

5. The Pyramids of Sudan
   http://www.m-huether.de/sudan/bajr.htm

   a. *Where* in Sudan are the pyramids?
   b. *When* were they built?
   c. *Who* built them?
   d. *Why*?

EXERCISE 3 **Choosing your topic**

Review the information you found on the Internet. Then, choose the topic you find most interesting to write about in your essay.

EXERCISE 4 Brainstorming questions

*With two or three classmates who chose the same topic, brainstorm
WH- questions that should be answered in your essay in addition to the
four questions you answered in Exercise 2.*

*In the examples below, two students brainstormed questions about
another mystery, Machu Picchu. The questions on the left had been assigned
by the instructor.*

Muang and Choua's Questions about Machu Picchu

Where is Machu Picchu?

Who discovered it?

Who built this city?

Why did they build it?

How was the city built?

Who lived there?

Where did these people come from?

What did they look like?

Where do their descendants live today?

What does Machu Picchu look like now?

Why was it abandoned by its founders?

When was it abandoned?

Who lives there now?

How do you get there?

EXERCISE 5   **Generating ideas**

With a classmate who chose the same essay topic, choose one method you have learned in this book (for example: freewriting, brainstorming, listing, making a chart, drawing a fishbone map) to develop more ideas and to answer the questions you wrote in Exercise 4. Place your ideas in your writing folder.

EXERCISE 6   **Searching the World Wide Web**

In Chapter 4, you learned about choosing websites wisely ("Spotlight on Writing Skills: Selecting Websites"). Review that information, and then,

1. Go online to locate sources for your essay topic. A good place to start is a website that offers access to a variety of online magazines or links to other websites. See the suggested websites at our website: http://esl.college.hmco.com/students.
2. Review eight to ten online sources before selecting those you will summarize in your report.
3. Print the online materials you selected for your report.
4. Place the pages in your writing folder.

EXERCISE 7   **Doing a library search**

With one or two classmates who chose the same topic, go to the library to find additional sources for your report:

1. Select the most current sources because they are more likely to include the latest findings about your topic.
2. Start by researching magazines such as *Smithsonian*, *National Geographic*, or *Archaeology Magazine*. Ask a librarian for help if you do not know how to locate these and other magazines.
3. Look for other recent print sources that provide information about your topic.
4. To choose the best sources, look for information that answers your questions (Exercise 4) and relates to your ideas (from Exercise 5).
5. Remember to write down all source information, as you learned in Chapter 4. Also see the examples below.
6. Photocopy any articles or chapters that contain useful information. Place the copies in your writing folder.

Name of the author ⟶

Year of publication ⟶

Title of the book ⟶

Publisher ⟶

Place of publication ⟶

Book

Feder, K. L. (2001). *Frauds, myths, and mysteries: Science and pseudoscience in archaeology* (4th ed.). New York: McGraw Hill.

Year of publication
(no volume number
is given: include
season, month, or
month and day
designation) ⟶

Author ⟶

Page Numbers ⟶

Title of the article ⟶

Title of magazine
or journal ⟶

Journal or Magazine Article

Lange, K. (2004, January). The Himba people. *National Geographic,* 32–47.

EXERCISE 8 **Preparing to report information**

Review the materials you found on the Internet and at the library. Prepare to report that information by writing down the answers to the questions you brainstormed in Exercise 4.

EXERCISE 9 **Reporting information**

Form a group with two or three classmates who chose to research the same topic. Review the chapter's essay assignment. Then,

1. Give a one-minute oral report to your group about the information you found on the Internet. Only mention the most important information you found.
2. Take notes about the information you learn from your group. Use a different page for each presentation.
3. Keep your notes in your writing folder. You will need them for Exercise 10.

Here are two student examples of note-taking. Notice that Muang used informal writing in her notes.

Muang's Notes about Choua's Presentation

Machu Picchu-Andes, Peru
    Name = "manly peak" or "old peak"
Incas founded it in 1460s
    Mean warriors→conquered most of South America
    warrior leader and religious leader/high priest
    built many cities on mountains
    No prisons bc if you stole or sthg. they cut your arm off, poked
    your eyes, threw you off a cliff
MP really wasn't a city
    religious place of Incan king/ruler
    not many people lived in MP, mostly women & children
    New studies of bones show men lived there too (priests?)
Houses built with no mortar but very solid
    very thin knife cannot fit betw. stones
    heavy, 50 tons or more
    w/o knowing wheel, how did Incas carry stones? Mystery
    beautiful, architecture great
People cultivated the land, very self-sufficient
MP couldn't be seen from below→
    Spanish soldiers didn't find it
Why people lived in MP?
    training place for priests and priestesses?
    aliens _ large designs on ground were made to guide landing UFOs?
    more likely: astronomy place to observe sun, moon, stars
discovered in 1911 by American Hiram Bingham
    was looking for some other place but found MP instead

Muang's Notes about Sandra's Presentation

Machu Picchu found by Hiram Bingham in 1911
    thought he had found VILCABAMBA = last fortress of Incan
    empire. Most archeologists disagree w/HB
Not a city but a retreat for rich Incas
    or more prob. ceremonial site for priests
Incas used huge stones for walls and straw for roofs
    great structure, well organized streets, houses & buildings
    many buildings still okay
    scholars like to study architecture of place

VERY IMPORTANT: column of stone on top of stone block
    called INTIHUATANA = post for "tying the sun"
    religious ritual 4 winter solstice→priest tied string to column
    to keep sun in place
    some scholars say priest tied string during equinoxes, not
    just solstice
    Equinox→sun's right above column and casts no shadow
    priests prob. tried to keep the sun longer by doing ceremony
Spanish CONQUISTADORES destroyed columns in other Incan places
    Conq. never found MP→didn't destroy column
Some people think MP's very spiritual
    if you touch column with your forehead, can feel one with spirit
    world @ MP also Temple of the Moon (cavern)—not sure what
    was for goddess temple?

Note: For more on note-taking, review note-taking skills in Chapter 3.

EXERCISE 10 **Making suggestion charts**

For each classmate's presentation, suggest which information might go in the background paragraph and which would be better in the body paragraphs.

1. Create a suggestion chart similar to Muang's charts below for each presentation.
2. Give the charts you completed to your classmates.
3. Place the suggestions charts from your classmates in your writing folder.

Muang's Chart for Choua

Background paragraph	Give info about the Incas or maybe put it in the intro and talk about how the place looked instead.
Body Paragraph 1	Talk about Bingham, how he discovered Machu Picchu, what he found.
Body Paragraph 2	Talk about the importance of the place—architecture, stones without mortar and what scholars have learned about Incas from studying MP.

Muang's Chart for Sandra

Background paragraph	Give info about Machu Picchu, like where it is, who built it and why.
Body Paragraph 1	Give info about Bingham and that he thought he had found another city. Tell about his expedition there.
Body Paragraph 2	Talk about the religious stuff like the column and the ceremonies, why they were important to the Incas and why they are important today.

POWER GRAMMAR

Parallel Structure

Parallel structure means that the same parts of speech (all nouns, for example) are used in a sentence to show that two or more ideas are equally important. By using parallel structure you make your ideas clearer and easier to read.

When listing ideas in your thesis, be sure the ideas follow a similar grammatical structure. Notice the parallel structures in the thesis statements below.

Thesis Statements	Explanations
<u>This essay</u> *describes* Machu Picchu, *tells* about its discovery, and *explains* the historical importance of this "lost city."	The subject ("<u>This essay</u>") is followed by three phrases that start with a verb: **1.** *describes* Machu Picchu, **2.** *tells* about its discovery, and **3.** *explains* the historical importance of this "lost city."
This essay <u>describes</u> *the Cave of Chauvet-Pont-D'Arc, its discovery, and its historical and artistic significance.*	The verb "<u>describes</u>" is followed by three noun phrases: **1.** *the Cave of Chauvet-Pont-D'Arc,* **2.** *its discovery,* and **3.** *its historical and artistic significance.*

Parallel Structure (cont.)

Thesis Statements	Explanations
In this report, I will show that the Vikings were not just raiders, but they were also farmers, explorers, and settlers.	The word "also" is followed by three nouns: 1. *farmers,* 2. *explorers,* and 3. *settlers.*
In this essay, I will explain *who* Otzi the Iceman is, *how* he was found, and *why* his discovery is important to the field of anthropology.	The verb "will explain" is followed by three WH- clauses: 1. *who* Otzi the Iceman is, 2. *how* he was found, and 3. *why* his discovery is important to the field of anthropology.

EXERCISE 11   Noticing errors

In the following thesis statements, the students did not use parallel structure in their lists of ideas. With a classmate, read each statement and correct the underlined form so that it matches the other forms in the parallel structure. The first sentence has been completed for you.

1. This essay gives a detailed description of Orrorin Man, discusses its discovery, and it explained the effects of this discovery on anthropology. *explains*

2. This paper reports on the Melungeons, explains their European origins, and discussing their place among Appalachian cultures.

3. In this paper, I will report about Orrorin Man, the discovery of his remains, and I will talk about the importance of this anthropological discovery.

4. The purpose of this paper is to describe the ancient city of Copan, how it was discovered, and its archeological and historical value.

5. This essay explains about Copan, the way it was found, and it is also about the reason this city is important in history and archeology.

EXERCISE 12 Identifying errors

With two or three classmates, read the following sentences and correct the errors in parallel structure. (Hint: Each sentence has one error.) The first sentence has been completed for you.

1. Copan is important because it was a large Mayan city, ~~its sudden and mysterious collapse~~, and it still ~~contains~~ many clues about Mayan life. *it collapsed suddenly and mysteriously*

2. The possible causes for the decline of Machu Picchu were the frequent wars among Inca tribes, diseases, and the Spanish conquerors invaded the Incan empire.

3. To make sure the prehistoric paintings in the Cave of Chauvet-Pont-D'Arc were real, scientists looked at animal representation, crystallization, and they also looked at line continuation.

4. The discovery of Chauvet-Pont-D'Arc has great archeological value because a large number of prehistoric animals are represented in the murals, the painting techniques are very sophisticated, and the esthetic quality of the paintings.

5. Orrorin Man created a huge controversy among anthropologists because he predates the first human ancestor (Lucy), shows evidence of walking on two legs, and Orrorin man comes from a densely forested area of East Africa.

WEB POWER

For more practice with parallel structure and sentence structure in general, go to
http://esl.college.hmco.com/students.

○ Focusing and Organizing

EXERCISE 13 **Writing a working thesis**

Reread the essay topic, your suggestion chart, and the materials you collected. Then,

1. Write a working thesis statement for your essay. Your thesis statement is a statement of intent that explains what information you will cover in your essay. Here are some ways to state your intent: "This paper describes . . ." "This essay explains . . ." "In this essay, I will discuss . . ."
2. Use a parallel structure for your thesis statement (see Sandra's and Choua's examples below).
3. Compare your thesis statement to the essay assignment to make sure it answers the assignment. Notice how well Sandra and Choua answer the essay assignment in their thesis statements.
4. Circle the controlling ideas in your thesis statement.
5. For each controlling idea, write three to five questions you plan to answer in the body paragraphs.
6. Place your working thesis in your writing folder.

Sandra's Working Thesis

In this essay, I will report about Machu Picchu, and I will also explain how it was discovered in 1911 and why it is an important discovery for historical and religious reasons.

Choua's Working Thesis

This essay describes Machu Picchu, tells about its discovery, and explains the historical importance of this "lost city."

EXERCISE 14 **Writing your essay map**

Review your working thesis statement, the materials you found on the Internet and at the library, and your classmates' suggestion charts. Then,

1. Write topic sentences for two or three body paragraphs. Write each topic sentence on a different sheet of paper. In each topic sentence, refer to one or more controlling ideas in your working thesis statement.
2. Circle the controlling ideas in your topic sentences.

3. Under each topic sentence, list WH- questions that you will answer in the paragraph.
4. Answer each question, and list the source(s) of your supporting evidence.
5. Compare your map to Sandra's map below. What can you learn from reading her essay map?

Here is Sandra's essay map, where she also listed the evidence for her introduction. Many of Sandra's notes are incomplete sentences and phrases. Notice that she did not include a source for the last piece of information in body paragraph 3 ("To prolong summer season, harvest season"). Therefore, her classmate put an asterisk next to the information so that Sandra would remember to add the source(s). Also, her classmate suggested that Sandra split paragraph 3 into two—one about the historical importance and one about the mystical importance of Machu Picchu. This is a good suggestion because Sandra lists a lot of supporting evidence in this paragraph.

Sandra's Essay Map

INTRODUCTION: Explain who the Incas were and how religion influenced them (Internet article, "Inca")

THESIS STATEMENT: In this essay I will report about Machu Picchu, and I will also explain how it was discovered in 1911 and why it is an important discovery for historical and mystical reasons.

BACKGROUND PARAGRAPH: Machu Picchu is a famous archeological site built at the time of the Incan empire.

What is Machu Picchu? A retreat for rich Incas, a ceremonial site or most likely both (Internet, Ziegler's article and Bingham's book, Lost City of the Incas)

Where is it located? The Andes of Peru, 7,000 feet above sea level. Semi-tropical area overlooking Urubamba river (Bingham)

Why did the Incas build it? Most likely, a ruler needed a place to perform religious rites (Internet article, "Machu Picchu, Peru")

BODY PARAGRAPH 2: Machu Picchu was discovered in 1911 by an American explorer.

How was Machu Picchu discovered? The Yale University Peruvian expedition stumbled upon it while looking for Vilcabamba, the last fortress of the Incan empire (Bingham)

Who discovered it? Hiram Bingham, American explorer (Bingham)

When was it discovered? 1911 (Bingham)

Why hadn't it been discovered before? Spaniards didn't see it because of vegetation, hard to get there. Even among Incas probably few knew about it (online article, "Machu Pichu")

BODY PARAGRAPH 3: The discovery of Machu Picchu has historic and mystical meaning.

Why does Machu Picchu have historic importance? Architecture of the time is well preserved, other aspects of everyday life here are evident (Bingham, "Machu Pichu")

What artifacts have been found? Tombs, even recently, bones, metal tools and other artifacts, buildings (Online Reuters News)

How has this knowledge helped understand Incas? Understanding of agricultural system and architectural structures helps see level of development in Incan empire ("Machu Picchu, Peru," Bingham) Religious rituals are clearer because of intact Intihuatana (same sources)

Why is the site significant from a mystical point of view? New age movement tries to re-create ancient rites (Machu Picchu, Peru")

What rituals were performed? Equinox and solstice rituals (same article)

Why were rituals performed? To prolong summer season, harvest season *

CONCLUSION: Recap main points and predict that further study of ruins will bring more knowledge of Incan culture and religious beliefs.

EXERCISE 15 Evaluating a classmate's essay map

Exchange essay maps and supporting materials with a classmate. Then,

1. Carefully review your classmate's thesis and topic sentences. Do the controlling ideas in the topic sentences correspond to the controlling ideas in the thesis statement?

2. Put an asterisk (*) at the end of each piece of information that needs to be cited.

3. Choose the most effective topic sentence, underline it, and explain why it is the most effective (example: topic sentence #2 is the best because it is very specific and well supported with evidence).

4. Give two or three suggestions that can help your classmate improve her or his essay map. Write them at the end of the essay map.

5. Return your classmate's essay map.

6. Thank your classmate for the feedback.

POWER GRAMMAR

Modals of Possibility

The sources you use in your essay will refer to scientific studies. Scientists study evidence such as concrete objects, facts, and data and then draw conclusions by interpreting this evidence. Sometimes the evidence is not enough to reach a solid conclusion. Therefore, in commenting about research findings, scientists will use adverbs, report verbs, and modals to express their ideas.

In Chapter 2, you learned about report verbs. In this chapter, you will learn about the modals *may, might*, and *could*.

Sentences with Modals	**Explanations**
A smallpox epidemic *may* **HAVE** *caused* the decline of Machu Picchu.	Modals with past meaning are used to interpret an event that occurred in the past:
The collapse of the cave *could* **have been brought** on by torrential rains.	*modal* + **HAVE** + **past participle** of the main verb.
The collapse of Copan *might* **HAVE been** the result of a long draught.	
The carving *may* **represent** the founder of Stonehenge.	Modals with present meaning are used to interpret current information and evidence:
The paintings *could* **be** the work of a prehistoric artist.	*modal* + **verb** (no endings).
The faint markings *may* **indicate** an earlier construction stage.	

EXERCISE 16   Noticing modals of possibility

With two or three classmates, read the following sentences and underline the modal verb in each sentence. Use the list in the Power Grammar box above to identify them. The first sentence has been completed for you.

1. Some anthropologists believe that Kennewick <u>could</u> be a Native American of Caucasian descent.

2. Copan's collapse could have been caused by excessive farming and illness, especially anemia.

3. A colder climate may have been a major factor in the decline of mountain settlements.

4. Kennewick man may have arrived in America before Asian settlers.

5. Chauvet-Pont-D'Arc's paintings may be considered the most detailed prehistoric art known today.

EXERCISE 17 Noticing modals of time

With a classmate, circle the past modals used for past time meaning in the sentences below. Underline the modals used for present time meaning. Use the list in the Grammar Box above as a guide. The first two sentences have been completed for you.

1. Early settlers (may have abandoned) the site after a few years.

2. The large stones <u>may symbolize</u> the hours of the day.

3. The first people to settle in Stonehenge may have come from Germany.

4. The massive limestone sarcophagus may be the work of a master sculptor.

5. The many clay soldiers could have been placed in the tomb to stand guard.

6. An earthquake could cause the collapse of the cave.

7. The erosion evident on the wall of the tomb might be the result of water damage caused by an early flood.

8. The mummies may have been made to look like warriors to ward off evil spirits.

WEB POWER

For more practice with modals, go to
http://esl.hmco.com/students.

○ Writing, Revising, and Editing

SPOTLIGHT ON WRITING SKILLS

Reviewing Summary Skills

This chapter essay assignment requires you to summarize a lot of information. Here is a quick review of the steps for writing a good summary that you learned in Chapter 2.

1. Read the paragraph you want to summarize.
2. Circle the keywords and phrases.
3. If you do not understand some of the main words, look them up in a dictionary or ask your instructor.
4. Use synonyms for the reporting verbs in the original text.
5. Use synonyms for some of the less important terms and phrases.
6. Use different sentence structure.
7. Compare your summary with the original text to make sure the meaning is the same.

The following paragraph comes from the online article "Machu Picchu. How They Kept the Secret," by Gary Ziegler. A student summary follows the passage.

Original Text

Actually, Machu Picchu was not a city at all. It was probably built by Pachacuti Inca as a royal estate and religious retreat in 1460–70. Its location—on a remote secondary road in nearly impassable terrain high above the Urubamba River canyon cloud forest—almost ensured that it would have no administrative, commercial or military use. Any movement in that direction to or from Cusco and the Sacred valley would have been by other Inca roads, either the high road near Salcantay or by the Lucumayo valley road. Travel was restricted on these roads except by Inca decree. [98 words]

Other information is written in the student's own words.

Keywords are the same as the in original. The sentence structure is different from the original.

Student Summary

Machu Picchu was probably the estate of the Incan rulers. It was built around 1460 on a mountain above the Urubamba River. *The Incas would have used other roads. And even to travel on these roads the people received permission from their rulers.* [43 words]

EXERCISE 18 Evaluating a summary

With one or two classmates, read the paragraph below from Ellie Crystal's webpage "Machu Picchu" and the student summary after it. Then, complete the steps that follow.

Original Text

Another possibility is that a novice priest defiled one of the sacred Virgins of the Sun. Garcilaso de Vega, the son of a Spaniard and an Inca princess, wrote exhaustive commentaries on Inca customs. According to him, anyone found guilty of sexually violating an "ajilla" was not only put to death himself, but servants, relatives and neighbors, inhabitants of the same town and their cattle were all killed. No one was left . . . The place was damned and excommunicated so that no one could find it, not even the animals! Was this, then, the fate of the inhabitants of Machu Picchu? [101 words]

Student Summary

Maybe Machu Picchu was destroyed by the Inca rulers for religious reasons. Garcilaso de Vega was the son of a Spanish conquistador and an Inca princess. In his notes, he told about an Incan rule: if a man had sex with a sacred Virgin of the Sun, he was excommunicated and then killed along with his family and entire village, including the livestock. [63 words]

1. Circle the keywords in the summary that are the same in the original text.
2. Notice the report verb *wrote* in the original text. What report verb is used to replace it in the summary?
3. Mark the subjects (S) and verbs (V) in the first two sentences of both texts.
4. Bracket each clause in the first two sentences of both texts. What differences do you see in the sentence structure of the two texts?
5. Eliminate nine or ten words to make the summary shorter. You may rewrite some sentences.

EXERCISE 19   **Practicing with paraphrase**

Review "Power Grammar: Paraphrase" in Chapter 3. Then, with two or three classmates, read the original text below from Martin Gray's webpage "Machu Picchu, Peru" and the student examples of paraphrase. Finally, complete the steps that follow.

Original Text

Invisible from below and completely self-contained, surrounded by agricultural terraces sufficient to feed the population, and watered by natural springs, Machu Picchu seems to have been utilized by the Inca as a secret ceremonial city.

Student Paraphrase 1

Machu Picchu was probably built as a religious center. It could not be seen from the canyon below and was completely independent. Its inhabitants had built terraces in the mountainside where they grew enough produce to feed themselves. Water was supplied by nearby springs.

Student Paraphrase 2

Invisible from below, agriculturally self-sufficient, and watered by natural springs, Machu Picchu seems to have been utilized by the Inca for secret ceremonial purposes.

Student Paraphrase 3

Machu Picchu was built by the Incas. The city had natural water springs, beautiful terraces, and enough food for the whole population. The Incas built Machu Picchu so that they could perform secret religious ceremonies.

Student Paraphrase 4

The Incas most likely built Machu Picchu for ceremonial purposes. The area was well hidden from outsiders. The people tilled the soil surrounding the area, obtained water from local natural springs, and were generally a self-reliant community.

1. Circle any keywords in the paraphrases that are the same in the original source.
2. Compare the students' paraphrases to the original text. Which examples of paraphrase are the most effective? Why? (*Hint*: Look at word choice and sentence structure.)
3. Which paraphrases are the least effective? Why?
4. What have you learned from this exercise that you can apply to your writing?

EXERCISE 20   Noticing synonyms

Form a group with two or three other students, and then do the following:

1. Student paraphrases 1 and 4 above have synonyms in place of some words and phrases in the original text. Circle three words or phrases that are different from the original.
2. Student paraphrase 2 is too similar to the original text. On separate paper, revise the paraphrase.
3. Compare your revision with another group's. Which one do you find more effective? Why?
4. What have you learned about paraphrasing that you can apply to your writing? Discuss your answers with your group.

WEB POWER

For more practice with paraphrasing and summarizing, go to http://esl.college.hmco.com/students.

○ Writing, Revising, and Editing

EXERCISE 21   **Analyzing a student introduction**

With two or three classmates, read Hoa's introduction below. Then, answer the questions that follow. If you have difficulty answering any of the questions, ask your instructor for help.

Hoa's Introduction

Key terms

Many people all over the world are fascinated by *megaliths*. These are huge stone monuments that are found all over Europe, especially in Great Britain, France, and Italy, and go back to prehistoric times. Some areas only have one megalith, called a *menhir*, while other areas have many megaliths placed in a row, called *megalithic alignment*. The last type of megalithic structure is the *stone ring* or *stone circle*, where the stones are placed at intervals next to each other to form an enclosure. Even though it is called a stone circle, it is not always circular in shape (Arosio & Meozzi). The purpose of all these megalithic structures is uncertain, but based on recent scientific studies, many archeologists now agree with Forbes, a famous archeologist who believed that these structures may have been used to observe the moon and stars (as cited in Michell, 2001). One of the most famous stone circles is Stonehenge. In this paper, I will explain about Stonehenge, the investigation of this site and its archeological importance.

When quoting from a secondary source, write "as cited in" followed by the author and date of the secondary source.

Always cite all your sources on the References page, including the sources used in your introduction.

References

Arosio, P. and Meozzi, D. (n.d.). Stonehenge. Stone circle, henge and standing stone. Retrieved December 2, 2003 from http://stonepages.com/england/ england.html

Michell, J. (2001). Sacred science and the megaliths. Retrieved December 2, 2003 from http://www.britannia.com/wonder/ michell0.html

1. What is the purpose of Hoa's introduction?
2. How many sources does she cite?
3. Is the author's name mentioned with each citation? Why?
4. Are page numbers given for each citation? Why?
5. Circle the controlling ideas in Hoa's thesis statement. What questions do you expect her to answer in her essay? Write them on separate paper.
6. Do you find Hoa's introduction interesting? Why or why not?
7. What other information could be added to Hoa's introduction?

EXERCISE 22 **Writing your introduction**

Review your essay map and your thesis statement. Then, write an introduction for your essay. Be sure to:

1. Introduce the topic to your readers.
2. Define any terms the reader may not know.
3. Add some interesting or surprising information to attract readers' attention.
4. Revise your working thesis statement so that it flows with the rest of the introduction. Make sure your thesis has a parallel structure.
5. Place your introduction in your writing folder.

EXERCISE 23 **Responding to an introduction**

Exchange introductions with a classmate who wrote about a different topic. Answer the following questions at the end of your classmate's introduction paragraph.

1. Does the introduction begin with a general statement that introduces the topic of the essay?
2. Does the introduction contain interesting information that makes you want to continue reading?
3. Does the writer define any unfamiliar terms related to the essay topic?
4. Write one or two suggestions to help your classmate improve her or his introduction. Sign your name, and give the introduction back to your classmate.

EXERCISE 24   Analyzing a background paragraph

Read Joanna's background paragraph below. Then, complete the steps that follow.

The paragraph has
4 parts:

1. Topic sentence

2. The story of
the discovery of
the caves

3. Information about
the caves

4. **Concluding
sentence**

Joanna's Paragraph

The **Cave of Chauvet-Pont-d'Arc** was discovered accidentally by three French people, and it contains beautiful prehistoric art. On December 18, 1994, Jean-Marie Chauvet, Eliette Brunel, and Christian Hillaire decided to explore a small cave in an area called Pont d'Arc near the Ardèche River in France. The three friends had explored many caves before, and they had already been to this cave. But this time they decided to dig a passage through some fallen rocks. They discovered a huge cave filled with rock formations and animal bones. On their way out, their flashlights revealed some mammoth drawings on one of the rocks. The three friends continued their exploration and discovered hundreds or rock paintings. The three *spelunkers*, amateur cave explorers, were experienced enough to cover their footprints with plastic sheets and create a path, so they would not step on any more bones and other remains. A few days later the spelunkers told the French authorities about their discovery. Ten days later an official expedition was sent to study the caves (Clottes & Féruglio). Radiocarbon dating shows that some of the paintings are 35,000 years old. Surprisingly, the cave was not used as a dwelling. As Clottes states in the article "France's Magical Ice Age Art: Chauvet Cave," "People never lived in Chauvet. Prehistoric master artists, children, perhaps ritual participants—all came to experience the power of this subterranean sanctuary" (Clottes, 2001, p. 111). **When the entrance to the cave collapsed, the paintings were preserved until discovered by Chauvet, for whom the cave is named, and his two friends.**

References

Clottes, J. (2001, August). France's magical ice age art: Chauvet Cave. *National Geographic*, 104–121.

Clottes, J. and Féruglio, V. (n.d.). The cave today: The discovery. Retrieved December 2, 2003 from http://www.culture.gouv. fr/culture/arcnat/chauvet/en

1. The paragraph has four parts: the topic sentence, the story about the discovery of the cave paintings, information about the cave, and a conclusion. In which of these parts do you find the present tense verbs? Highlight or circle them.
2. Why did the writer use present tense verbs in a paragraph about things that happened in the past?
3. Put an asterisk (*) in the margin next to the supporting details that interested you the most. Write the reason(s) for your choice here:

    _____

    _____

4. Compare your answers to items 1 to 3 with a classmate's.

Note: The quotation in Joanna's paragraph is followed by an in-text citation. This includes the author's name, the date, and the page number. Page numbers are given only for direct quotations. If the page number is not given on the website, just give the author's name and the date of publication.

POWER GRAMMAR

Writing about the Past

Two important rules about verb tenses:

1. Use past tense verbs to tell about something that happened in the past.
2. Use present tense verbs to talk about something that is always true.

Read the examples below from Joanna's paragraph to learn about shifting tenses correctly.

Sentences	Purpose of the Sentences
The Cave of Chauvet-Pont-d' Arc **was discovered** accidentally by three French people, and it <u>contains</u> beautiful prehistoric art.	Topic sentence for a paragraph about the history of ancient paintings and their modern discovery: The **past tense** is used to tell the past time story (what happened). The <u>present tense</u> is used to explain why the cave is important now.

(Continued)

Sentences	Purpose of the Sentences
On December 18, 1994, Jean-Marie Chauvet, Eliette Brunel and Christian Hillaire **decided** to explore a small cave in an area called Pont d'Arc near the Ardèche River in France.	The story begins. The past tense is used to tell about the past time story.
The three friends **had explored** many caves before, and they **had already been** to this cave.	The writer goes back to a time **before the story**. She gives background information about the people in the story.
But this time they **decided** to dig a passage through some fallen rocks. They **discovered** a huge cave filled with rock formations and animal bones.	These sentences are in the past tense. The past tense is used to tell the rest of the story.
Radiocarbon dating **shows** that some of the paintings **are** 35,000 years old.	Now the writer changes from telling the story to telling us about the paintings. The present tense is used for general truth.
Surprisingly, the cave **was not used** as a dwelling. As Clottes **states** in the article "France's Magical Ice Age Art: Chauvet Cave," "People never **lived** in Chauvet. Prehistoric master artists, children, perhaps ritual participants—all **came** to experience the power of this subterranean sanctuary" (Clottes, 2001, p. 111). When the entrance to the cave **collapsed**, the paintings **were preserved** until **discovered** by Chauvet, for whom the cave **is named**, and his two friends.	These two sentences explain how the caves were used in the Ice Age by the people who made the drawings. The word *states* is in the present tense because the quotation is still true. The quotation uses past tense for the past time activities of the prehistoric artists. The concluding sentence connects the prehistoric past to the modern discovery. It then includes information about the name of the cave.

EXERCISE 25 **Noticing tenses**

With two classmates, read the sentences below. Underline the verbs. Which verbs are past? Which are present? Why? Ask your instructor if you are not sure.

1. Machu Picchu is in Peru, in the Andes, which are the highest mountains in South America.
2. Machu Picchu was founded in 1460 by the Incas, who were destroyed when the Spanish conquered South America.
3. The Incas were warriors who conquered most of South America.
4. The ruins of Machu Picchu are easy to see from the air, but they are hidden from the people in the valley.
5. Not many people lived in Machu Picchu, and they were mostly women and children.
6. However, new studies of human bones from Machu Picchu show that men lived there too.
7. Today, nobody knows for sure why Machu Picchu was abandoned.
8. Some archeologists think that Machu Picchu was a training place for priests and priestesses.

EXERCISE 26 **Finding the errors**

With a classmate, highlight or underline the verbs in the sentences below. Correct the verb tense errors (one error per sentence). The first sentence has been corrected for you as an example.

1. Machu Picchu was discovered by Hiram Bingham in 1911, but he thought he ~~finds~~ found VILCABAMBA, the last fortress of the Incan empire.

2. The Incas used huge stones for the walls and straw for the roofs. Many of these walls were still in good condition today.

3. Machu Picchu was an Incan ceremonial site, and a ceremonial stone, the *Intihuatana*, is used by the Incas to "tie the sun" during the winter solstice.

4. The Spanish conquerors destroyed the ceremonial column in other Incan places, but they never found Machu Picchu, so they do not destroy its column.

5. Nowadays, some people believed that if you touch the *Intihuatana* with your forehead you can get in touch with the spirit world.

6. The Temple of the Moon was recently discovered at Machu Picchu. Some archeologists think that the Incas use it to worship one of their goddesses.

7. Machu Picchu was self-sufficient because the people who lived there tilled the land and grow crops.

8. Many tourists visit Machu Picchu every year even though they had to hike for hours to get there.

WEB POWER

For more practice with verb tenses, go to
http://esl.college.hmco.com/students.

EXERCISE 27 **Writing your background paragraph**

Reread your essay assignment. Then, review your working thesis statement, essay map, and other materials in your writing folder. Begin writing your background paragraph. Include information about the following:

1. *What* was discovered (Lascaux, Otzi, Copan, Orrorin, or Sudan's pyramids)
2. *When* the discovery was made (the exact date if possible)
3. *Who* made it (an explorer? a passerby?)
4. Other *historical* data related to the discovery (Joanna, for example, gives information about the French government sending an official expedition to study Chauvet Cave.)
5. *In-text citations* (at least six)
6. Definitions of terminology associated with the topic (For example, Joanna gives a definition of *spelunkers* in her paragraph.)
7. Additional information that you think will help the reader understand the essay (for example, Joanna explains *how the cave was discovered* in her background paragraph because she discusses *how the cave was studied by experts* in her second body paragraph.)

EXERCISE 28 Responding to a background paragraph

Exchange essay maps, background paragraphs, and supporting materials with a classmate who chose the same essay topic you are writing about. Then,

1. Circle the controlling ideas in the topic sentence of the background paragraph.
2. Highlight or underline:
   a. *what* was discovered
   b. *when* the discovery occurred
   c. *who* made the discovery
3. Draw lines between the main points in the paragraph and the controlling ideas in the topic sentence.
4. Put an asterisk (*) in the margin next to the most interesting supporting details.
5. At the end of the background paragraph, write one question that your classmate might also answer in her or his background paragraph.
6. Return the materials to your classmate.

EXERCISE 29 Evaluating feedback

Read your classmate's feedback. Then,

1. Ask that classmate any questions you have about her or his comments.
2. Thank your classmate for the feedback.
3. Make changes to your background paragraph as your classmate suggested.
4. If you need more information for your paragraph, look through the sources in your Writing Folder to locate the information. Make a note at the end of your background paragraph to remember which source has the information you need.
5. Place your background paragraph with your classmate's comments in your writing folder.

EXERCISE 30 Evaluating Hoa's body paragraphs

Review Hoa's introduction, especially her thesis statement (Exercise 21). Then, read her body paragraphs and complete the steps that follow.

Hoa's Body Paragraphs

This paragraph explains what: Stonehenge.

Paragraph development: definition and explanation

Historical data is given as support.

Stonehenge is in England, and it has been studied for many years. Stonehenge is located about two miles from the village of Amesbury, England. The name Stonehenge comes from the Old English Stanhenge, which means "hanging stone." Nobody knows exactly why the site has such a strange name. Some people think that criminals used to be hanged at Stonehenge. Others think that the name came from the fact that from a distance, the stones seem to hang in the air. Whatever the origin of its name, Stonehenge has been studied for centuries. The oldest written record about Stonehenge goes back to 1066. The author was the Norman Archdeacon Henry of Huntingdon, who wondered how the huge stones could stand so straight and who had put them there. The first serious study of Stonehenge was done around 1620 by the English architect Indigo Jones by order of King James I (Sullivan, 1998). After this time, other archeologists studied Stonehenge through the centuries, so they could learn more and more about the megalithic structure. Recently, Archeologist Terence Meaden discovered the carving of a face on the side of one of the megaliths. During an interview with a BBC reporter, Meaden claimed that no one had noticed the carving before because the face can be seen only when the

Always introduce, interpret, and/or describe the figure.

Insert the figure right ──────➤ sun hits the stone at a certain angle (see Figure 1).

below the part of the essay that refers to it.

Figure 1

Center the figure, and place the caption below the figure. Include an in-text reference.

Face Carving

Other scientists have confirmed the authenticity of the carving. As we can see, the long history of studying Stonehenge continues today (Whitehouse, 1999).

This paragraph explains *what*: stages of construction.

Paragraph development: classification

After all these years of study, archeologists are now sure that Stonehenge was built in four stages, not three as previously thought. During these four stages that spanned more than 1400 years, different structures made of dirt, wood, and stone were built, dismantled, and rebuilt. The first stage of construction, called *Pre-Stonehenge*, occurred over 8 million years ago. At that time four pits with big pine posts were set a few hundred meters from where Stonehenge is now. The next stage, *phase I*, occurred around 2900 BC when the circular bank, ditch, and Aubrey Holes (a circle of 56 pits) were created. In *phase II*, beginning in 2500 BC, cremated human remains, pottery, and animal bones were placed in the ditch and some of the Aubrey Holes. In *Phase III*, the final stage, a number of stones were erected while some holes were dug but never filled (Arosio & Meozzi). *Phase III* is the most complex stage in the building of Stonehenge, and it has been divided in three sub-phases: *a*, *b*, and *c*. In *Phase IIIa* Stonehenge was shaped the same way it is today. However, some of the *Bluestones*, the type of stone used at Stonehenge, were removed and then replaced during *Phases IIIb* and *c*. Other stones were also added, and the most important was the Altar stone which now stands in the middle of the semicircle of Bluestones. Many symbolic carvings can be seen on the stones. Scientists are still determining more details of the four-stage construction of Stonehenge (Witcombe).

This paragraph explains *why*: the reason(s) Stonehenge was built.

Paragraph development: reasons/causes

Archeologists consider Stonehenge a very important place, but they do not really know who built Stonehenge or why. For a long time, many people believed a theory introduced in the 19th century that claimed the *Druids*, a people that lived in England before the Roman invasion, had built it as a temple. Many Druid sects were created, and they visited the site for ritual ceremonies. In fact, so many Druids visited the site that they actually caused serious damage to some of the stones. Later, archeologists were able to date the stones and realized that Stonehenge had been finished more than a thousand years before the Druids even existed. Probably, Stonehenge was built by the indigenous people that lived in the area in order to study the heavens. The astronomer Gerald Hawkins studied the site extensively, and he recently realized that Stonehenge is aligned with solar and lunar phases and can even be used to predict eclipses. Instead of being a temple, Stonehenge was more likely an "astronomical calculator" (Witcombe). However, the stone additions in Phase III do not seem to match astronomical events. For this reason, some archeologists believe that the site was first used to corral cattle and possibly perform rituals involving animals. With time, the site became exclusively a religious place (Krystek, 1998). In spite of all these theories, Stonehenge, its founders, and its purpose are still a mystery.

References

Krystek, Lee (1998). Stonehenge and the rings of rock. Retrieved December 2, 2003 from http://www.unmuseum.org/stonehen.htm

Sullivan, N. (1998). Welcome to Stonehenge. Retrieved December 3, 2003 from http://www.fortunecity.com/roswell/blavatsky/123/stnhng.html

Whitehouse, D. (1999, October 15). Stonehenge face mystery. *BBC Online*. Retrieved December 3, 2003 from http://news.bbc.co.uk/1/hi/sci/tech/474977.stm

Witcombe, C. (n.d.) Stonehenge. Retrieved December 3, 2003 from Sweet Briar College website http://witcombe.sbc.edu/earthmysteries/EMStonehenge.html

Always give your references in alphabetical order.

Remember that only the initial letter of the first word is capitalized in the title, but do capitalize proper nouns.

1. Underline the topic sentences.
2. Circle the controlling ideas in each topic sentence.
3. Circle the main points in each paragraph. Do the main points in each paragraph match the controlling ideas in the topic sentence? You may draw lines to connect each main point to the corresponding controlling idea to make sure they match.
4. Look at Hoa's last paragraph again. Does she refer to events that are happening today or that happened in the past? How can you tell?
5. Discuss your answers with a classmate.

EXERCISE 31 Analyzing in-text citations

With two classmates, do the following:

1. Highlight the in-text citations given in parentheses. What information does Hoa provide? Why?
2. Which supporting details do you find most interesting? Why?
3. What information does Hoa provide for the figure?

EXERCISE 32 Drafting your body paragraphs

Review your essay map, supporting materials, introduction, and background paragraph. Then,

1. Compose your body paragraphs.
2. Compare the controlling ideas in the topic sentences with the controlling ideas in the thesis statement. Make sure they match.
3. Review each paragraph's main points to make sure they relate to the paragraph's controlling ideas.
4. Review the evidence in each paragraph to make sure it supports the paragraph's main points.
5. Put your introduction, background paragraph, and body paragraphs in your writing folder along with your other materials related to the essay assignment.

EXERCISE 33 Organizing your paragraphs

Review your essay, and then do the following on separate paper:

1. Consider the overall organization of your essay and paragraph sequence. Write one sentence explaining why you chose to order your paragraphs in this way.
2. Consider the organization of each paragraph. Explain what WH- question(s) you answered in each paragraph.
3. Check the citation information in each paragraph. Make sure it follows APA format.
4. Place the paper in your writing folder.

EXERCISE 34 **Writing questions**

You have had many opportunities in this course to receive and give feedback. In this exercise, you will create your own peer review questions. On separate paper, write five to seven questions you would like to ask a classmate about your body paragraphs' content, organization, citations, grammar, and vocabulary.

1. **Content**—Ask questions about your topic sentences, main points, supporting evidence, and citations. Examples:
   a. I'm not sure the controlling ideas in body paragraph 3 match the thesis statement. How can I improve my topic sentence?
   b. Is the supporting evidence in my first body paragraph sufficient? If not, what should I add?

2. **Organization**—Ask questions about the order of your paragraphs, of each paragraph's main points, and of the supporting details in each paragraph. Examples:
   a. I changed the order of my body paragraphs. Paragraph 1 used to be paragraph 2. Do you think I should change them back?
   b. Body paragraph 2 classifies the types of remains found at the archeological site. Should I add more information about each type?

3. **Citations**—Ask questions about the number of citations, the amount of support for each controlling idea in the topic sentence, and the citation information. Examples:
   a. Source 1 in the third paragraph does not have an author or date of publication, so I used the title, but it is very long. Is it OK to give only part of it in parentheses?
   b. Am I supposed to give the page number for the quotation in paragraph 4? What if I do not know the page number?

4. **Grammar**—Ask questions about your sentence structure and transitions. Examples:
   a. Do I need a comma in paragraph 2's topic sentence between *discovery* and but?
   b. I use *however* three times in my third body paragraph. What other transition can I use instead?

5. **Vocabulary**—Ask questions about your word choice and spelling. Examples:
   a. Do I need there or their in the last sentence of paragraph 3?
   b. What other word can I use in paragraph 2 in place of interesting?

Follow the example below to type or write your own form on separate paper. Leave enough room for feedback under each question.

Give your form
this title. ──────────────────────────────────➤ **Chapter 5**
                                                   My Peer Review Form

                                                   Writer Hoa   Reader Sandra
Type your name. ────────────────➤ ────────────────────────➤

Leave room for
reviewer
information.

Leave room after ──────────➤ *Yes. You give details about studies done before the 17th century and*
each question for   **Question 1:** In my first body paragraph, I talk about the studies
your classmate's   done at Stonehenge. Should I give more information?
answers.
                         *Yes. You give details about studies done before the 17th century and
                         then you jump to recent times. Maybe you can write about one
                         major study done in each century until Meaden's discovery.*

                         Question 2: I really like the organization of paragraph 2, but I'm
                         not sure about the concluding sentence. Do you think it should
                         be revised?

                         *I like your concluding sentence. I think this classification paragraph is
                         very strong.*

                         Question 3: Do I give enough supporting details in paragraph 3?

                         *You do a good job. I am just a little confused when you mention
                         "indigenous people." Who were they? I think you should tell
                         something about that.*

Ask at least one ──────➤ **Question 4:** I'm not sure about the figure captions. Are they
question about your   supposed to be at the top or bottom of each image? Are my
figures.   captions correct?

                         *I wasn't sure about this, so I asked our instructor. She said you did it
                         right, but in other classes you may be given different directions.
                         Always ask the instructor.*

Ask at least one   **Question 5:** Did I give the correct information in parentheses for
question about your   my citations?
citations.
                         *Yes. At first I thought your citations for Witcombe were missing the
                         date, but then I checked your References and noticed that there was
                         no date at all. So it is OK.*

Ask at least one ────────▶
question about
your grammar.

Your classmate may
notice something
you did not ask
about. Leave some
room for additional
suggestions. Notice
that Hoa asks
specific questions
about aspects of
her paper she is
not sure about.
Avoid general
questions such
as "Are my body
paragraphs well
developed?"

Question 6: Many of the sentences in paragraph 3 start with a transition word. Should I get rid of some of them?

If you use the same sentence structure all the time, your writing will be boring. I think you can change or combine a couple of sentences. For example, the sentences about the Druids can be combined together to get rid of "In fact": "Many Druid sects were created, and so many Druids visited the site for ritual ceremonies that they actually caused serious damage to some of the stones."

Please write two or three suggestions that can help me improve my body paragraphs:

1) *In paragraph 2 you should change the definitions for bluestones from "the type of stone used at Stonehenge" to "the large boulders used at Stonehenge."*

2) *You use a lot of big words in the part of Par. 3 that starts with "Surprisingly" and ends with "a religious place." So I checked your source but I did not find those exact words. Did someone help you write this part? Our instructor said we should not get help in writing the paper. If you wrote it all by yourself, your sentence structure and vocabulary are GREAT!!!*

EXERCISE 35   Reviewing body paragraphs

Exchange body paragraphs and all the materials in your writing folder with a classmate. Hand her or him the peer review form you wrote in Exercise 34.

1. Read your classmate's body paragraphs carefully.
2. Read and respond thoughtfully to each question in your classmate's peer review form.
3. Add comments that can help your classmate improve her or his body paragraphs.
4. Return all materials and the completed peer review form to your classmate.
5. Thank your classmate for the feedback.
6. Put your classmate's feedback in your writing folder.

EXERCISE 36 Evaluating Hoa's conclusion

Read Hoa's conclusion below with two or three classmates. After you read,
answer the questions that follow.

Hoa's Conclusion

Hoa begins with a
concluding phrase

No new main points
or supporting details
are introduced in
the conclusion.

The words <u>may</u> and
<u>perhaps</u> express
uncertainty.

<u>As this report shows</u>, the mystery of Stonehenge has fascinated many people over the centuries. Archeologists have been studying the megalithic structure for a very long time. However, nobody has been able to find out exactly who built the structure and why. We only know it was built and rebuilt for thousands of years, and it <u>may</u> have been a cattle enclosure originally, then an astronomical observatory, and finally a religious site. <u>Perhaps</u>, one day archeologists will be able to answer more questions and piece the information together better as technology improves.

1. What word does Hoa repeat in the first sentence of the conclusion that is also in the last sentence of the last body paragraph (Exercise 35)?
2. What main ideas does Hoa summarize in the conclusion? Underline or highlight keywords that refer to these ideas.
3. What concluding technique(s) does Hoa use (prediction, recommendation, solution, evaluation)?
4. What other idea(s) might Hoa summarize in her conclusion? Write your suggestion(s) here:

_____

_____

_____

5. Compare your answers with two or three classmates'.

 EXERCISE 37 Writing your conclusion

Reread your essay, especially your introduction and thesis statement. Then,

1. Begin your conclusion with a concluding word or phrase.
2. Write a sentence that connects with the last sentence of the last body paragraph.
3. Add a brief summary (two or three sentences) of the essay's main ideas.
4. Use a concluding technique to leave the readers with a final message.

EXERCISE **38** **Evaluating a student essay**

With two or three classmates, read Sandra's essay below. Cover the comments in the right margin with a ruler or a piece of paper. Then, complete the steps that follow.

Sandra's Essay

Machu Picchu: a Religious Retreat

Machu Picchu was founded by the Incas. They were a fierce warrior people that ruled a large area of South America from around A.D. 1200 to A.D. 1535 when the Spanish *conquistadores* took over the area. Even though they were an aggressive people, the Incas were very religious.

Unfamiliar terms are in *italics*. ⟶

Therefore, religious rituals were very important to the Incas. These rituals were usually performed on the highest point in the village because this point was closer to the sun, called *Inti* or *Sun God*, the most important god in Incan religion. The Inca rulers built religious retreats high on the mountains to be closer to *Inti*. Machu Picchu is one of these retreats (Crystal). In this essay, I will report about Machu Picchu, and I will also explain how it was discovered in 1911 and why it is an important discovery for historical and mystical reasons.

In-text citations are added after any quoted, paraphrased, or summarized information.

Machu Picchu is a famous archeological site built at the time of the Incan empire. It is located in the Andes of Peru, 7,000 feet above sea level. This semi-tropical area is surrounded by a jungle and overlooks the Urubamba River. It was a religious retreat where rich Inca rulers performed religious ceremonies. Machu Picchu was built on the top of the Old Peak, which is what Machu Picchu means in the Quechua language (Ziegler, 2003). All around the citadel, Machu Picchu farmers carved terraces in the sides of the mountains and planted crops, mostly potatoes and corn (see Figure 1).

Figure 1

Number each figure as it is presented in your essay, and add a caption below each figure.

Machu Picchu (Crystal)

Place figures in the text.

The phrase "In Crystal's words" introduces the quotation.

Sandra connects the quotation to the next idea (intense studies) with a transitional expression that refers back to the quotation.

The buildings were carefully planned and built with huge stones that weighed around 50 lbs. each. The walls were built so well that not even a thin knife blade can be inserted between the stones ("Machu Pichu," 2003). In Crystal's words, "The citadel is a stupendous achievement in urban planning, civil engineering, architecture and stonemasonry." Archeologists world-wide agree with this statement and the site is still the center of intense studies. New artifacts are still being found at Machu Picchu, and in 2002 a tomb was unearthed by Peruvian archeologists (Vargas, 2002). That is why Machu Picchu is such an important archeological site today.

Machu Picchu was discovered in 1911 by an American explorer. His name was Hiram Bingham, and he led the Yale University Peruvian Expedition in search of Vilcabamba, the last fortified city of the Incan empire. When he accidentally found Machu Picchu, Hiram thought he had found Vilcabamba. **However**, most scholars today are convinced that he was wrong. At the time Bingham discovered Machu Picchu, some people still lived around the area to avoid paying taxes to the Peruvian government or to escape army recruiters ("Machu Pichu," 2003).

For in-text citations, give the name of the author and the date whenever possible. Sometimes for online sources you have to go to the main page or homepage to find this information.

Nevertheless, nobody actually lived at Machu Picchu, which was uninhabited for hundreds of years. Some people are puzzled by the fact that the Spaniards did not find Machu Picchu, but the area was well hidden by the jungle below and the mountains around it. **Besides**, the Incas themselves probably did not know that Machu Picchu existed. Only the ruling class knew about ceremonial sites like this one (Ziegler, 2003). Therefore, Machu Picchu was forgotten until Bingham's discovery.

Machu Picchu has great historical meaning. Its 200 buildings are in good condition, and archeologists can study the architecture of the time. Machu Picchu has "polygonal masonry, characteristic of the late Inca period ("Machu Pichu," 2003). Most houses were built in groups of ten around one large courtyard. Some houses were built on narrow terraces and connected by narrow alleys. Also, many artifacts such as axes, knives, textiles, and jewelry were found in Machu Picchu. Archeologists have been able to recreate the everyday life of the Incas based on these artifacts. The Inca people worked hard as masons, metalworkers, farmers, and cooks. However, they also spent a lot of time feasting and partying, and they drank a lot of *chicha*, corn beer, during these feasts and religious ceremonies. At the Carnegie Museum of Natural History, visitors can explore the Machu Picchu exhibit and learn about the citadel and its inhabitants. At this exhibit, visitors can also view a lab where artifacts and bones are analyzed with the most up-to-date technology ("Unveiling the Mystery").

If possible, in your essay mention current exhibits or studies that relate to the topic as Sandra does.

The historical significance of Machu Picchu is only matched by its mystical significance. Many important religious ceremonies were performed at Machu Picchu, but the most important was the "tying of the sun." Because the Incas worshiped the sun and the moon, they had an astronomical observatory in Machu Picchu. A stone post on top of a block of stone called an *Intihuatana*, indicates the exact date of the two equinoxes, the winter solstice, and other celestial events (see Figure 2).

Figure 2

Intihuatana, Machu Picchu (Gray, 2003)

During the equinoxes, the priest performed a religious ritual where a string was tied to the column to keep the sun in place, probably to prolong summer and the harvest season. At this time, the sun is right above the *Intihuatana* and casts no shadow. In December, the priests performed a similar ceremony and tied the sun to the post so that the sun would stay longer in the sky. When the Spanish *conquistadores* invaded the Inca empire, they destroyed all the *Intihuatanas*. But they never found Machu Picchu, so they did not destroy it there. Some people think that Machu Picchu is still a very spiritual place. According to Gray, "Shamanic legends say that when sensitive persons touch their forehead to the stone, the Intihuatana opens one's vision to the spirit world" (Gray, 2003). Not just the Intihuatana, but the whole area was considered sacred by the Incas. The sacred peak of Huayna (or Wayna) Picchu contains the *Temple of the Moon*, which is located in an underground cave on the northern side of the mountain. The temple was discovered only recently, so archeologists are not sure what ceremonies were performed there. The temple and the *Intihuatana* are still important to the new age movement, which explores mysticism and ancient rituals. Thus, the mystical significance of Machu Picchu is great even today.

The conclusion
begins with a
concluding phrase
and summarizes the
essay's main points.
It ends with a
prediction about
further studies.

Remember to
double space
your references.

If the article or
webpage has no
publication date,
write n.d. in place of
the date.

If no author is listed,
begin the reference
with the title of the
article.

List all your sources
in alphabetical
order.

Always remember
to give the date
you printed or
downloaded the
information.

In conclusion, mystical as well as historical reasons make Machu Picchu one of the most important archeological sites of our time. Because it was discovered so late, Machu Picchu was not destroyed like many other Incan sites. Archeologists and anthropologists continue to explore this site and find more human remains and artifacts. Further study of these remains will bring more knowledge of Incan culture and their life at Machu Picchu.

References

Crystal, E. (n.d.). Machu Picchu. Retrieved November 20, 2003 from http://www.crystalinks.com/machu.html

Gray, M. (2003). Machu Picchu, Peru. Retrieved November 17, 2003 from http://www.sacredsites.com/2nd56/21422.html

Machu Picchu: Unveiling the mystery of the Incas. (n.d.) Retrieved December 1, 2003 from http://www.carnegiemuseums.org/cmnh/exhibits/mp/artifacts.htm

Machu Pichu. (2003). Retrieved November 17, 2003 from Minnesota State University, Mankato, E-museum http://www.mnsu.edu/emuseum/prehistory/latinamerica/south/sites/machu_picchu.html

Vargas, M. (2002, October 12). Peru finds Inca burial site at Machu Picchu. *Silicon Valley News*. Retrieved November 20, 2003 from http://www.siliconvalley.com/mld/siliconvalley/news/4271801.htm

Ziegler, G. (n.d.). Machu Picchu: How they kept the secret. Retrieved November 17, 2003 from http://gorp.away.com/gorp/location/latamer/peru/machu.htm

1. Circle the controlling ideas in the thesis statement.
2. Circle the controlling ideas in the topic sentences (the background paragraph has been completed for you). Do the controlling ideas in the topic sentences match the controlling ideas in the thesis statement?
3. In the fourth paragraph, draw lines to connect the controlling ideas in the topic sentence and the main points in the paragraph. Does each main point relate to one or more controlling ideas?
4. Sandra did not write a concluding sentence in the fourth paragraph. On separate paper, try to write one for her. Compare your group's sentence with that of another group of classmates. Which one do you like more? Why?

EXERCISE 39 Analyzing in-text citations

With a classmate, look at the in-text references in Sandra's essay. Notice that she listed only the sources she actually cited in her essay. One source listed in her essay map (see Exercise 14) is not listed here because she did not refer to it in her essay. Also, she added more sources to her list because she needed more supporting details.

1. How many sources does Sandra cite in each paragraph?
2. What information does she provide in parentheses?
3. Why does this information vary? For example, why does she give the author's name sometimes and at other times she does not?
4. What is Sandra's purpose in citing sources?

 EXERCISE 40 Writing your References page

Write a complete reference for every source you cite in your essay (see Sandra's References page):

1. Type your references on the last page of your essay.
2. Double space all lines.
3. Begin each reference flush with the left margin of the page.
4. Indent five to seven spaces after the first line of each reference.
5. List your sources alphabetically.
6. Put your References page in your writing folder.

WEB POWER

For updated information on APA style for citing sources, go to **http://esl.college.hmco.com/students**.

 EXERCISE 41 Writing your cover page

Follow Hoa's example on the next page to create your cover page:

1. Begin your paper's title about one-third of the way down from the top of the page.
2. Write your title, your name, the course title, your instructor's name, and the date.
3. Place your cover page on top of your essay.

Hoa's Cover Page

The Mystery of Stonehenge

Hoa Xiong

English 101, section 4

Professor Brown

October 1, 2004

EXERCISE **42** **Revising your essay**

Reread the essay assignment, your essay draft, and all the other materials in your writing folder, especially your classmate's feedback about your body paragraphs. Use this checklist:

—— Your introduction gives general information about the essay topic.

—— Your introduction captures the readers' attention with interesting information about the topic.

—— Your thesis statement controls the rest of your essay.

—— Your topic sentences relate directly to the thesis statement.

—— The main points in each body paragraph relate to the topic sentence.

—— Each paragraph's supporting evidence explains the paragraph's main point.

—— The information from online and print sources is properly cited (APA format).

—— Your conclusion summarizes the essay's main ideas and uses a concluding technique (recommendation, prediction, solution, evaluation).

—— Your References page lists all the sources you cited in your essay, including figure information.

EXERCISE 43 **Self-editing your essay**

Print your essay. Then, do the following:

1. In your essay, underline two or three words or phrases that express uncertainty about scientific conclusions (examples: "Results suggest that the area was settled in prehistoric times." "The area was probably settled in prehistoric times." "The area *may* have been settled in prehistoric times"). Are there other places in your body paragraphs where you can add or change words or phrases that express uncertainty?

2. Do you need to add transition words and phrases at the beginning of each body paragraph?

3. Does each of your sentences have a subject and a verb?

4. Do you use the past tense appropriately? For help, review "Power Grammar: Writing about the Past" in this chapter.

5. After you finish editing your essay, print three copies—one for your writing folder and two for peer reviews.

EXERCISE 44 **Rewriting your essay**

Reread your essay carefully. Then,

1. Consider your classmates' responses:
   a. Which suggestions can you incorporate that will improve your essay?
   b. What did you learn from reading your classmates' essays that can be applied to your writing?

2. Rewrite your essay.

3. Place your draft in your writing folder. Include your previous drafts with peer responses, your essay map, and all the other materials you developed for Essay Assignment 4.

4. Give the folder to your instructor.

EXERCISE 45   **Analyzing your instructor's response**

When you receive your essay back, read your instructor's comments carefully and:

1. List your essay's strengths on an index card or separate paper.
2. List your essay's weaknesses on the back of the card or paper.
3. Keep the card or paper in your writing folder.
4. Circle any instructor comments that confused you. Make an appointment with your instructor or go to her or his office during office hours to ask for help. Remember to bring your writing folder with you.

EXERCISE 46   **Writing one more draft**

If your instructor requires a final draft for your essay, revise according to each of your instructor's comments. Put your final draft with all the other materials related to this chapter's essay in your writing folder. Include all drafts, exercises, and materials related to your essay. Give your writing folder to your instructor.

○ Additional Assignments for More Practice and Assessment

Assignment 1: Write about Learning

Review this chapter's objectives, and complete the checklist. Then, choose two objectives you have not learned well. Write one or two paragraphs explaining:

- Why these objectives have been difficult for you
- What specific steps you will take to improve in these areas.

Assignment 2: Write a Summary

Summarize one article you cited in your essay. Paraphrase one or two sentences from the article. Follow the summarizing strategies you have learned in this textbook.

Assignment 3: Evaluate Writing Assignments

Write a one-page essay in response to these questions:

1. Of all the essay assignments in this course, which assignment did you like the most?
2. Why did you like it?
3. What was easiest about this assignment?
4. How has this assignment helped you improve your writing? (Think of what you learned by completing it.)

WEB POWER

You will find additional exercises related to the content in this chapter at **http://esl.college.hmco.com/students.**

Appendix 1

○ **Peer Response 1-1**

Writer: _____

Reviewer: _____ Date: _____

Read the topic sentence. Write four questions you expect the paragraph to answer that are based on the topic sentence. (Examples: Are any young people in the ad? What is the ad trying to sell? What does the ad say?)

_____

_____

_____

_____

Paragraph Format and Organization

1. Is the paragraph's first line indented and the first word of each sentence capitalized?	☐ Yes	☐ No
2. Does the topic sentence clearly identify the ad and state the controlling ideas?	☐ Yes	☐ No
3. Does the paragraph have at least two main points?	☐ Yes	☐ No
4. Do specific supporting details explain the main points?	☐ Yes	☐ No
5. Is there a concluding sentence?	☐ Yes	☐ No

Paragraph Content

Give your classmate some *suggestions* that will help her or him improve the paragraph. Don't just say, "Your first supporting point does not explain the main idea." Be specific. For example, you could say, "Your first supporting point does not seem to explain the main idea, which is that the ad is very sensual. You should talk more about the shape of the perfume bottle and the fact that it is shaped to resemble the curves of the woman's body." Write your comments on the lines under each question.

6. Review the main points. Do they answer the questions you wrote at the top of the page?

_____

_____

_____

_____

7. Do the supporting details clarify and explain the paragraph's main points?

_____

_____

_____

_____

8. Does the concluding sentence refer to the paragraph's controlling idea?

_____

_____

_____

_____

Appendix 2

○ Peer Response 1-2

Writer: _____

Reviewer #1: _____

Reviewer #2 _____

Reviewer #1: Write your name in the space above. Then, read your classmate's paragraph and answer the questions below. After you finish, pass this form to Reviewer #2.

1. Underline the topic and circle the controlling ideas in the topic sentence. Does the topic sentence answer the essay question? Does it identify the ad and state the effects of the stimuli? Why or why not?

   _____

   _____

2. What questions based on the topic sentence do you expect the writer to answer in the paragraph?

   _____

   _____

   _____

3. Do the main points refer to the controlling ideas? Explain why or why not.

   _____

   _____

4. Does the evidence in the paragraph answer your questions? Explain.

   _____

   _____

Reviewer #2: Write your name in the space provided at the top of the previous page. Then, read your classmate's paragraph and answer the questions below. After you finish, give this form back to the writer.

1. Highlight or circle keywords and phrases that refer to the controlling ideas circled by Reviewer #1.

2. Should the writer change some of the key terms? Why or why not?

    _____

    _____

    _____

    _____

3. Are any words or sentences confusing? Mark them with an asterisk (*). At the bottom of the paragraph, suggest how the student could revise the confusing words and/or sentences.

4. Does the paragraph have a clear concluding sentence? Explain.

    _____

    _____

    _____

    _____

Appendix 3

○ Revision Checklist

Read the list below carefully. Check (✓) each item as you review your essay. Revise any part of your essay that does not conform to this checklist. When you finish, place this checklist in your writing folder.

Introduction

——— The essay topic is mentioned in the first sentence of the introduction.

——— The introduction grabs the reader's attention with a description, a dialogue, a surprising fact, a thought-provoking question, or an interesting anecdote about Web design.

——— The **thesis statement** mentions the websites and Web design criteria that will be discussed in the essay.

Body Paragraphs

——— Each body paragraph has a **topic sentence** that states the paragraph's controlling ideas (= Web design criterion/criteria). Keywords and phrases from the thesis statement are used in the topic sentences.

——— The topic sentence controls the main points of each body paragraph. This means the Web design elements mentioned in the topic sentence are the main points of the paragraph.

——— Each body paragraph's main points are supported with enough relevant details (facts, personal experiences, examples, observations, etc.) to make the paragraph clear to the reader.

——— The in-text citations follow the correct format shown in Chapter 2.

——— Each body paragraph has a concluding sentence that refers to the paragraph's controlling ideas.

Conclusion

—— The essay has a clear conclusion that summarizes the essay's main idea and main points (paragraphs' main ideas). The conclusion does not introduce Web design criteria that were not discussed in the body paragraphs.

References Page

—— The end-of-text citations follow the correct format shown in Chapter 2.

Appendix 4

○ **Essay Format**

Follow this format for all your typed drafts unless otherwise directed by your instructor. Bring your printed drafts to class, but also save a copy of your essay on a disk.

1. Use 12-point size Times New Roman font.

2. Use 1.25-inch margins so that you or your group members have enough space to write questions and comments.

3. At the top left-hand corner of the first page, consistently use this heading, single-spaced, unless otherwise instructed:

   Your name (First Last)

   Class, section

   Name of instructor

   Date

   First/Second/Final Draft

4. Center the title of your essay.

5. Double space your essay.

Appendix 5

⭕ Read-around Peer Review

Writer: _____

Reader #1: _____

Reader #2: _____

Reader #3: _____

Read the instructions below carefully. If you have trouble understanding one or more steps, ask your instructor for help.

Reader #1

1. Underline the thesis statement, and circle the controlling ideas. Do the controlling ideas answer the essay assignment?

2. Underline the topic sentence of each paragraph, and circle the controlling ideas.

3. Draw a line to connect a controlling idea in the topic sentence to the same idea in the thesis statement.

4. Put an asterisk (*) in the margin each time you find effective supporting details.

5. Write two suggestions that can help your classmate improve her or his thesis statement, topic sentences, or supporting details:

   _____

   _____

6. Sign your name at the end of the paper as **R #1**.

Reader #2

1. Put a check mark (✔) in the margin next to each confusing or unclear sentence.

2. Identify any words you think are misspelled or used incorrectly. Put a question mark (?) above each incorrect word.

3. If you know the correct word, write it in parentheses next to your question mark.

4. In the margin beside the conclusion, indicate which concluding techniques the author used.

5. Write two suggestions that can help your classmate improve her or his conclusion:

   _____

   _____

6. Sign your name at the end of the paper as **R #2.**

Reader #3

1. Highlight the quotation(s) used in the essay.

2. If a quotation does not seem to support the paragraph, put a question mark in the right margin. Explain why the quotation does not work well.

3. Check the format of the in-text citation(s). If you think a citation's format is correct, put an asterisk (*) next to it. If you think a citation's format is incorrect, write your suggestion for improvement above the citation.

4. Read the end-of-text reference information. If more than one reference is given and the references are not in alphabetical order, put a check mark (✔) in the margin.

5. If the format is incorrect, suggest how the end-of-text references can be improved:

   _____

   _____

6. Sign your name at the end of the paper as **R #3.**

Appendix 6

◯ Read-around Peer Response

Writer: _____

Reader #1: _____

Reader #2: _____

Reader #3: _____

Reader #1

1. Underline the <u>thesis statement</u> and circle the controlling ideas. Do they answer the essay assignment?

2. <u>Underline the topic sentence</u> of each paragraph and circle the controlling ideas. Do the controlling ideas in the topic sentences correspond to the controlling ideas in the thesis statement?

3. Circle the words in the body paragraphs that relate to the controlling ideas in the topic sentences. Do the main points in each body paragraph correspond to the controlling ideas in the topic sentence of that paragraph?

4. Write two suggestions that can help your classmate improve her or his thesis statement, topic sentences, or supporting details.

   _____

   _____

5. Sign your name at the end of the paper as **R #1**.

Reader #2

1. Read the body paragraphs. Should the paragraphs be in a different order? If so, use arrows to suggest a different order for the paragraphs.

2. Underline the words or phrases (transitions) that connect one body paragraph to the next.

3. Draw an arrow in the margin where you think a transition is needed.

4. Indicate in the margin beside the conclusion which concluding techniques the author used.

5. Write two suggestions that can help your classmate improve her or his transitions and/or conclusion.

   _____

   _____

6. Sign your name at the end of the paper as **R #2**.

Reader #3

1. Put an asterisk (*) in the margin by each sentence where you find effective supporting details.

2. Write P above each paraphrase or summary and Q above each quotation.

3. Highlight the report verbs that introduce the cited information.

4. Highlight the in-text citations. Do they support the paragraph's main points?

5. Put a check mark (✓) next to the in-text citation you find most interesting and effective.

6. Write two suggestions that can help your classmate improve her or his in-text citations and/or end-of-text references.

   _____

   _____

7. Sign your name at the end of the paper as **R #3**.

Appendix 7

○ **Peer Review of Sources**

Writer: _____

Reviewer: _____

Reread the essay assignment your classmate has chosen to write about. Read your classmate's materials. Then, answer these questions:

1. Who is the author? _____

2. What is the website's domain? _____

3. When was the website last updated? _____

4. Are any experts cited on the website? Does the website provide a summary and discuss research results or statistics? Explain why the information is or is not reliable.

   _____

   _____

5. Put a check mark (✓) next to the most important information your classmate can use to support her or his essay.

6. Give your review to your classmate.

7. Read your classmate's review of your materials. If some of the feedback is unclear to you, ask your classmate to explain those comments.

8. Thank your classmate for the feedback, and place your classmate's suggestions in your writing folder

Appendix 8

○ **Two-Part Peer Review**

Writer: _____

Reviewer #1: _____

Reviewer #2: _____

**Read your classmate's essay. Then, do Part I if you are Reviewer #1.
Do Part II if you are Reviewer #2.**

Part I: Content

1. Compare the controlling ideas in the thesis statement to the controlling ideas in each topic sentence. Do the controlling ideas in the topic sentences correspond to the ideas in the thesis statement?
2. Write one or two suggestions in the margin that can help your classmate improve her or his thesis statement or topic sentences.
3. In each body paragraph, underline the main points or keywords.
4. Draw lines to connect the main points to the controlling ideas in the topic sentence. Do the main points correspond to the controlling ideas?
5. Write one or two suggestions in the margin that can help your classmate improve her or his main points.
6. Put an asterisk (*) in the margin each time you find effective supporting details.
7. Write one or two suggestions in the margin that can help your classmate improve her or his supporting details.
8. Write **Reviewer #1** at the bottom of your classmate's essay and sign your name. Give this form to Reviewer #2.

Part II: Citations

1. Write P above each paraphrase or summary and Q above each quotation.
2. Put a check mark (✓) next to the most interesting in-text citation.
3. Put a question mark (?) next to material you think should be cited.
4. Underline the reporting verbs in each paragraph. Write R where you think the writer should add a reporting verb.
5. Check your classmate's References page. Put a question mark in the margin next to a reference that does not seem to follow APA guidelines.
6. Write two or three suggestions at the end of the essay that can help your classmate improve her or his in-text citations.
7. Write **Reviewer #2** at the bottom of your classmate's essay and sign your name.

Index